MW01487521

All he wants
is to become
world famous.
How hard can
it be?

DON'T YOU KNOW...
WHO I AM?

Failure

Tony James Slater

ISBN: 978-1720111788

Copyright © Tony James Slater 2017

All rights reserved. No part of this publication may be reproduced, stored in a retrieval system or transmitted, in any form or by any other means without the prior written permission of the author, nor be otherwise circulated in any form of binding or cover other than that in which it is published and without a similar condition being imposed on the purchaser.

Although this is a work of non-fiction, some names have been changed by the author.

An e-book edition of this title is also available.

Paperback edition published by **Various Things At Different Times**
Cover Design by **Various Things At Different Times**
Formatted for paperback by **Tony James Slater**

Please visit the author's website for a selection of photographs that accompany this book:

www.TonyJamesSlater.com

Books by the same author:

Travel Memoirs:
That Bear Ate My Pants!
Don't Need The Whole Dog!
Kamikaze Kangaroos!
Can I Kiss Her Yet?
Shave My Spider!

Science Fiction:
Earth Warden

Contents

For Roo

My beautiful, amazing wife… who has had to read,
re-read, edit and proofread, every gory detail of
every relationship I had before I met her.
And she still loves me.
At least, I hope so…

On Prequels

This is the story of my attempted journey into the world of acting.

Before you read any further, you should know something: this book is a prequel.

If you've never read any of my books before, congratulations! You've missed absolutely nothing. But I should probably mention that, if you're reading this hoping it will describe the path to becoming a world famous actor, then you've come to the wrong place. At the risk of a slight spoiler, I never actually became world famous. Which is a bit of a shitter, but I've tried to accept it philosophically.

If you have read my other books, don't worry – this will help you to understand the occasional references, which I've scattered liberally throughout just for you. I guess you could say that this book is kind of a sequel-prequel. And the really great news is, you don't have to suffer through as much of it; this book turned out to be a fair bit shorter than the others.

It's an unequal sequel prequel.

So, the first-timers can feel free to skip ahead, Choose-Your-Own-Adventure style, to the next paragraph. The rest of you will have to unlearn what you have learned about me.

Forget the suave, debonair adventurer that I never quite became, and cast your mind back to a simpler time, when I was... well, simpler. A time before mobile phones and Facebook, before cafés became bistros, when the Spice Girls were cool and shell-suits roamed the Earth. For me it was a period of innocence; a time when my dreams were still intact, and I had yet to realise the depth of my inadequacy as a world traveller.

Most of all, no matter which camp you fall into, it's important that you manage your expectations. Because one thing we can all agree upon about prequels, is that they're rubbish.

Now, the difficulty with writing a prequel is knowing where to begin. I mean, I don't remember much of my time as a foetus, and I can't imagine anyone else really cares at what age I learnt to go pee-pee on the potty. The only truly interesting thing about my very early life is that my first words, when they emerged, were in the form of a complete sentence. Having never before uttered anything, one day when I was around 18 months old, I watched my mother taking out her handbag. "Are we going shopping, Mummy?" I asked.

At which point she probably shit herself and called an exorcist, but she was kind enough to leave that part out when telling me the story.

In truth, she was over the moon. She spent the next decade prophesying my greatness, citing this as irrefutable evidence to anyone who would listen that she'd given birth to a genius.

Whereas in reality, I'd just peaked early.

Poor woman. She must have been gutted.

But my point is, I started waffling on when I was a year and a half old, and they haven't been able to shut me up since.

For more evidence, read on....

The End Of Innocence

People often ask me, "when did you first realise you were a Thespian?"

This is a bit of an awkward question, because the truth of the matter is I don't think I *am* naturally a thespian; I mean, don't think I was *born* this way.

As with many alternative lifestyle choices, you have to look far back into my childhood to understand what happened.

Which is, my parents forced me to do it. Almost certainly against my will. And the resultant trauma caused my mind to block it out, so that for many years I couldn't even remember what I'd done. Even now, my memory of that period is hazy, and just thinking about it makes my tummy go all squibbly.

But this is, after all, a story about beginnings, and so I will recall it as best as I can. And you, dear reader, can judge for yourself what damage was done.

I can't have been more than six years old, the first time it happened.

In small North Yorkshire villages like the one I grew up in, there isn't a whole lot to do outside of putting live ferrets down your trousers. Some people attempted to outdo one another in the growing of unnecessarily large vegetables; the rest mostly drank tea and talked excessively about the weather. The bi-monthly Tupperware party was the height of the social calendar. But a small group of deviants found an outlet for their unnatural, exhibitionist urges – in Amateur Dramatics. The local players put on four shows per year. Three plays, with dubiously comedic titles like *Don't Get Your Vicars In A Twist*, and one raucous pantomime. Each ran for a week, and pretty much the entire population turned up to one show or another. The village hall was always packed with a sell-out crowd; you have no idea how badly rural Yorkshire needed cable TV in the 1980s.

The Hambleton Players Society was like a cult. You could join, but you could never leave. And once involved, under substantial pressure from fellow Thespians, you inevitably dragged your family members in, one by one.

Mum had been recruited at playschool. Whilst picking up my three-year-old sister, Gillian, she'd let slip her secret fascination, and was immediately pounced on by the woman that ran the place.

She was drafted into the chorus, which for anyone not familiar with Am-Dram is a large-ish bunch of people, mostly middle-aged women, who do group songs and dances to pad out the show. To be honest, it's where they stick the people with more enthusiasm than talent, but it's the first rung on the ladder for the newly initiated.

And so it began.

With his passion for hot beverages, Dad was an easy convert to tea-lady, whilst my little sister Gill and I spent the twice-weekly rehearsal evenings sitting at the back of the hall, colouring in.

Of course, at that age my brain was like a sponge. It still is, in some ways. Mostly in the way that it's filthy and squidgy and I keep finding bits of it in the sink. But at six years old, sitting through rehearsal after rehearsal, I rapidly memorised the entire play. During the performance, Dad, Gill and I always came to watch Mum. We got seats in the front row, as befits the family of the cast, and I would do what I'd always done in rehearsals – shout out any lines the players on stage forgot.

Quite possibly it was this disconcerting habit that got me liberated from the audience and press-ganged into the upcoming pantomime. Perhaps the higher powers thought I'd be less disruptive on stage than off?

Ha! How wrong they were.

That panto was *Mother Goose.*

I was added to the ranks of a special Children's Chorus – most likely created as a crèche for all the kids of the regular chorus, thus allowing the adults to perform their duties with no excuses. It was a tough gig. All I really remember is being taught to fight hand-to-hand, trained in weapons and explosives, and sent out into the community as a heavily-armed sleeper agent.

Although there is a slight possibility that this is an alternate reality I created to avoid acknowledging the trauma of what really happened in that group.

Which is, we were taught to dance.

See? I'll take ninja-spy school any day.

The dances we learned were each choreographed around a theme. In one we would be woodland creatures, in another, evil skeletons. Don't ask me why there were skeletons in *Mother Goose* – it's just one of those things you have to accept. What happens in panto often defies all rational explanation.

It's a bit like Vegas in that respect.

For Mum, that show formed one of the highlights of her acting career. Decades time later, Dad still loves to remind her of it. Along with the other ladies of the chorus, dressed in a canary-yellow leotard, matching tights, and yellow-feathered wings, she performed a beautifully-synchronized rendition of 'Ever So Goosey-Goosey-Goosey Gooooo-sey!'

I'm not sure it was meant to be a comedy number, but the audience certainly thought so.

As for me, as my debut approached, I began to feel an emotion I'd never experienced before: *Stage fright.*

Although young, it wasn't lost on me that everyone I'd ever known would be out there, watching me. Friends and family, bitter enemies from across the road, future wives and girlfriends – every pair of eyes from miles around would, at some point that week, be focussed on me. But at that age, you do what you're told – at least, in those days, we did. Mostly.

So I swallowed my nerves, donned my festive green streamers, and followed the rest of the kids into the spotlights. I can't remember if that first dance went well or not, because what happened next eclipsed it forever.

There was a rapid costume change between the two dances, a chaos of confusion in the dim light of the dressing room. The dances had been practised endlessly, but the quick change between them had not. We were low priority; the costume ladies had only finished sewing our various garments two days before opening night. All our costumes were on racks, and we fought to get to them, and into them, before we were due back on stage. This night was no exception. I struggled out of my woodland nymph outfit and grabbed for the shapeless black net that turned me into a skeleton. The thing was bundled over its hanger, and my panicked fingers only succeeded in knotting it further. I hauled it on anyway, desperate to get out of the dressing room, but nothing could dislodge the coat hanger sticking out of my shoulder. Time was up; I scurried through the passage behind the scenery, still tugging at my costume, well aware that I looked more like a jumble of bones than a skeleton. I arrived in the wings just in time, and was shooed onto the stage. But as I scrambled out, the protruding coat-hanger hooked into one of the other kid's costumes, dragging him along by the neck. He fought me – fought the invisible force which fastened him to me – but it was no good. The stage was a pool of inky darkness in preparation for our dance, and I was struggling just as hard to untangle myself from the opposite direction.

And then the lights came up, the cymbals crashed, and our dance began.

But we couldn't dance. Neither me, nor the poor kid I was shackled to, could do any thing more than flail our legs. We moved apart, and were pinged back together again, nearly ending up on our arses. The dance went on around us, but hopelessly out of sync, as we blundered around in the centre, bashing into other kids. There were hoots and shrieks from the audience, as they started to notice what was going on. Scattered laughter, building into a roar as more people spotted our predicament. It was like a slow-motion nightmare, from which there was no escape; we were the epicentre of a day-glow disaster.

Oh, because, did I mention? This dance was being done entirely under UV lights.

Our costumes were all black, save for the cardboard bones stitched onto them, which glowed dully. But they paled into comparison beside the incandescent star of the show: the bright white plastic coat-hanger, hooking the two of us together centre-stage, doing a merry dance all of its own.

They never asked me to be in another pantomime.

I still have nightmares about it.

And I turn forty next year.

That was my last foray into the world of acting for almost a decade. The closest I came to performing was at the village fete two years later, when I won the kids costume competition dressed as He-Man. I had a woollen mop on my head and an arsenal of tin-foil weaponry lovingly crafted by Mum. She also drew He-Man's rippling abs onto my stomach with eye-liner; over twenty years later, they remain the most convincing muscles I've ever had.

And there you have it! An insight into the vagaries of life in a remote corner of Yorkshire, together with a slightly inauspicious foreshadowing of my acting career.

Amateur dramatics had been the beginning of my tale, and I was to flirt with it several times on my path to (or not *quite* to) super-stardom. It would produce many more unforgettable moments – along with several that, try as I might, I will never *be able* to forget.

Quite a few of those came from *Mother Goose,* actually.

Including the sight of eighteen-stone (250lbs) Mr Barry – an enormous bloke by anyone's standards, and twice as hairy – prancing around in fishnet tights, pink wings and a sparkly tutu, singing (rather campy), "It's hard to be a fairy when you're 40…"

I think that scarred me for life.

Especially as I went to school in the village, and Mr Barry was the headmaster.

School Daze

As this is a story of beginnings, why don't we do a brief recap of my school life?

Sorry, that's a rhetorical question, given that this book is already written. What I should have said is, 'I'm about to force you to read a brief recap of my school life.'

But honestly, feel free to skip ahead. I'll never even know.

I started out at Hambleton Primary School, a tiny place that had supplemented its bricks and mortar classrooms with Portacabins. In these, I was to spend most of my days playing with stickle-bricks and Lego; it was a delightfully innocent time. The honeymoon period ended when I found myself on the wrong side of the school gang. We can't have been more than six or seven years old, but pack mentality had obviously started to assert itself. I remember weeks when I was definitely *in* the gang, and weeks when I was decidedly *out*. It was all down to some kid called Mathew, for no reason I could understand. After asking him to explain why the in/out decision was solely his, and what he based his choices on, I found myself permanently out. Maybe he saw my questions as a challenge?

He certainly wasn't pleased about it.

Under Mathew's direction, the gang formed a line in the playground, backing me up against a high brick wall in the middle – and threw stones at me. They were only small stones, but sharp-edged, and there were a lot more of them than there was of me. I protected myself from the stinging hail as best I could, but then something snapped. I reached down and grabbed the first thing that came to hand – it speaks volumes about the safety standards of the school that this was half a brick – and launched it at my principle adversary.

My aim was true.

Mathew was taken to hospital to have his face rebuilt, and if he ever came back to that school, I never saw it. I didn't see much of anything, as I began a months-long stint of punishment for my actions, forced to spend every playtime and mealtime sitting on my own in the entrance hall. Eventually Mum got wind of this, decreed it unfair, and had some kind of battle of wills with the teachers. Believing they had it in for me, she pulled me out of that school and sent me to the Catholic school in the next town over. Thus, my first attempt at education didn't go entirely as planned.

It wasn't all bad, though. I have distinct memories of a homework assignment where the teacher wrote a bunch of words on the blackboard. I copied them out and handed them in, only to receive a bollocking for not understanding the assignment. Apparently we'd been meant to write a *story containing* those words. This concept, when explained, excited me so much that I went home that afternoon and wrote a story about time-travel that blew the staff away. As a reward they gave me a whole day off classes, sending me out onto the playground. A team of painters had been hired to create games for us, and I got to be their model. I hop-scotched, and they drew the hop-scotch around me. I jumped as high as I could on the wall, and where I touched became the centre of concentric circles. An alphabet snake was created following my path and gait... funny. I wonder if it's all still there? That paint lasts a damn long time. It was probably made of lead and arsenic.

My spell in Brayton Roman Catholic Primary School was a

much happier one.

It was also my first encounter with the pervasive myth that wet grass is somehow dangerous. That school was blessed with a gigantic playing field, a hundred times bigger than the school itself. Acres and acres of shimmering green grass; it went on forever, a child's idea of heaven. But we were never allowed on it. If the grass was wet – a condition which was decided by the teacher on duty – it was forbidden. Now, this was North Yorkshire. It rains three-hundred days a year up there. The only time the grass wasn't wet from either recent precipitation or nightly dew, was a few weeks over midsummer – during the school holidays! Looking back, I think this perma-wet grass was really a conspiracy to keep us in check. I mean, if we'd all gotten out onto that vast expanse of grass at the same time, who knows if we'd ever come back?

There was also a climbing frame – an epic structure, as I remember, though that image may be tinged with reverence for an object simultaneously as near as the school gate, yet as far away as the dark side of the moon. Clearly, climbing frames are extremely hazardous activities. We only got to go on the grass a handful of times in my years there; I never once set foot on that climbing frame.

My sister Gill began her schooling at Brayton, though tragically the infants (her) and the juniors (me) were segregated, even having our own playgrounds. We'd become inseparable at home, and were always scheming sneaky ways to hang out at school. We shared a bedroom, decorated half in Care Bears wallpaper, and half in Superman. We spent most of our time playing with Star Wars and Transformers toys – I think I corrupted Gill away from girly games quite early on. She did have an impressive collection of My Little Ponies, complete with their Show Stable, but she rarely got chance to play with them. I did concede to watching the original My Little Pony movie with her. It featured a brilliant villain in the form of 'The Smooze' – an unstoppable purple liquid that covered everything, and sang about it the whole time! Kind of like global warming, only with a sense of humour and lots of eyeballs. From then on, every time we played with her ponies, she'd beg me, "Please Tony, don't make The Smooze come!" of course, I'd promise not to. Until the ponies were all unpacked, at which point I'd cry: "Oh no! Gill – it's The Smooze!"

Poor girl – it terrified her so much, I think if I called that out now, she'd still pee herself. The onset of The Smooze forced all the ponies to make a rapid dash for cover in the Show Stable. At which point I'd say, "Well, seeing as how they're all packed away now, we might as well play Transformers..."

We fought a lot. Inevitably, at three years older, I was her main antagonist. But I also defended her aggressively. Chief amongst her memories of that period is one where she'd been chased by several older kids, and they'd caught her and tied her up to a lamppost. I must have been out looking for her, and when I found the kids I flew at them with a vengeance, chasing them down the road with a stick. Then I came back to console Gill – only, finding her predicament suddenly hilarious, I decided to leave her tied up...

It was the first thing she mentioned, when I told her I was collecting stories for this book. I've a feeling she's never quite forgiven me for it.

My own scuffles with older kids in the village sort of blend in together, except for one. It happened in an area widely known as 'The spooky place': an abandoned barn behind a crumbling, ivy-clad brick wall. My best friend Adam and I had made several daring raids into the overgrown interior; we counted them amongst our most high-risk missions. Even being there meant we were more than twice as far from home as we were allowed; the only reason we hadn't been expressly forbidden from exploring the structure was because none of our parents knew it existed. The Spooky Place was an area of myth amongst the kids, and Adam and I were at our most daring when we ventured into those creepy confines. Unfortunately, older kids liked to hang out in there sometimes, and a group of them caught us once. They quickly stripped us of our bravery charms, which for me meant my favourite teddy bear. Laughing, the lads threw the bear to each other over my head, before tiring of the game and pitching him up onto the rusting roof of the barn. Leaving me in tears, inconsolable, the older kids left, and I made my sorrowful way back home. Thus, I received the lesson early on, that exploring new territory could have unexpected consequences. Obviously I didn't learn from it, but I never claimed to be smart.

In a delightful twist of humanity, a couple of days later there was a knock at our front door. There on our doorstep, shaking, bruised and covered in dirt and cuts, was one of the kids from the group that had tormented us. He held out my teddy bear, filthy and soggy but otherwise intact, and scarpered when Mum thanked him. I found out later that, feeling bad for what his friends had done, he'd gone alone into The Spooky Place and climbed onto the roof of the barn. The whole structure had collapsed under him, and he'd emerged unscathed only by the miracle that protects kids until they're old enough to know better. It was a fantastic example to me that decency exists even in the people you least expect it.

But my favourite episode from that time was convincing Gill that I was magic.

We both loved these tiny ice-lollies made of frozen milk. Mini-Milks, they were called, and as a special treat, we were allowed one each when the ice cream van came around. We'd hear that familiar, haunting melody, and rush to the bedroom window. Sure enough, the ice cream van hove into view on the street below. "Wait here," I told Gill, "I'm going to demonstrate my special powers. You keep watching out the window. I'm going to go to that van and buy us a Mini-Milk each – but I'm going to turn invisible. You won't be able to see me at all!"

Gill stared out of the window, and was stunned when I returned a few minutes later with a pair of Mini-Milks. She hadn't even seen me leave the house.

I displayed this ability several times more, before losing interest in magic and moving on.

More than fifteen years later, I was having a drink with Gill when she dredged up this memory. "I never figured out how you did it," she admitted.

"Oh, it was easy," I told her. "I went shopping with Mum, and bought a whole box of Mini-Milks. I was only fetching them from the freezer."

Her jaw dropped open. "Oh my God!" she said. "All this time... I... I honestly believed you were magic!"

Highs and Lows

Our time in the sleepy village of Hambleton came to an end when I was nine.

I've written elsewhere about the disastrous transition from Yorkshire to Lancashire, so all I'll say is that the kids in our new county were mean in a way we'd never experienced before. Both Gill and I were heavily picked on, by the kids in our village as well as those at our new school. Due to a discrepancy in school ages between the two counties, I was tested and ended up skipping a year of primary school, becoming the youngest and smallest in a class of intimidating strangers. After only one year there, I followed this class to the much bigger High School, where instead of bonding with my erstwhile classmates, I became the whipping boy for the entire first year.

Was it my fault? I certainly had a penchant for screwing up, giving my detractors all the ammunition they needed.

Invited to another kid's birthday party, I found myself in the middle of the park, desperate for a pee. I've never been that great at holding myself, but I was way too meek to ask someone else's parents for help. I'd have been fine, except I was too slow getting off a slide; the kid behind me slid down and crashed into me, and as we tumbled to the ground I felt myself letting go…

The spreading wet patch on my jeans was just small enough for me to hide with my hands. Before long we were all in the car, heading back to the birthday boy's house.

"Can anyone smell piss?" one of the other kids said.

I shrugged – without moving my hands from my lap.

Get back. Get to the bathroom. Soak myself with water. Complain about the taps.

It was my mantra, and all that was keeping the panic down.

I made it as far as the front door, making sure I was walking well ahead of everyone else. This meant I reached the door first, and as I reached up for the handle I inadvertently revealed the stain for all to see.

"Look! Slater's pissed himself!"

It took me quite a while to live that one down.

In fact, I never really did – just, newer embarrassments took over as the source of taunting. For a little while it was the sudden rampant growth of hair on the side of my face. Strange, eh, the things kids find to pick on?

"Waheey! Check out Slater's side-ies!"

"No WAY! It's Sideburn Slater!"

Looking back, it's hard to see why this would even bother me. I mean, in the grand scheme of things to be teased about, this must be the least hurtful. But I'd been steadily working my way back from the brink of pariah – or so I thought. I wasn't going to let my unruly hairline get in the way. I went home and enlisted Mum's help to completely obliterate the errant facial hair.

I showed up the next day with a secret inner-grin. I knew they'd be waiting for me... and now they had nothing to go on. I couldn't wait to see their faces!

"There he is!" I heard the cry. "How's the side-ies, Slater?"

I just shrugged, and let them notice in their own time.

"Fuckin' 'ell! He's shaved 'em off! What did you use, Slater, your Mum's Ladyshave?"

"Urrrr... no? I used scissors..."

"LADY-SHAVE! Check it out, Slater used a Ladyshave to shave his side-ies!"

"No, really, I just used —"

"LADY-SHAVE! Nice work, *Ladyshave.*"

And that was my nickname for the next two years.

I didn't even know what a Lady-Shave *was*. I doubt Mum did, either, but that didn't make one iota of difference.

"How was school?" she'd ask, and I'd respond with the ubiquitous, "Fine."

I mean, at thirteen years old, how do you tell your mum you're being victimised for allegedly stealing her feminine grooming products?

Thirteen was an awkward year for me.

Fourteen, on the other hand was positively tragic.

A school trip had been organised to Paris, France, and for once my folks were in the position to afford it; Dad's job was doing well, and he was now running a whole office full of people in Sale, near Manchester. The school trip to Paris was going to be epic. I could hardly believe I was going. It says something for my optimistic personality that, even though I was hating every minute of the six daily hours I had to spend at school, I still couldn't wait for the trip. Maybe that was an indicator of just how exciting travel would become for me later on? It represented... I don't know. Escapism? The possibility for re-invention? No matter what kind of educational lean the teachers tried to put on it, this was a holiday. And I'd always secretly believed that, if the kids at school ever got to know the real me, it would be a whole new ballgame.

Paris would be incredible!

And it was.

Apart from getting tear-gassed by a gang of French youths, but no-one could have seen that coming. Looking back, I can't imagine any modern school group would be allowed to find themselves lost at night in some random backstreets of Paris, where we must have inadvertently wandered into the wrong kind of neighbourhood. Still, what doesn't kill you makes you stronger, right? It damn near killed one of the boys in our group, as he had terrible asthma and got engulfed in the cloud spilling out of the grenade thrown at us. But we dragged him clear and calmed him down, by which point our assailants were long gone.

Which was probably for the best, as a vengeful rampage through the backstreets of Paris by a group of hopelessly lost fourteen-year-old lads was never going to end well.

I've a feeling that evening's activities never made it onto the report sheet provided to parents.

During our visit to *Notre Dame* Cathedral, I slipped away with another lad called Rick. We found a tiny shop in a back alley, and managed to buy six cans of beer each. We stashed the ice-cold cans, straight from the fridge, in our jacket sleeves, and headed back to re-join the school group.

Only to find – with horror – that instead of getting back on the bus, and returning to the hotel, we were walking along the banks of the Seine to take a tour around the *Palais De Justice*. Within minutes, both Rick and I were shaking. Who knew that keeping icy cold cans in your armpits could make you hyperventilate?

When we finally made it back to the hotel, the now warm beers were passed around an illicit gathering in one of the larger rooms. Rick and I were hailed like conquering heroes. For a few fleeting moments, I was *cool.*

But when we got back to school, nothing had changed.

It didn't help that I developed possibly the worst case of acne the world has ever seen. Even my scabs had scabs, affecting not just my face but my back and chest, and lasting for three of the most miserable years of my life.

The acne was so severe that Mum took me to the doctor, and he proscribed a new drug called 'Roaccutane'. It was powerful but experimental, and I agreed to submit to a battery of blood tests every few weeks. I didn't care – even being phobic about needles didn't deter me. I hated that acne more than anything in my life, before or since, and I was determined to be free of it. The side-effects were surprisingly vicious, but I endured them; nosebleeds that never ended, causing me to miss several days of school simply because the amount of blood streaming from my nose made Mum want to take me to the ER. I suffered all sorts of minor ailments, but the most debilitating was the joint pain. *Arthralgia,* in doctor-speak, it began in my knees, making walking so painful that I crabbed my way along walls, using doorframes, window ledges and bannisters to take the pressure off my legs. At home I got around by bracing my arms against the walls and furniture – at least until the pain spread to my wrists. As anyone who's used crutches will know, your arms aren't meant to support your bodyweight. My wrists were the weakest link in a dramatically over-stressed chain, and they couldn't take the pressure. As my tally of complaints added up, my school days lost 'through illness' became substantial. Several times I was sent home by teachers, concerned when my nose bled uncontrollably, or after observing me making my agonising, tearful way down a long corridor. For me, the pain paled into comparison when compared to the embarrassment; take any fifteen-year-old lad into school with both wrists bandaged up, and just see how much shit he gets!

Eventually I graduated, against the odds, and had managed to retain my straight 'A' average in spite of the less than ideal situation. My doctor decided to discontinue the Roaccutane, but the drug had done its work. The last of my acne dried up practically overnight. At the school graduation ceremony, I was awarded the 'Hilda Mogden Memorial Shield for Strength in Adversity'. I guess it was an award they'd had knocking around for kids who lost their parents to cancer or something, and I felt like a fraud when they called me up to accept it. I'd done nothing special; my problems were all of my own doing, both in accepting the experimental drug and in failing to convince the other kids that I was really an okay guy.

I like to think that the teachers, who'd witnessed my journey first-hand, had given me the shield to acknowledge the incessant bullying I'd had to cope with, rather than out of sympathy for the side-effects of a drug I'd carried on taking regardless.

The award did little to lift the veil of depression I was under, but that was okay; I had my family for that. Always close, my parents and my sister had become my best friends. My home life was a beautiful, shining beacon to ward away the darkness of my time at school.

Interestingly enough, depression was later discovered to be a major side-effect of Roaccutane. The drug was withdrawn from sale in the US, pending a large number of law suits from patients and their parents. It's still available on prescription in the UK, but has been linked to over twenty teen suicides in the last few years.

Say it with me, now: *Drugs are bad, m'kay?*

Friends With Benefits

I'm a big believer that people come into our lives when we need them the most. Dave, an obese kid from high school, had come into my life when I needed a bulwark against the relentless onslaught of bullying. He took a lot of the flak, as he was – sorry Dave – a rather large target. He was also one of the best friends I ever had, and without him I seriously doubt I'd have survived high school.

It all changed after graduation – which in the UK, happens at 16 years old. From there, roughly half the kids carried on to college, a completely separate institution and a stepping stone to university.

College offered significantly more freedom, allowing us to choose the subjects we wanted to study, and placing the responsibility for going to classes in our own hands. This is where Dave and I diverged, as our subjects, and thus our timetables, differed completely. Mostly because I didn't have a clue what I wanted to do with my life!

I still don't, as it happens.

The only lesson we shared was English Language. Concentrated into one uber-lecture, stretching for three hours on a Monday morning, we'd assumed it would be an extension of the creative writing we'd both excelled at in school. It was not to be. English Language was (apparently) the study *of* language; how it evolved over time, its rules and morphology, and other shit so mind-numbingly boring I can't even bring myself to spell it out. Sitting through three consecutive hours of it should have been outlawed by the Geneva Convention.

Luckily, college provided a nifty solution to this: self study. Dave and I convinced the teacher (a walking skeleton who must have been at least a hundred years old) that we needed time in the library to research our various projects. What we actually did is drove to Blackpool in the tiny yellow car he'd just learned to drive, and spent our lesson time in bars and amusement arcades.

Consequently, we were both kicked out of English Language towards the end of our second year, and given a temporary tutor to oversee our final coursework. I've always found coursework and exams quite easy, so completed my thesis in a week, and walked out of the exam with an hour left on the clock.

A few months afterwards, I met the teacher who'd kicked me out of class, in a bookshop of all places. She glared at me, and grudgingly admitted, "You covered yourself in glory." – like it was an accusation! I just nodded my thanks, because making her admit that my score of 99% was theoretically impossible seemed a bit harsh.

At a time when my friendship with Dave was leading me into an increasingly sedentary lifestyle, a new lad moved into our tiny village. Pete hadn't come far; his parents had relocated from a small town a few miles away. But this still cut him off from all his old friends, and rather than trying to fight his way into existing cliques, it was much easier for him to befriend the other new kid – which, despite having lived there for six years at that point, was me.

Pete was restless, athletic, and competitive by nature – the perfect antidote to the exercise-free-zone I'd been living in.

This new friendship coincided with the start of college, and the introduction of 'free periods' into our timetables. Dave preferred sitting in the cafeteria, playing cards, and we did that quite a bit – but more often than not, Pete convinced me to walk almost an hour across town to the sports centre, hire a badminton court, and play as many games as we could fit in before starting the hike back.

It was the single best thing that could have happened to me at that point.

Even though I was crap at badminton.

Pete also led me into my lifelong fascination with kung fu.

He'd discovered a local class, and blatantly started taking lessons without telling me so that he'd be better than me when I joined. He needn't have bothered; I was never any good at it. I loved it, though.

Our instructor, or *Sifu,* was another Dave – but he was a real diamond in the rough. His gruelling regimen of push-ups (on our knuckles, on the hard wooden floor) and sit-ups, were the first intentional exercise I'd ever done. *Sifu* Dave worked us hard, telling us, "Last ten press-ups!" – then after we'd done them, saying, "I lied! Ten more!" He made me work harder than I'd ever believed possible.

Once, for a demonstration, he brought me to the front of the class and kicked me in the head.

"How tall are you?" he asked me.

"Urr... about six foot," I replied.

"You see?" he told the class. "I'm only five-nine, but I've got a six-foot kick!" And he kicked me in the head again to prove it.

And once, after getting heavily stoned before the lesson, he followed the regular pattern of push-ups with, "Right, everyone lie down on the floor."

We all scrambled to comply, mentally bracing ourselves for another round of sit-ups, as he lay down in front of us.

"And... just chill out," he told us. And promptly fell asleep.

Kung fu gave me a new outlet, and a new circle of friends. Although, as locals born and bred, the others always treated me with a certain wariness. Mum had worked hard to make sure neither Gill or me picked up strong accents as children, and always used correct pronunciation. This caused the rest of the kung fu crowd much hilarity.

"E talks dead propa, 'im," said Corin, one of the few girls in the class. "Dun't 'e talk dead propa?"

There was a chorus of "Aye"s and "Arr"s.

Apparently I was studying kung fu with a bunch of pirates. Who knew?

Pete was also a fan of drinking. At 16 years old, it was a natural desire. I've always looked older than I am, and had already discovered that I could get served in almost any bar, no questions asked. With Pete's encouragement we began clubbing (by which I mean, dancing in nightclubs, not bashing baby seals). One morning I woke up with a sore nose. It got worse over the coming days, so I went to the doctor, who pronounced it broken. I couldn't figure out what had happened, so I called Pete.

"Shit!" he said, when I told him. "How did you break it?"

"Dunno. That's why I'm asking you!"

"Ohhh… did I do it last week, while we were dancing to 'Kung Fu Fighting'?"

"Yeah, probably…"

The intersection of these two interests was always a volatile one.

On another night out in Preston, we invited the whole kung fu class. After several drinks, we were explaining to one of the younger lads how impressed women were by our ability to do the splits. Taking our advice to heart, he immediately pushed his way onto the packed dance floor. Approaching a pretty girl from behind, he tapped her on the shoulder. As she turned to look at him, he performed his party trick – spinning around and dropping straight into a full splits from standing. Two people walking behind him tripped over his violently outstretched back leg, sending their drinks flying into the crowd. His front leg took out two of the girl's friends, felling them like an axe-blow to the knees. Chaos spread around him as people collapsed onto each other like dominoes… Needless to say, it was around this time that Pete and I legged it.

The next great friendship to enter my life was with a Danish lad called Anders. We worked together at the Games Workshop in Preston. It was a dream job – we sold an infinite variety of toy soldiers, and got paid to paint them and play games with them. What more could a boy want? Anders had relocated from Denmark for the opportunity.

As he was far from home, living in a tiny rented flat in the centre of Preston, my parents invited him to spend that Christmas with us. We had a great time, especially Gill, who was smitten by this charismatic, blue-eyed stranger.

Eager to impress, she played the piano for him. We'd both taken lessons, but I'd given up early, acknowledging that Gill had inherited both our shares of musical talent. Anders spent a fascinating Christmas morning drunkenly trying to convince my sister that the keys on Danish pianos went up to 'H'.

His Danishness came out in the most amusing ways. His command of English was probably better than mine, but he couldn't pronounce the letter 'V'. It's not a letter that gets used a lot in casual conversation, and I only noticed because our drink of choice at the time – because it was the cheapest – was Virgin Vodka.

Whilst working together at Games Workshop, we found ourselves doing a stock-take. Anders was calling out the products, and how many of them we had left on the shelves, and I was frantically writing it all down. We'd finished tallying up the Elves, and moved along to the next shelf. Anders crouched down to get a closer look at the packaging.

"Wampire."

"A… I'm sorry, *what?*"

"Wampire."

I repressed a snigger. "Okay, how many… Vampires… have we got?"

"Seven."

"Okay. Next?"

"Wampire Lord."

I came close to pissing myself in public for the second time in my life, as I realised that the next entire product line was vampires, and Anders was going to read out every single one of them.

He rarely talked about Denmark, though. To me it sounded like a mystical and exciting place; I couldn't believe anyone would voluntarily leave it for Preston in Lancashire, which I considered to be the armpit of the UK. I asked him about it once.

"So, what the hell made you want to come all this way just to work at Games Workshop?"

"Easy!" Anders struck a heroic pose. "My ancestors were Wikings!"

"Ah… you mean, Vikings?"

"Yes! So you see, it makes perfect sense for me to come to your country, study your war-games, take your English money and steal your women!"

"Um, Anders… you know we work in a toy shop, right?"

Drama Queen

It was around this time that the tentacles of amateur dramatics began to envelop me once more. Tentative at first, they soon wrapped me around and sucked on me like... I'm sorry, I'm not sure where I'm going with that metaphor.

Let's just say that, once again, it was Mum's fault.

Pete was most definitely *not* a Thespian. In fact, the merest suggestion that he was would probably have resulted in a punch in the face.

Dave, on the other hand, was more questionable. He'd been known to prance.

As for Anders... I don't think that word was in his Wocabulary.

But for me, the change had come.

Mum never mentioned how they'd got to her. 'Helping out' is usually the gateway drug; you start by offering to sew a few costumes, and before you know it you're up on stage in a frilly dress singing 'Hello Dolly'.

I should state for the record that neither of those things ever happened to me.

But following the usual progression of such things, Mum lured Gill into the fold, and the pair of them became hopelessly enmeshed in rehearsals for the upcoming musical production of *Brigadoon.*

At this stage I was in no danger of getting involved. I could neither sing nor dance (Pete had famously described my best moves as resembling a centipede with fifty broken legs), and I had all the musical inclination of a dead aardvark. Inevitably though, I had to go and watch at least one performance.

If you're not familiar with the story, it follows two American tourists hiking in the Scottish highlands who get hopelessly lost, and stumble upon the mysterious village of Brigadoon. One of them falls in love with the place's quirky charm, and literally in love with a beautiful girl – only to be let in on the secret that Brigadoon only appears for one day in every 100 years. He is given the choice to stay, or to leave – in either case, forever. It's a beguiling tale of love's triumph over magic, and in this case the hero Tommy was played to perfection by local legend John Sangster.

But that's not what entranced me.

No, what caught my attention was the sheer quantity of cute girls who joined Mum and Gill in the chorus, wearing kilts and doing a dance over crossed swords. My recollections of Am Dram began and ended with Mum in her yellow goose costume and Mr Barry in his fishnets. The notion that attractive young women would be involved in such shenanigans had never occurred to me.

Suddenly, my imagination was in overdrive.

You have to remember that, in addition to the usual mix of teenage hormones, there was the utter hopelessness of my romantic prospects. I was now seventeen, an age at which a significant portion of the UK population is already pregnant – and I'd never been kissed. No girl had looked at me without scorn since before puberty…

Maybe this was my chance?

It was perhaps not the most solid of motivations for setting the course of my life.

But those of you who know me from previous books will appreciate one very important factor which comes into play here: I'm an idiot.

So when Mum was asked to relay an offer to me, of a small role in the upcoming play, the decision was completely out of my hands.

That is how I found myself treading the squeaky boards at St Ambrose Church Hall in Leyland, dressed in brown slacks and an old tweed coat from a charity shop. I was playing the character of young *Freddy Beanstock,* in a painfully old and unfashionable play called *Hobson's Choice.*

One of my fellow players was a man called Alan Green. A wiry little bloke about my dad's age, he skittered around the rehearsal room with a mischievous grin, cracking jokes at a speed most professional comedians would envy. Playing *Doctor Macfarlane,* a character described as a 'domineering Scotchman of fifty', he came in late to the process. He only had one scene, right at the end of the play, yet he carried the entire show with it. Determined to save the lead character *Mr Hobson* from a slow death by alcoholism, Alan's doctor ratcheted up his Scotch brogue at the same rate as his temper. By mid-way through his scene, he was noo'ing and nae'ing with such fiery fervency that you had to concentrate pretty hard just to figure out what he was saying. And then he came to a line which has stuck forever in my memory.

"Mister Hobson," he declared, "Ah judge yer daughter's not the sort ta
want the truth wrapped aroond wi' a feather-bed for fear it hits her hard."

I was drinking coffee at the time, and I choked on it, spraying the liquid in as wide a circle as humanly possible. All eyes shifted to me, mostly out of concern that I'd had some kind of seizure.

The director rolled his eyes at me, waved his hand, and Alan glanced down at the script in his hand.

"Wrapped 'roond wi' a feather bed," he repeated, "For fear it 'its 'er 'ard..."

And that was it. The entire cast collapsed in gales of laughter, including Alan, up on stage.

What I'd heard – and what everyone else now heard – was unmistakable. Alan's strident Scottish accent stripped most of the leading 'h's from his words. The result?

"For fear 'er tits are hard."

It was perfect.

It wasn't until the following rehearsal that we realised something else; we were all going to have to stand on stage every night, radiating concern and anxiety, waiting for him to deliver this line, whilst trying to keep our faces straight.

It was impossible.

Mostly because Alan made damn sure it was.

He was a veteran of the am-dram scene, and he squeezed that line for every penny. It was delivered so fast, I don't think our audiences ever figured out why the entire cast burst into hysterical giggles halfway through that final, emotional act.

Whereas I took to the stage clad in a delightful brown-on-brown ensemble depressingly appropriate for the period, my beautiful co-star Crystal, playing Freddy's fiancé, got two changes of outfit. A drab shop-girl dress was worn for most of the play, but in preparation for her sister's wedding she was required to don her 'Sunday Best'. This was a rather more elaborate satin dress with a very prominent bustle, which had to be attached separately. It's not hard to guess my reaction to this; of course I hid the bustle at every opportunity, and when she came storming up to me demanding to know where it was, I'd say, "But I thought you were wearing it…"

This earned me a slap on no few occasions, but our good-natured horseplay was one of my sweetest experiences to date. Of course, her pranks on me were every bit as subtle.

In one scene, we all sat in Mr Hobson's parlour, sipping tea. The tea was brought fresh from the kitchen at the back of the church hall, and I'd begged the volunteers to put two sugars in mine. They forgot on the opening night, but I choked the bitter beverage down and pleaded with them afterwards to make a note of it somewhere.

The following night, my tea was sweetened to perfection, and it actually helped me to relax into character, swigging the brew as though there wasn't over a hundred upturned faces just beyond the lights, watching my every movement.

On the third night, I mentally crossed my fingers when we reached that scene and took a sip. I gagged on the sudden sweetness, covering my reaction with a cough, and shot a look at Crystal. Her eyes twinkled with mischief as she stared back at me. Damn her! It was her character's job to bring the tea on to stage for us, and she'd spiked it. She must have put at least twelve sugars in there. And unlike the rest of the cast, I had to drink the whole thing.

The next night it was worse.

By the time our final performance rolled around, I tipped the cup and a solid cake of sugar fell out and hit me in the face. From the noise Crystal made I hope she was wearing incontinence panties under that bustle, because she was absolutely pissing herself.

Crystal was the first girl I fell in love with. I mean, I'd fancied loads of girls at school, but none of them would piss on me if I was on fire, so I didn't think they counted. But here was a stunning young woman who would do *way* more than piss on me. Okay, that came out wrong. What I mean is, she was prepared to talk to me – she had to, actually, as the script kind of made it essential.

It is entirely possible that being cast opposite such an attractive girl was the single strongest influence behind my decision to become an actor. I mean, it all made sense; if girls wouldn't talk to me normally, all I had to do is become an actor, and they'd have no choice!

For the first time, this infatuation inspired a piece of ball-shrivellingly bad poetry – the first of many, which naturally I will be sharing with you throughout this book.

NO! It's okay! I'm only messing with you.

No-one needs to read that stuff.

Not *ever*.

In fact, it doesn't even exist anymore.

Anywhere.

So don't even bother looking.

The end of Hobson's Choice plunged me into the lowest of lows. It had been a ridiculous amount of time and effort committed to prepare for a run of less than a week, but such is the case with amateur shows. Next week there would be something else on in that church hall – Morris Dancing perhaps, or a flower festival. But those months of rehearsals had been so much fun. I'd met people from entirely different circles, and I'd been free to reinvent myself in their presence. I'd been part of a team, striving towards a common goal, helping and supporting each other along the way, but not afraid to muck around and break a few rules in the name of enjoyment. I still can't decide if I was a natural extrovert that was bullied into introversion, or a natural introvert whose only defence was clowning around to draw attention in a way I could control. I guess it doesn't really matter. What did matter, at that time, was just how utterly, pant-wettingly terrified I was of stepping out of the wings and onto that stage. I swear my life flashed before my eyes on several occasions. And yet, being out there with everyone watching, feeling their eyes on me and their reactions to my antics, gave me a greater high than any drug I've ever known. It was euphoric, ecstatic, and emotionally overwhelming. I bloody loved it.

After each performance, the high stayed with me for hours. I felt like I was soaring, or glowing; like people on the street outside would point to me and whisper to each other in awe. In pure biological terms it was an adrenaline rush, but one that sustained me all throughout the show and for ages afterwards – no forty-second roller-coaster ride could ever come close.

Consequently, the crash, when it came, was severe.

I didn't help that Crystal wasn't interested in me.

I spent a week in my bedroom, and felt like all possibility of joy had been exterminated from the universe.

Hopelessly addicted to the surge of emotion I'd felt, and devastated by the prospect of a life without it, I made a choice that seemed at the time to be a complete no-brainer.

I decided to become an actor.

No matter what it took, I would dedicate my entire life to the pursuit of that singular, exquisite pleasure. Because without it, there was nothing.

I was going to become famous.

Now all I had to do was tell my parents…

The Beginning

My parents supported this snap decision wholeheartedly.

I've said it before, and I'll say it again: I owe them everything.

Without their constant help and encouragement – to say nothing of regular cash injections – I wouldn't be where I am today.

I also wouldn't be where I'm not, only for entirely different reasons. If you see what I mean.

No? Okay, that was a bit obscure.

What I mean is, I never would have had the chance to try acting at all were it not for their belief in me. Admittedly, that belief was somewhat misplaced, as I ended up jacking it all in and buggering off around the world, but they even supported me in *that*. Amazing, eh?

Mum and Dad – thank-you very much indeed.

Oh, and if you're reading this... can I borrow a tenner?

With my mind made up, a certain weight was lifted from me. This was because I was entering a stage at college where university applications are submitted. Actually, I was nearing the end of that phase – and I still hadn't picked which universities to apply to.

Or what subjects I was applying to study...

It has been noted that I'm not the most organised of people. Or the most decisive.

Now, suddenly, the problem was taken out of my hands.

Under the 'UCAS' system, I was allowed to make six applications. It wasn't hard to narrow down the field; as luck would have it, only six acting courses were eligible. The big name schools, like RADA (Royal Academy of Dramatic Art) and LAMDA (London... Accumulates Many Dying Aardvarks?) – all considered themselves way above the public system, and had appropriately far-fetched price tags. I needed a course that was pure acting, as the million-and-one 'drama' degrees out there lead to a career in teaching drama degrees, and not much else.

The acting industry, at least in the UK, is a closed shop. The only way to gain entry is by attaining membership of Equity, the British actors' union. Perversely, the only way to become a member of Equity is to work professionally as an actor. It's a tricky little situation that effectively screws all but the most intrepid before they've even left the starting blocks. But there is one chink in this otherwise impenetrable façade; Equity Student membership. Enrolment on a suitably accredited acting course allows one to apply for this, and graduating allows for conversion from student to full member status. This was the route I discovered, and the only one realistically available to me. Hence, the limitation of my choices; if I wanted the government to pay my tuition fees (a thing that was standard at that time, except for those attending special institutions, like Oxford and Cambridge) – there were precisely six options.

I applied for all of them, safe in the knowledge that at least one of them was bound to come through. Because I *was* going to be an actor, damn it! No matter what the statistics said. They weren't pretty, by the way. I'd come across these nuggets during my research, only they weren't filled with the Colonel's chicken – they were deep-fried dog turds dipped in misery.

Apparently, 92% of all actors in the UK were out of work at any one time, and of those lucky enough, or tenacious enough, to achieve Equity membership – more than half of them earned less than £6,000 per year. Put in perspective, that's about £1,000 below the minimum wage for the era – barely enough to eat, much less pay the kind of rent required to live in London, where almost all the work is.

It wasn't the most promising news, but I didn't let it bother me.

I'd always felt that there was something different inside me, some piece of raw determination that would see me through in spite of the odds. In fact, the odds made me hopeful; surely by discouraging others, they would narrow the field for me?

And I would triumph.

Because I was magic.

So, with that problem solved, there was one other matter to attend to.

Auditions!

That's what I'd be facing – assuming the various institutions let me get that far.

And to date, my entire body of acting experience comprised a handful of lines as Mr Freddy Beanstock, and getting tangled in that bloody coat-hanger.

I think it's fair to say, I was playing catch-up.

There would be other hungry souls fighting me for a place on those courses – hundreds of the buggers, I imagined – and it was hard to imagine anyone starting out with less expertise.

I needed some practice, and I needed it quick.

I needed to get on TV.

Now, this wasn't as impossible as it sounds. I'd heard rumours that there were agencies out there, that supplied untrained people for crowd scenes. I'd seen adverts in newspapers for 'TV Extras' – usually right next to the ads for 'Visiting Massage Services' and 'Escorts For Hire'. I'd been tempted to apply, but I didn't think Mum would approve of me becoming a prostitute.

I figured that any agency advertising in the paper would be inundated with applications from glory seekers just like me. It didn't seem likely to result in actual TV work. So I accessed my meagre store of initiative, pulled out a pen, and wrote a letter.

I know, right? A letter! In my best handwriting, too. If that doesn't date this book, nothing will.

I wrote to the BBC, as they owned two of the four channels currently available on television. The funny thing is, it never even occurred to me that they wouldn't write back. I mean, that's how it works, right? Or how it used to work. You write a letter, and someone else responds. In this case the later was addressed 'To Whom It May Concern', but by pure chance – or perhaps the actions of whatever power it is that watches over me – it found its way into the hands of someone who *was* concerned.

A week later I had my response. I'd asked for the contact details of the company that supplied the 'extras' for their shows; accompanying my reply was a document so precious that I still have it. It was a four-page long print out of all the legitimate agencies that employed 'Walk-On and Supporting Artists' in the UK. Fate definitely shone on me that day. In later months and years I was to photocopy this list and give it to dozens of people. To many more, I recommended writing to the BBC and requesting it for themselves, but of those who got back to me, not a one had ever been sent such a list. "We apologise, but we are not at liberty to disclose those details," was the standard response. I don't know if I was the last in a long line of hopefuls to be sent that list, or if it had never left BBC Headquarters before. Hell, maybe someone got in trouble just for posting it out?

Regardless. With the list in hand, and all those glorious phone numbers, I wasted no time in calling every single one of them.

That's how I wound up on the books of *Pan Artists,* the premier Supporting Artist agency in the north of England. Pan was run by Dorothy and Wendy, a mother-daughter tag-team. They were once described to me as, "a pair of middle-aged women, sitting chain-smoking in the spare bedroom of their flat in Manchester." I can't verify this opinion, however, as I never met them. Our business was conducted entirely over the phone, except for my payment, which I received by cheques in the mail.

To me, Pan Artists will forever remain a mystery; a disembodied female voice, polite, husky, and straight to the point. I guess time is money when the BBC need you to find 100 people for a crowd scene by tomorrow morning. Most of our calls consisted of only one sentence from each of us; I don't think a single one of them lasted more than thirty seconds.

I worked for Pan Artists for the best part of a decade.

From the forty-odd agencies I'd called, many had been regional, only working in their immediate vicinity. Many more had required me to be based in London, and the greatest number of them had simply told me that their books were closed. Like all of them, Pan Artists never advertised. Their existence was a secret carefully guarded from the outside world, yet they still received enough applications by word-of-mouth to keep their roster chock-a-block. I was incredibly lucky that they had space for a young man, as the majority of people working as extras tend to be middle-aged. I didn't have to pay any fees, or sit for an expensive photo-shoot. I just filled out their application form, sent it back with a decent snapshot of myself, and waited. And a week later, I got a phone call.

"Tony, it's Dorothy from Pan Artists, can you do *Hollyoaks* on Friday?"

I was so excited, it took me until Friday to get my breath back.

Walk On, Walk Off

Hollyoaks, for those that don't know, was the UK's fourth-most-popular soap opera.

Filmed on a shoestring budget compared to the big boys like *East Enders* and *Coronation Street,* it featured a cast of mostly teenagers, and was shown on Channel 4.

Glamorous, it was not.

But you know what? Who cares! *I was going to be on TV!*

For my first gig, Mum dropped me off at the entrance to what appeared to be a small country estate of the outskirts of Liverpool. A very small, innocuous sign on the gatepost was my only clue to what lay within; the beating heart of Mersey TV Studios. It made sense, of course, not to advertise their presence with a ten-foot billboard. People tend to have an insatiable curiosity about the TV industry, and nothing disrupts the smooth running of a shoot like crowds of fans trying to break in and storm the set.

As I walked down the long, curving driveway, I had no idea what to expect. I wasn't even sure I was in the right place until I rounded a bend and caught sight of several boxy vans, parked haphazardly, with cables trailing out of them. That's one of my prevailing memories of the industry, in fact; there are bloody cables *everywhere.* As someone who is not perhaps the most graceful of individuals, I tripped over more cables in any given month than most electricians do in a lifetime. And roughly ninety percent of the time, my fall was followed immediately by a rather obsolete warning from the nearest technician; "Watch out! There's a cable there."

Yeah. Thanks for that. *Let me show you where you can stuff your cables…*

But none of that happened on Hollyoaks. No, it was a slick operation, military-like in its precision and organisation. I arrived, was processed, instructed, prepared and positioned so smoothly I hardly knew it had happened.

HAHAHAHAHAHAHA! Fooled you!

No. In fact, it was anything but.

The production side of any TV show, as a general rule, is a bit like a terrorist attack on a petting zoo, only with less shit and machine guns. There are people running, people walking, people crouching, and people stood looking around themselves in complete confusion. Sudden noises, random outbursts of swearing, machinery vibrating, ladders clanking, cables dragging, bright lights flashing without warning – not a good place to be epileptic, come to think of it.

And all this is to describe a regular, harmonious, well-run TV set.

By comparison, filming Hollyoaks was like holding a haemophiliacs convention in a shark tank. It was a fucking bloodbath.

My first hour on set was spent trying to find anyone who even gave a shit that I was there. That person, when found, turned out to be a skinny man not much older than me, wearing ripped jeans and a crumpled t-shirt. He was also wearing two headsets, and trying to listen to each one alternately. Trying, and failing, because at least one of them – possibly both – were broken. He regarded me with confusion, like someone presented with a pizza they didn't remember ordering, then sent me off to stand with a huddle of people in a corner of the set.

"Wow! Pretty chaotic!" I said, to the first person who made eye-contact.

"Nah," he replied, "it's always like this. This your first time?"

"Yes! Can you tell?"

"Ha. Yeah. You still look like you're enjoying yourself."

I decided to take this as a complement. "So... what are we doing today?"

"Dunno."

"Oh! Right. Should I ask, do you think?"

"I asked. That dude with all the headphones, he's the Third AD, the third Assistant Director. It's his job to tell us what to do."

"Ah! So you asked him what we're doing today?"

"Yup."

"And what did he say?"

"Dunno."

As instructed by Dorothy from Pan Artists, I'd taken a bag full of the blandest clothing I owned – no logos, no bright colours, nothing that might catch the eye of the viewing public and distract their attention from what was going on in the foreground. The idea of the job was to be as close to invisible as possible, whilst still going about whatever tasks we'd been given; standing around, mostly, with the odd bit of walking.

The morning routine of a supporting artist, which I came to know quite well, generally involved introducing myself to the 3rd AD, signing paperwork to prove I'd arrived, then getting a quick check-over by the make-up and costume departments. Sometimes this became a lengthy process, as outfits had to be tried on, swapped and tried on again, or battle-damage applied to my face or limbs. I also encountered a few beards and a wig or two during my time. Once make-up and wardrobe gave the OK, I'd join my fellow extras in whatever holding pen had been allocated to us. This ranged from a corner of the pavement if filming outside, to a double-decker bus in the car park, to a seat in the canteen if filming in a studio. The comfort of the accommodation varied dramatically from set to set and from show to show, but they had one thing in common: we spent a lot of time in it. Starting at 7am, and quite often pulling twelve-hour days, still there were occasions when I did absolutely nothing. It was quite surreal, being an oasis of calm amidst the frantic and desperate busyness. I felt like I was sitting reading my book in the middle of the motorway, with drivers charging past honking and cursing on all sides.

On this first gig, I spent most of the day stood in the corner of a café set. Long hours of doing nothing were punctuated by short bursts of doing nothing but with the cameras rolling. I'd been hastily directed into the corner by the headset guy, and either he forgot I was there, or it took them an entire day to film a five minute café scene.

I didn't need my carefully prepared bag of clothing. I simply wore what I'd shown up in, and no-one asked me about it. That was hardly surprising, as the colour of my t-shirt seemed to be a fairly low priority amidst the seething, roiling crucible of chaos that comprised the set. Everywhere I looked, there were people. Old men with dubious personal hygiene rolling cigarettes they'd never get chance to smoke; camera operators that were dressed for work on Bondi Beach; lighting guys and sounds engineers in ripped jeans and trainers, and at least a dozen other characters that looked like they'd wandered in from a Pink Floyd concert twenty years ago and never left. What they did, beyond twiddling the odd dial and scratching themselves more than was strictly necessary, was a mystery.

There was a glorious inefficiency to it all. Everyone who passed through the set would move something, only for the next person to scurry in and move it back. There seemed to be a constant war between those who laid the cables everywhere, and an equally dedicated group who went around removing them. Lights were moved, cameras were moved, then they were moved back. One of the cable guys would reappear, confused as to why the bits he'd just laid had vanished. Boxes of equipment and ladders would materialize spontaneously in the middle of the set, and sound engineers walking backwards would crash into them and curse. But no-one seemed to know who owned them, or where they'd come from and why. Eventually the harassed 3rd AD would rush in and drag them away, trying three different locations before he found a place he could leave them without being sworn at. Then the lights would come on, one bulb would explode, and an electrician would stride onto set carrying his toolbox, calling for a ladder. Someone else would be sticking stripes of coloured masking tape onto the floor, only to have it peeled up by the cable guy and used to secure his latest stretch. This would prove to be in the way of the electrician's ladder, so he'd ruthlessly rip it up, and it would be long gone by the time he carried his tools off, leaving the ladder centre-stage. At which point the cable guy would dangle a wire from the ceiling, and would look like he was about to cry when it reached the ground and he found there was no longer anything there to plug it into.

The director was noticeable by the imminent-heart-attack-red of his face, and by the fact that he did most of the shouting. If his tone of voice was anything to go by, the day's shoot was not going very well. The other members of the production hierarchy were eventually identifiable by their tasks; the First Assistant Director, or 1st AD, gave most of the orders and seemed to exist solely to prevent the director from screaming himself into an early grave. The 2nd AD had the equally unenviable task of trying to corral the cast. The cast members themselves could be distinguished from the rest of us because they were all in their mid-twenties, but dressed as though they were teenagers; they wore five times more make-up than any human being I'd ever seen – including the boys; and because they spent most of their time mucking about, yelling, pushing each other and calling each other names, but no-one told them to stop.

Oh yes… chaos was putting it mildly.

By the time Mum picked me up ten hours later, my veneer of enthusiasm had worn thin.

"SO! How was it?" she gushed.

"Ah… not bad."

She must have thought I was being all nonchalant, the budding TV star playing it cool. "Ooo! Exciting! So are you going to be on telly?"

"I… I don't know for sure."

"Were   you   on   camera?"

"Well, I could *see* a camera. But I don't know if it could see me. I had my back turned most of the time."

"So, what did you do?"

"Well… I stood talking to this guy in the corner of a café."

"Ahhhh! And what else?"

"Um… that was it, really."

"Oh! What was the storyline about?"

"Ah… two people were pissed off at each other… And… it was in a café?"

"Oh. Right. Never mind. Do you know when it'll be on TV?"

I slumped back in the car seat and shook my head.

I never saw myself on Hollyoaks. Because, try as I might, I could never quite bring myself to watch it. My kind of TV featured car chases and explosions, as much sex as I could get away with watching, and the occasional ninja.

Whereas Hollyoaks was about a bunch of stroppy teenagers going to school, moaning about school, picking on each other, arguing, and occasionally eating chips. Watching it was like being forced to relive the worst bits of high school – and people did this *voluntarily?* Like, it wasn't enough to actually *be in* school for half your life, you had to come home and watch the same damn thing on TV?

It blew my mind.

At that point, peak audience figures for Hollyoaks in the UK was around 4.1 *million*. It was also showing in Sweden, Serbia, Finland, Bosnia, Iceland and South Africa.

I know, right?

Ridiculous.

My back was going to be *so* famous…

Extra Time

I did a lot of Hollyoaks, at first. The work was sporadic, a day here and there with sometimes weeks in between. But it slowly increased, and Pan Artists sent me on an ever-expanding variety of gigs as Dorothy grew to trust me.

It's crazy, really, that there was any need for this kind of proving process. I mean, the job, in keeping with most I've done, was incredibly simple. No special training was required; just basic common sense.

For starters, you had to accept that any given day could be long, almost certainly boring, and quite possibly uncomfortable.

Beyond that, it was easy; just show up, do exactly what you're told, and try not to annoy anyone.

But it's amazing how difficult some people found this. They'd disappear for a cigarette thirty seconds before they were needed on set, sparking a half-hour man-hunt. Or they'd buttonhole the director with a lengthy complaint about the car parking situation. Or they'd be too loud and exuberant on set, cosying up to cast members as though they'd been friends for years. I mean, the rules of etiquette were also no-brainers: don't keep asking the crew questions, as they have work to do. Don't expect set finishing times, or meal times, or complain about them being late. Don't try to persuade the ADs to give you a bigger role. Don't try to give yourself a bigger role, by acting up or talking on camera. Don't speak to the principal cast, unless they speak to you. And never, ever, *ever* ask them to sign anything – no matter how much your little boy loves the character they voice in his favourite cartoon.

And if at all possible, avoid being a racist, sexist, homophobic asshole at top volume in the middle of the cafeteria. I saw more people kicked off sets for this last problem than for anything else.

Of course, on Hollyoaks you could get away with practically anything. The crew were the youngest and least experienced of Mersey TV's employees, and anyone who attained any degree of competence was immediately pulled off the show and sent to work on *Brookside*. I did a couple of days on Brookside, playing a policeman, and whilst still chaotic, it was a world away from Hollyoaks. Still, that's where I spent the lion's share of my time. Surprisingly few young people do extra work, probably because it's so hard to discover how to, and Hollyoaks being aimed at teens, needed all of them.

At one point a special episode was planned, where a bunch of the younger cast members went on a trip to France. Before I could get all excited about the possibility of taking a paid trip over there, the mundane reality of Hollyoaks asserted itself. Via the 'magic' of television, a small corner of Calais was going to be portrayed by Liverpool's docks. It was much easier and dramatically much cheaper to keep everyone within a short bus ride of the studio, and knock up a bunch of French signs to hang over their English equivalents. But this depressing development was eclipsed by the most exciting news to date: I'd been given a tiny speaking part!

"You speak French, don't you?" Dorothy asked.

"Ah… yeah, sure," I told her. Not entirely truthfully, but it was on my CV. I'd graduated at the top of my class in high school French, with a starred A. It was only when I reached college and couldn't understand a single thing that I realised our school's standards must have been substantially lower than the others. I'd quit college French within the first two weeks; it was almost like a foreign language to me.

"They want you to play a French bartender," Dorothy explained, "so take black trousers, white shirt, and some spare bits and pieces."

It was a grey day, in a grey part of a grey town. The docklands of any English city are rarely attractive places, and Liverpool had the added advantage of being a shithole to start off with. It was going to take serious magic to convince a viewing audience they were looking at the coast of France. Then again, the show was aimed at teens; I doubt most of them would know or care what France looked like. This universal disinterest was typified by the storyline; the three young lads of the cast that had come to France had only one goal on arriving – finding booze.

In the end, I had just one microscopic scene in the show. I was a Calais café owner; the young boys had wandered into my place to try and buy beer, and I had to throw them out.

"Just say something in French while you do it," the director told me. I don't think he knew or cared what. So as we moved through a series of rehearsals, fine-tuning the camera placement and testing the sound recording, I pushed the lads away from the café, shouting, *"Vous n'avons-pas dix-huit ans!"* This, as far as my limited high school French informed me, meant, "You're not 18!"

Not that that would have mattered in France, where the boys would in reality have been able to buy beer without question. Much as I had on my school trip there.

But the lads were joking around as always, and their mischievous attitude began to rub off on me. I started ad-libbing a few insults, to see if anyone complained at me, but I was delightfully beneath their notice. So as we set up for a take, I made my decision.

Be a rebel!

I mean, come on. You've got to have some fun in life, right?

We blew through three takes in rapid succession, until the director was happy. I'd been increasingly violent with my ejection of the boys, as requested, and I must have finally got the balance right.

"*Vous n'avons-pas dix-huit ans!*" I called out, as I shoved them through my doors and off my patio. "*Va te faire foutre!*"

Which means, in layman's terms, "You are *not* 18. Fuck off!"

And no-one said a word to me about it. The director even thanked me personally – I guess it was fairly rare, on a show like Hollyoaks, for people to show up and actually do the job they'd been hired for.

Mum wasn't too happy when I told her what I'd done. Everyone else thought it was hilarious. I'd almost have watched the show to see this bit – but not quite. Mum still wanted to tape my speaking debut, so she scoured the TV listings for weeks, trying to find out when the episode would air. Sadly, it never did; it was released as part of a holiday special video, which I was certainly not going to buy. So I'll never know if my sneaky little quip made it into the final version or not. I guess it depends on whether or not any of the editors spoke French... and if they did, whether they had a sense of humour.

I didn't mind the soap days. They paid well, and I started to develop a rapport with crew members from the different shows. But far more interesting were the one-off jobs, the drama series, or documentaries, or TV movies.

One of my first was a show called 'My Wonderful Life' – which was so wonderful it sank into oblivion almost before it was shown. I was playing a policeman, which seemed to happen a lot. Something about the shape of my face must have suggested seriousness or responsibility. Or maybe I just looked old?

In this show, a bunch of hippies were protesting a new road, and had occupied a stand of trees. I was picked from the group to be the officer tasked with grabbing the lead cast member, and pulling him down out of his tree. This meant for great exposure, and I was allowed to ad-lib a few lines, of the 'Come with me, sir," variety. But best of all? The person I had to accost was none other than Time Team's Tony

Robinson – better known (at least in the UK) as Baldrick, from the iconic British comedy series *Black Adder*.

I've never been good with celebrities. I don't mean I treat them badly, or chloroform them; quite the opposite, in fact. I'm just not interested in them. I know these days there's a cult of celebrity worship, so strong that certain reality TV stars can parlay their dubious popularity into running entire countries... But I don't have a lot of brain capacity to spare. I have difficulty just remembering the names of friends and acquaintances. When it comes to celebrities, nine times out of ten I don't have a clue who they are. I wouldn't recognise Kim Kardashian if she bitch-slapped me with a Gucci handbag, much less the apparent stars of random TV shows.

But I friggin' *loved* Black Adder.

Tony Robinson was a lovely man, and very committed to his role.

He kept telling me to be more aggressive when dragging him away. "I'm going to fight you," he warned me, "so be ready!"

But he's a tiny bloke; the idea that he could hurt me was laughable. I was just terrified I'd break him.

It's a shame, really, that I didn't have more of a drive to collect celebrities. It could get you into trouble in this industry, but most extras treasured their stories of brief interactions with household names. I didn't care, because I honestly didn't recognise most of them. But Tony Robinson I did know, and he'd have been easy to collect; he would almost have fit in my pocket.

It was the highlight of my career as far as Dad was concerned. He's never shut up about it. Even twenty years later, when I told him I was writing this book, his first reaction was, "Are you going to write about pulling Tony Robinson out of that tree? Hey, you could call the book, 'My Wonderful Life'!"

Thanks Dad! As requested, please find the story above.

But as for using *My Wonderful Life,* as a title... I've a feeling it's been taken.

One of the most exciting phone calls I had from Pan Artists

was when Dorothy disclosed an opportunity to me. "There's an opening for a regular on *Coronation Street*," she explained. "It's a big step up. If we put your forward for it, and they choose you, you'll have to agree to be available to work at least one day every two weeks, and they expect you to be very professional on the Street."

"I can do it!" I told her. "I'm always available. And I'm always professional."

"Yes, I know," she said. "That's why we put you forward for it last week, and they called today to say they've chosen you. So, Coronation Street tomorrow morning, seven am in the Rovers Return pub, take three changes of clothes."

I was lost for words.

Life on the Street

Coronation Street was undoubtedly the most exciting event in my acting career so far.

And, simultaneously, by far the most boring.

As the UK's no.1 TV show, with ratings in the tens of millions, it felt like I'd been catapulted into the big leagues. I mean, we had our own friggin' Green Room for crying out loud!

It wasn't green, though.

The set – actually many different sets – were built inside a gigantic warehouse. All were composed of hardboard wall sections on timber frames, which could be slotted together to create whichever room was required. Several sets, such as the interior of the corner shop and the Rovers Return pub, were permanently erected. They were constructed the same way though, so any given wall could be removed in minutes, allowing cameras to film from angles that wouldn't be possible inside an actual shop. You'll appreciate this issue if you've ever tried to take a photo of your living room, and found yourself halfway down the road before you can get it all in. Wouldn't it be awesome if you could just pull the front wall off your house? In TV-land, you can. Or rather, several burly stage hands armed with power drills and wheely trolleys can.

The set I spent most of my time in was the afore-mentioned Rovers Return. For those who know nothing about the show, it follows the lives, loves and fortunes of the residents of Coronation Street – a fictional road in Manchester lined with tiny, Edwardian-era terrace houses. It started out in black and white, in 1960, and has been on the telly continuously ever since, making it the longest-running soap opera in the world.

Unsurprisingly, the production process was somewhat slicker than the other shows I'd worked on. The *Corrie* crew actually seemed to know what they were doing – and better than that, they seemed to know what each other was doing. This unprecedented level of teamwork and communication, coupled with actors who could act (and seemed to want to), made filming both easy and monotonous.

The cast and crew were so friendly, and treated their supporting artists so well, it seemed like there was less of a divide than in other shows – less of a 'them and us' mentality. Which, to my way of thinking, meant that bridging that gap was bound to be easier. Surely someone would recognise this talent lingering in the background, and take a chance on me…

Surely?

It never happened.

And I worked on Coronation Street once every two or three weeks, for over seven frikkin' *years.*

I never stopped hoping, though. Very occasionally, my professionalism and enthusiasm was rewarded with a microscopically more prominent piece of the background to stand in. I even got the odd word in, but the *Corrie* crew were notoriously cagey about this – it meant paying us extra, you see, and they spent these 'upgrades' frugally.

For me, it was all about exposure; in my mind I was building up to something, one snatch of dialogue at a time. But for the other extras, the jaded veterans of many years, it was all about the cash.

Some were militant about it, demanding the nearest AD note down any chance utterance. It was an opportunistic world; these guys would climb over each other's dead bodies to stand by the serving counter in the corner shop, and say

"Thank-you!" when handed a newspaper. This single word could easily be parleyed into an upgrade to coveted 'Walk-On 2' status, whereas 'Walk-On 3' required that you take individual direction, feature prominently in a scene, or speak a full line of unscripted dialogue. We were hired on Equity-based contracts, and Equity had negotiated a price for *everything*. From partial nudity to accidental beheading, you could be sure there was a clause to cover it – and a pay scale to match.

And these guys knew all of them.

They were experts at exaggerating the tiniest of details into life-threatening situations that demanded a pay increase. If someone spotted a dead mouse in a corner of the warehouse, there'd be a hurried conference with low voices, during which they'd declare the place unsanitary, meaning they could claim the 'Dangerous Working Environment' penalty rate.

And then they'd go and pester the 3rd AD about it.

Poor bloke. He was already the most overtaxed member of the crew, forever chasing missing props, missing people, and missing lunch orders. The last thing he needed, while the director was screaming at him in one headset, the riggers were hounding him on the walkie-talkie and his phone was buzzing with missed calls from the production office, was a skinflint walk-on artist trying to squeeze another drop of blood from his stones.

"You were standing *near* the hose, but I can't give you a 'Wetting Down' allowance for that," he'd say.

"I don't know, my shoes got soaked..." would come the reply.

"Frank, you *know* the water has to cover a third of your body to qualify!"

On Corrie, they did things on an industrial scale. When they hired extras, they didn't pinch pennies and call us in for the scenes we'd be featured in. They booked us by the day, content to let us sit or stand around for hours so we'd be instantly accessible when needed. I didn't mind; that was the job. I came well-prepared, with books, magazines, my Walkman, my journal, usually a half-finished essay or two...

but for some reason, most of the others brought nothing to occupy themselves. Just food, and maybe the free newspaper that was handed out on station platforms. Then they'd spend most of the day bitching about being bored…

I feel like I lived half my life in that Green Room.

It was on the third floor, but in a rather serious design flaw, shared a back wall with the top of the studio space where filming took place. Apparently noise carried rather well from our end, so anywhere between three and fifteen times per day, depending on the rowdiness of the group, one of the Assistant Directors would poke their head into the room and ask, beg or yell at us to be quiet.

But penning upwards of a dozen old blokes into a tiny room for anywhere from six to thirteen hours was not a recipe for tranquillity.

Most of the regulars had spent years in the entertainment industry. They were comedians, musicians, performers of one sort or another – not the kind of people known to ignore an audience. And it might just be my failing memory, but I'm fairly sure they were all called either Frank or Jeff.

Their debates, generally revolving around previous gigs they'd done, were endless and spirited. They had encyclopaedic memories of their pay-upgrade triumphs, and nursed grudges for every time they'd been denied. I sat through them in disbelief, eyes staring blankly at my book, unable to tune out the incessant noise.

Jeff: "So, I'm wearing the penguin outfit, and I'm thinking, okay, so this means costume-rate, and obviously I'm under individual direction, as a penguin, so it's Walk On Three…"

A rumble of assent from the surrounding veterans confirmed this fact.

"…but then I'm asking myself, is this Special Skills? I mean, I'm *impersonating* a penguin. Not just anyone can do that…"

Nods all round, and a mutter of, "Mm, Jeff's right, his penguin is pro-quality."

"…so, whaddaya reckon? Should I call my agent?"

"Oh, I dunno, Jeff," Fred would speak up. "Remember when I played that gorilla at the fair in *Emmerdale?*" He paused for nods and grunts of recollection. "They'd written, 'Juggling Gorilla' on the call-sheet."

"I didn't know you could juggle, Fred?"

"No, I couldn't actually juggle, not in those big gorilla hands! But the point is, I was a *juggling* gorilla. So that's Special Skills right there."

"Aha!" Jeff crowed. "Thought so! Did they pay it?"

"Damn right they did! Tried to weasel out of it, but I was on to my agent like a shot. *Juggling* gorilla, I told her, not your common-or-garden gorilla. Which is why I'm saying, check the wording first. If 'penguin' was on the call-sheet, they could say it was a standard requirement. No disrespect to your penguin, Jeff. I'm sure it's excellent."

"Mm-hm," Jeff agreed, "it's all in the hips, the penguin." He'd spring up and swagger around the room for a few seconds, in an act that would probably have been easier to appreciate if he'd been dressed as a penguin. A chorus of approving murmurs would seem to make his mind up. "Sod it, I'm gonna call my agent," he'd say, heading for the door.

As it closed behind him, a collective sigh would go out from the group. Silence would reign for a few seconds, until someone else interjected, "Jeff's penguin is shit."

Aside from keeping quiet, the other thing most extras are terrible at is miming. Which is bizarre, because some days that was literally their whole job. I'd be stood in the Rover's Return, facing a fellow extra, having a casual conversation just over the left shoulder of one of the principal cast. The director would remind us all that *miming* was the order of the day, what with the highly sensitive microphones trained on us from above. Then he would call 'Action' (yes, that really does happen) – and I would begin mouthing silently to my partner, pausing for their simulated reply. Only, nine times out of ten, what I got was a whispered "what?" To which I would reply, of course, in silence (after I had overcome the urge to roll my eyes at them, something very noticeable on camera). Inevitably, my second bit of mime would be met with a slightly louder, "What?" from the person opposite me. Sometimes they'd even tap their ear, or do that stupid finger-wiggle that signals, 'I didn't hear that.' I would have to fix them with a glare, and mouth, "QW-EYE-ET!" In response, they'd stage-whisper "Sorry, what did you say...?" At which point the director would bawl "CUT!" and then admonish us all for being too loud.

It made absolutely no difference.

In all my years on Corrie, I only met a handful of people who could carry on a mimed conversation. It's like some weird psychological block people have; even the ones who managed to stay quiet usually did it because they were reciting 'Mary Had A Little Lamb', or constantly mouthing, "Me-me-me-me-mo-mo-mo-mo-mu-mu." Here's a tip for anyone planning a career as a background artist: that shit is SO obvious! Next time you're in a coffee shop, check out the people chatting on the table next to you. See how natural they look. Now imagine what it would look like if one of them was saying, "Mi-mi-my-my-mo-mo-moo!" over and over. Reckon it would look like a proper conversation? Or like they'd been possessed, and were about to start projectile-vomiting excrement at any moment?

The other popular alternative – which I have to admit to being guilty of myself a time or two – is overly emphatic gesturing. When you have no clue what the other person is saying, and particularly when you're talking silently yourself, it's almost like the body wants to fill that communication gap with hand waving and extreme facial expressions. One person mi-ma-mo-ing for all they're worth, while their partner shrugs and frowns so hard it looks like he's trying to shit out a basketball... Now that really *does* look weird on camera.

Doesn't stop it happening, though.

Take a close look at the people in the background, next time you watch telly. I guarantee you'll see the weirdest facial expressions outside of clown school.

Especially if one of them is me...

Amateur Hour

Most people who decide to dedicate their lives to show business do it fairly early on. Some have parents in the industry, some just demonstrate an extraordinary talent in school plays and follow what they feel good at. Typically, acting students progress from drama classes in high school to those in college, often by way of handy extra-curricular activities like actually *being in shows*. The lucky ones get private after-school tuition, usually singing and/or dancing lessons too, and grow up with an encyclopaedic knowledge of plays, musicals, great actors of the past few decades and, invariably, ridiculous vocal warm-up techniques.

I had none of this. High school had been spent specifically trying *not* to draw attention to myself. Fannying around in tights would have been a sure-fire way to get beaten up. Even the merest suspicion of latent thespianism would have been cause for a serious ass-kicking behind the bike sheds.

As I recall, the school only put on one show during the five years I attended. It was a musical about the plight of the Amazon, called 'Yanomamo', and the closest anyone came to acting in it was the school nerd Ian flapping around dressed as a bat, murdering a song about eating figs. I'd dropped drama before it had even started, choosing instead to try my luck at art.

Man, I was crap at art.

At college, alongside those delightful English Language classes, I'd taken Business Studies, which I spent most of trying to chat up the very attractive girl who sat next to me, and Computing – where they taught us to program in 'PASCAL', a language that was obsolete before we started learning it.

So when it came time to put this burning new passion of mine into practice, the vast sum of experience I had to draw upon was my five minutes of on-stage glory in Hobson's Choice, and getting tangled in that bastard coat hanger when I was six.

So.

With a few days of extra work under my belt, I allowed myself to be sucked back into the incestuous world of amateur dramatics. Rehearsals for St Ambrose's next play, *Wait Until Dark,* were held almost exclusively in the pub. Not for everyone else, mind; Alan Green and I had tiny roles, showing up right at the end of the final act. I was a policeman, along with a portly bloke called Lee, and Alan played an absent husband returning with the cops to find his wife at the mercy of two robbers. I had relatively few lines, which was lucky, as I was usually too pissed to remember anything complicated. Mum, bless her heart, didn't have a clue. She dropped me off at the start of rehearsals, not being in this show herself, and I hung around while Alan did his part in the opening scene. Then we nipped down the road for a few pints, returning two hours later for our triumphant finale. Curtain; applause; pass out in alcoholic daze while being chauffeured home. Now *that* was show business!

I appreciate that I might not be giving a very good impression of my dedication here, but I want you to understand that I was embracing the acting lifestyle *holistically.*

Which is to say, I was sixteen, and I was mostly in it for the chicks and the booze.

After the show was done, my fellow policeman Lee asked

Alan to play the lead in a ridiculous comedy he was directing. He asked me if I could do an American accent, and to my surprise I found I could. Mum had once been freaked out to hear two loud American voices emanating from the bedroom I shared with my sister; it turns out that whenever we played with our Transformers toys, we both impersonated their cartoon equivalents, adopting flawless American accents. I counted this as an easy win, and agreed to play an American werewolf called Harry 'Hairy' Talbot, in a play called *House of Frankenstein.*

Now that was a fun show.

It was absurd and hilarious, and we laughed our way through two months of rehearsals. Alan played Baron Victor Von Frankenstein, and the story revolved around his creation of an elixir meant to cure various afflictions suffered by creatures of the night. The cast included Frankenstein's Monster-slash-butler, Count Dracula pursuing his runaway bride the Countess Ilona Bathory, a Valkyrie named Frau Lurker, and the surprise appearance – at the very end of the show – of the Invisible Naked Man.

We began the show robed and hooded in black, carrying tall candles, processing ominously through the theatre to the strains of *Carmina Barana* (famous as 'The Omen' music – even though it wasn't actually in the film). Alan had spent the pre-show mingling with the audience, dressed in his lab coat, cackling madly. Every show without fail, just as we were about to go on, he'd scamper past our sombre line-up. And every time, he'd stop and look at us, curiously. Then he'd point at us, and say, "You've all got a monk on."

This is an obscure Northern slang expression for being grumpy – or, occasionally, for having an erection…

Suffice to say, we all pissed ourselves laughing, only seconds before we had to shuffle on stage in our creepy procession. Every. Damn. Day. We *knew* it was coming, but that only made it worse; it was bastard impossible to keep a straight face after that.

I should probably mention, for anyone who may be wondering, that there is no evidence of me in ANY of these productions. In fact, there never was. No film was ever made of any of them, and even if it had been, it would have been destroyed by age, or by people with good taste. But it wasn't, because IT NEVER EXISTED! Okay? So don't ask.

During *House of Frankenstein* I met Jane, a middle-aged lady who played the Hunchback of Notre-Dame. A fantastic actress, she was quite rotund, roughly as wide as she was tall, with breasts the size of my head. Noticing this rather prominent feature, Alan had gone off-script a bit, causing hysterics when he dubbed her the Hunch-front of Notre-Dame.

Jane had trained at RADA, possibly the most prestigious stage school in the world. She'd been a teacher for years, and offered to give me a few lessons ahead of my upcoming university auditions. I accepted wholeheartedly, as no matter how strong my urge was to fulfil my destiny as an actor, I couldn't help but poo myself at the thought of what was to come.

One of Jane's first pieces of advice was that I get some singing lessons, and that I get them quick. In fairness, she gave that advice having never actually heard me sing; had that not been the case, she might have revised her suggestion to something like, "have you thought about a career in Accounting…?"

Lawrence Newnes was the tutor she recommended. He was the best in the area, apparently. Whether that was much of a distinction I wasn't sure; I couldn't think of anywhere in rural Lancashire that was famed for producing musical talent.

Nevertheless, Mum paid for a block of four thirty-minute lessons, each one costing the princely sum of £15.

Lawrence was balding, middle-aged and middle-sized. But he had presence; it shone from his eyes and boomed in his voice. He was definitely the genuine article – being greeted by him was like getting mugged by an orchestra.

"So, what can I do for you?"

"I can't sing," I explained, "At all."

"Impossible!" Lawrence declared, grandly. "Anyone can sing. You just need the correct instruction."

I looked back at Mum. She was shaking her head, dubiously. "He really can't sing," she confided.

"Nonsense! Sing this note." He struck one key on the piano, and the sound welled out of it.

"Laaaa…" I tried. Feeling more than a little sheepish.

His forehead creased slightly.

"Okay. Now sing this note." He hit another one.

"Laaaaa…."

His frown deepened. I braced myself for bad news.

But Lawrence was a professional. He wasn't going to give up that easily.

"You need to warm up," he said. "Let's work on some exercises."

He ushered Mum out of the room, and she drive off to the supermarket – ostensibly to buy things for dinner. But we both knew it was to spare me the humiliation of having her listen to me. Or possibly just to spare her from listening to me.

Once we were alone, Lawrence had me run some scales. We did breathing exercises, emphasising the diaphragm, and made a lot of nonsense syllables with our mouths.

"Meanie-Miney-Meanie-Miney-Meanie-Miney-Meanie-Miney-Meeeee…"

I was embarrassed on so many levels.

For one, I was in a room with a grown man, uttering gibberish.

In addition, I was *singing*.

But worst of all? Even though we were only chanting baby-language, I was *still* murdering it. How is that even possible? I was only singing one note at a time. But I was obviously singing the wrong one.

It was amongst the most painful half-hours of my life. And I've had surgery on my penis.

I was so relieved when Mum returned that I buried my shame in a hug.

"So, how did we do?"

Lawrence's eyes glazed over slightly. "He has a great voice." *Just not for singing,* his expression interjected into the silence that followed.

"That's lovely! Okay then, we'll see you next week."

The next three lessons continued in the same vein. After running through our nonsense routine, Lawrence would play notes on the piano and I would howl out the closest approximation I could manage. Poor bloke, he carried on striking those keys, as though *somewhere* on that piano he'd find at least one note I could hit. I mean, the damn keyboard looked long enough…

I was still waiting for him to attempt the 'teach me singing' part when Lawrence gave up.

He didn't tell me that's what was happening – he just conveniently forgot to ask Mum for more money. Never one to be stingy, Mum's decision not to press the issue was all the clue I needed. I wondered if she's been privy to a final report of some kind, delivered out of my earshot; a surreptitious phone call, perhaps. I could just imagine Lawrence's admission of defeat.

Mum: "So, what's the verdict?"

Lawrence: "He's tone-deaf, and he sounds like a dying ox with a foghorn stuck up its arse. But apart from that, he's great…"

Mum: "So, there's nothing more you can do with him?" (I knew she'd always try her best on my behalf.)

Lawrence: "You could consider gelding…?"

I like to think that I was his Waterloo; that he'd found in me the one immoveable object that defined his boundaries for students to come. They'd show up in tears, ashamed of their voices, and he'd sit them down with a tissue, and say, "You can't be that bad. Why, I had this one guy…"

I took a perverse pride in the fact that I couldn't carry a tune if it came in a briefcase. But it did start to prune away at my options somewhat.

For example, it didn't bode well for a career in musical theatre…

Trial By Jury

Dad drove me to my first audition.

It was for Rose Bruford College, a venerable and prestigious drama school set amidst acres of gorgeous leafy parkland in Kent. Although technically in London, it certainly didn't feel like it; the main building was a Grade II listed manor house, three stately stone stories overlooking a tranquil lake. More modern buildings tucked away behind it contained the rehearsal rooms, a pair of theatres, make-up and props workshops, sound studios, student accommodation and the bar.

All in all, it was a peaceful setting – completely at odds with the turmoil I was feeling. It's odd, but I'd never been nervous before my amateur performances. I mean, the last thirty-seconds before stepping out on stage were spent in the grip of ball-shrivelling terror, but that evaporated the moment I got out there. And in the hours leading up to the performance, I'd felt nothing bad at all – only excitement and anticipation.

Whereas now, I was absolutely crapping my pants.

I couldn't figure out why. Perhaps because the Am Dram stuff was exactly that – amateur – whereas this was for real? Or perhaps because this actually mattered; the whole course of my future hung on the two-minute speech I would deliver.

Or maybe just because, here I was alone, instead of surrounded by my friends. Here I was unsupported, facing a group of people who would be examining me minutely, evaluating every word and gesture, comparing me to others, watching for me to fail.

My new-found confidence crumpled like a tissue full of nervous vomit.

Dad *really* needed to get a bin in his car.

The Rose Bruford auditions were held in the Ball Room, which was much smaller than its name suggests. The lacquered wooden floor bore scars and scuffs from generations of past performances. A grand piano sat in one corner beneath tall Georgian windows. The room's ambience was so strong I could practically smell the sweat of the previous practitioners.

Or maybe that was me.

Yes, on second thought, that was definitely me.

My audition piece was thoroughly memorized. It was the one I'd been getting Jane Bell to help me with. I'd found it by taking the book she offered me, a Tom Stoppard play called 'Rozencratz and Guildenstern are Dead' – and simply flicking through without reading it until I found the first body of text substantial enough to be a considered a monologue.

The reason I was so haphazard in my consideration was something which, in hindsight, I probably should have taken as a sign: I *hated* reading plays.

I still do. Come to think of it, I'm not really keen on plays in general.

I mean, I like *being in* them, but I would never be arsed to go and see one.

They all seem so boring and old-fashioned. So full of Victorian sensibilities, conversations in the kitchen and the occasional whodunit. You almost never see a play with space battles or exploding ninjas in it. As far as I'm concerned, no ninjas = instant boredom.

Yet one of the main, defining traits of the vast majority of actors, is this: they actually *like plays*.

I know, right?

Bunch of freaks.

I rabbited my way through the speech, unable to stop myself delivering the words at twice normal speed. I barely had time to breathe; by the time my ordeal was over my mouth was dry, my hands were soaked and I was panting like a dog in heat. I bowed with a flourish – which was probably unnecessary – and braced myself to meet the gaze of my assessor.

"Tell me, Anthony," he drawled, pronouncing the 'th' (which I never do), "what made you choose this speech, exactly?"

Finally! Something I was good at. I'd been prepared for this question, and rapidly explained my empathy for the character, my understanding of his motivations and my entirely fictitious love for the underappreciated plays of Tom Stoppard.

"Yes, very interesting, thank-you," came the drawl.

He looked down at the papers in front of him and made a note of something. Then he looked back up at me. "I suggest you choose something different in the future. NEXT!"

And that was that.

I wasn't in tears when I re-joined Dad in the car park, but I was pretty close.

"How did it go?" he asked, with his usual blustery cheerfulness.

I faked a smile. "They'll call me later," I lied.

"That's great news! Well done, Tony!"

I was strangely quiet on the four-hour drive home.

I took myself to my second audition.

It was comparatively close by, at the Manchester Metropolitan University. One of only two regular universities on my list, I liked the thought of studying in a place where I'd be mingling with more than just acting students. There were other advantages, too – chief amongst them being, it was close enough to home that Mum could still do my laundry. Whilst part of me eagerly anticipated the chance to explore pastures new, the stronger, more cowardly part of me was more than happy to continue living in the bedroom next to my parents until the day I died.

Probably by strangulation for refusing to eat my vegetables.

Filing into a long auditorium, I found space on the top row of the sports-hall-style tiered benches. It was only after the panel of four judges sat down amidst the rest of us and called the first person onto the floor that I realised – this audition was going to be held in front of everybody!

Instead of being invited into a small room one at a time, close to fifty other students, all competing against me for a place on the course, would be watching my speech.

If that doesn't get your palms sweaty, I don't know what will!

As I studied the first few performances, I could clearly see the difference between those with strong self-confidence and those that, like me, were barely in control of their nerves. It was like night and day, and I suddenly had a very bad feeling about this. There was no way to fake confidence; at least, not that I knew of. I'd been searching for one my entire life.

It was nearly my turn. Only one more audition before me.

A slender girl stood up and made her way down the auditorium steps, gliding into position with perfect poise. She didn't seem remotely nervous as she turned her eyes up towards the panel of judges and delivered her name in an accent so cut-glass she could have stabbed them with it.

"If you don't mind," she continued, "I'd like to present a short piece from a show I've written and directed myself, and am currently starring in, in the West End."

My jaw fell open a bit.

My thought process went like this: 'Well, what the bloody hell is she doing here then?' It followed up with, 'And how is that fair?' And progressed rapidly to, 'I might as well go home right now.'

It was a tough act to follow.

Unsurprisingly, I wasn't asked back.

It was extremely demoralising, but I tried to find solace in the statistics; Manchester Metropolitan had received over 6,000 applications for their BA Acting course that year, and had narrowed the field down to just 200 auditionees – of which I had been one.

The next number in that sequence became my favourite shock-tactic whenever the subject of my auditions came up in conversation. I liked it, because it instantly absolved me of any blame for poor performance. Even though it was, in its own way, not the most encouraging of statistics.

6,000 had applied; 200 had auditioned.

And there were twenty-four places available on that course.

My audition at the Welsh College of Music and Drama was the one I'd been holding out for. I didn't know quite why, but I had this vibe; no matter how I pictured my future, I just couldn't imagine myself living in London. But Cardiff, the capital city of Wales, was a whole different ballgame. Busy, without being threatening; old and quaint and charming in its way, whilst still encompassing every modern convenience. Also, Cardiff was dominated by a beautifully-restored 12th Century castle, of which the Welsh College formed part of the grounds.

This was it! I knew it. I'd done my practice runs, got the jitters out. This was the place where I would *shine.*

Hopefully. Because I was starting to run out of options.

The day started well. Yet again, my parents were good enough to drive me two-hundred miles in each direction, eight hours in total down assorted motorways, for an audition that would barely top five minutes.

I resolved to repay them by doing the best I possibly could.

Which would still be a pretty crap repayment. I mean, your mortgage company is *never* going to agree to that one.

This time, I pulled out all the stops. My recent experiences had taught me to control my pacing, and observing other students in Manchester had given me a few new tricks. I strolled in like an Emperor gracing the court with his presence, and played with my speech – pausing to make eye-contact with my imaginary fellows, and even stopping dead for a few heartbeats to let emotion play across my face unimpeded. Basically, I acted my frikkin' socks off.

"Thank-you, Anthony," the tutor in charge said warmly.

I readied myself for the questions. Though I'd stuck with the same speech, I'd refined my reasons for choosing it. I'd created elaborate and carefully considered answers to every conceivable question. I'd even practiced the face I was going to make whilst I did the careful considering. There was nothing they could ask that could possibly faze me. This time, I was ready for anything.

"Tell me, Tony," he continued, pointing his pen at me like a wand. "Can you sing?"

Change of Heart

I didn't get into the Welsh College of Music and Drama.

Which was a bit of a bugger.

I'd sort of been pining all my hopes on the place, as somehow it had seemed more accessible, more plausible, than all the posh London drama schools I'd applied to. Now, halfway through my list of applications, I was facing an uphill struggle.

Dammit!

I really liked the Welsh College. I'd been able to see myself there, to visualize walking past the ancient castle walls on my way to class, entering via the classy but unassuming lobby, and following the simple, carpeted corridors to the battered parquet flooring of the rehearsal rooms. It was a tiny place, with no tower block of accommodation attached; a cosy place, where I could conceivably get to know every person in the building.

Or not, as it turned out.

Ah well! Moving on…

I'd made the mistake of telling Pete that I was driving to Wales for an audition, and he hadn't shut up about it since. "What do you call a sheep tied to a lamp-post in Wales?" he asked. "A leisure centre!"

I groaned.

"How do you tell a if sheep's a virgin? It can run faster than the nearest Welshman!"

And on.

So when I told him I was also applying to the University of Glamorgan, less than twenty minutes from Cardiff, I was amazed that he decided to come with me.

Pete wanted to study psychology, and Glamorgan was a proper university, offering every course under the sun. Suddenly I went from the prospect of moving on my own to a stuffy, pretentious stage school in London, to the possibility of chilling out in Wales for three years with my best mate... I really hoped Glamorgan would look as good in real life as it did on paper.

This time, Dad drove both of us down there, and Pete filled in the journey by telling me what to watch out for in Wales.

"People with Velcro gloves," he pointed out, "coz they help 'em hold onto the sheep. And welly-boots two sizes too big, so they can put the sheep's back legs in to stop them escaping..."

Jokes aside, this was bound to be a fun trip. Not only was Pete with me, but Glamorgan didn't require me to audition. Alone of the institutions I'd applied to, they accepted conventional applications, and offered places based on interviews and exam results. The lack of stress may have coloured my experience on that first visit, but from what I saw, it looked great. A thoroughly modern campus ranging up the sides of a steep hill, there was a clean, positive vibe about the place. Bunches of young people strolled to and fro, smiling, seeming carefree and relaxed. Our tour took in not one, not two, but *three* separate bars, including a miniature nightclub; Pete was sold already. A vast library, towering IT labs, plus (for me) a fully equipped black-box theatre, a TV studio, a radio studio and an extensive selection of camera equipment that could be hired out free of charge by students. My interview went well, and I re-joined Pete on a guided tour into one of the main buildings.

"Got a joke for you," he whispered.

"Oh God. What?"

"There's a Welshman taking his driving test. The instructor asks him, 'Can you make a U-turn?' The Welsh bloke says, 'I can make a ewe's eyes water!'

I stifled a snigger.

And at that precise moment, as we followed the corridor around a corner, a door opened to one side, and an electrician backed out, his overalls covered in tufts of pale-yellow insulation wool.

Pete looked at me, and the pair of us exploded.

Glamorgan had offered us even more than we'd expected. And there was one key reason for me applying to them in the first place: if I was to achieve a place on the course I wanted, all the acting classes would be taught not at Glamorgan itself, but over at the Welsh College in Cardiff!

It was almost too good to be true.

So when it came time to prepare for my next London audition, I started to get cold feet.

Guildhall School of Music and Drama was one of the top ten institutions in the world for performing arts. Around the same time I was making my applications, a young fellow called Orlando Bloom was doing the same; had I got in, we'd have been classmates. Daniel Craig also went there, as did Ewan McGregor.

But I didn't.

Partially because Guildhall was housed in the single ugliest building in the United Kingdom. A colossal concrete edifice resembling a block of flats from the 1960s, the school overlooked a stagnant pond with tall grass growing out of it. And that's being nice. Slap-bang in the centre of London, accepting a place there would require serious readjustment to the pace of life in The Big Smoke. And there was the small matter of the cost of living in London – which at the time, was reckoned to be triple the cost of living anywhere else in the country. At some stage, if I were to follow this path through to its logical conclusion, I would have to make the move to London. This was the depressing, yet inevitable reality of becoming an actor in England. But as a country boy, the big city filled me with terror. Where I lived, kids threw stones at me; in London, gangs roamed the streets armed with guns and knives. At least, my imagination, ever fertile, told me this. There was just something so *massive*, so overwhelming about the place... I certainly wasn't eager to make it my home. Not yet, at any rate.

The audition fee was £25; I couldn't ask my parents to drive me again, so the trip to and from London would cost me double that. It was a decent chunk of change for someone only working odd days, and would be wasted if my spectacular lack of success in auditions so far was any indication.

I weighed up all the pro's and con's, and made my choice.

Why bother adding another rejection to my pile?

Bollocks to that!

In the same glorious instant, I extended this decision to my one remaining option, the Central School of Speech and Drama. A much nicer-looking place, though still in London, I tried hard to find reasons for not wanting to study there. Their facilities looked excellent, their reputation was exemplary – Central had been one of the first drama schools in the UK, established in 1906, and amongst its notable alumni counted Sir Lawrence Olivier, Dame Judi Dench, both Dawn French *and* Jennifer Saunders – and Carrie Fisher.

Princess frikkin' Leia, man!

And yet... hand on my heart, I still didn't want to go there.

The reality was a secret I hardly dared admit, even to myself. I was worried – terrified may be a better word – that I wasn't good enough. With their glossy brochures and lists of famous graduates, their grand traditions and *Conservatoire* status... Even if I did, by some miracle, slip in, I had a horrible feeling I'd find myself the lowest in the pecking order, an outcast once more, despised for my lack of good breeding and artistry. The heavy Lancashire accent I'd adopted in a desperate attempt to fit in up north would mark me out as an unsophisticated, working-class buffoon with no training, no money, and few prospects.

I'd barely made it through high school, and the shame of being universally loathed and sneered at was still fresh in my mind. More than that, it influenced my thoughts and actions, imparting a desperate need to be liked. I'd become an entertainer, driven to make people laugh on my own terms, the better to prevent them from laughing at me maliciously.

In some ways I was a broken thing, newly put back together and still incredibly fragile. Only the love of my family had held my pieces together this far. Were I to leave their safety completely, and travel a hundred miles to the middle of an uncaring city, only to find my new classmates looked down on me with the same degree of disdain...

Well. I didn't know if I would survive that.

And so, my mind was made up. Instead of pursuing further auditions, stressing about them, paying for them, and being laughed out of them, I threw all my eggs into one basket. And sincerely hoped that the resulting University of Glamorgan omelette didn't have too much shell stuck in it.

I slept easier from then on. I felt sure I'd made the right decision, for several reasons. For starters, as a conventional university, I'd have access to way more courses, facilities and *people* than I would in a drama school. Living in Wales would be cheaper than London – by a factor of ten, I reckoned – and considerably less terrifying. Glamorgan also allowed new students to defer their enrolment for a year, which meant that Pete and I could both take a Gap Year and just hang out – an idea that was looking more attractive by the second. And one of the most exciting aspects of all was this: Glamorgan had been the only place where anyone even mentioned acting on camera. They had a TV studio, all the audio-visual equipment and video editing suites I could want. There was a separate degree program dedicated to the behind-the-camera side of film work, and another course for scriptwriters; students of all three disciplines were encouraged to collaborate, producing work which could form the basis of a professional portfolio or showreel. In sharp contrast, every drama school I'd visited had their emphasis firmly planted on stage work. Plays abounded; old Russian plays like The Caucasian Chalk Circle, older Shakespeare plays, contemporary plays which would doubtless require strobe lighting effects and unnecessary nudity; from prospectus to tutors to ex-student testimonials, they all ate plays for three meals a day.

Whereas I was already getting sick of plays. In fact, I was starting to think that plays could go screw themselves.

I already knew I'd never be lighting up Broadway with a song-and-dance extravaganza. Now I started to realise that, if The Royal Shakespeare Company had swooped down from their hallowed halls in The Globe and offered me a place amongst them, I probably wouldn't have taken it. I'm a tiny bit ashamed to say it, but that rambling old shit bores me to tears. A life spent endlessly rehashing the Scottish Play was very nearly as bad as having to get a real job!

I've said it before, and I'll say it again: what Shakespeare really needs is more ninjas.

I loved performing – loved being up on stage, loved being the centre of attention. Loved the applause, loved the adulation of the crowds...

Maybe I didn't really want to act at all?

Maybe I just needed a hug?

No. My stated aim was to replace Tom Cruise in the next Mission: Impossible movie. And to be honest, that was mostly because I wanted to do that stuff in real life. If Mission Impossible had existed, I'd *definitely* have put that on my UCAS form.

But it didn't – at least, as far as I knew.

So just to be on the safe side, I also applied to MI6.

(For my friends over the pond, this is the British equivalent to the CIA.)

It was surprisingly simple. Although this was 1995 and the Internet was in its infancy, the big government agencies already had websites. And much like any other international employer, they had a 'Careers' page.

I sent them a CV, slightly exaggerating my facility with languages and noting my ability, as an actor, to 'adapt to any role'. I also wrote an essay on why I believed I would be an ideal candidate for employment.

I *may* have mentioned ninjas, but then, who doesn't?

I never heard back from them.

Possibly because I'd fallen at the first hurdle; on the website, they strongly advise you not to tell anyone that you've applied. They are, after all, a spy organisation, and they recommend that applicants consider this secret as the first stage of training for the job.

I thought that was so cool, I told absolutely everyone.

And consequently, I am not now working as a spy for the British Intelligence Services.

Or... am I?

Best Laid Plans

The decision to take a gap year between college and uni was a no-brainer.

My plans for it were epic.

I was already working part time at the Games Workshop store in Preston, a job which mostly involved playing with and painting toy soldiers. It was a job I loved, and I was looking forward to going fulltime.

I would earn vast quantities of cash, and equip myself in such style that when I went to university, I would take the place by storm.

Free from the shackles of studying, I would spend all my time with Pete and Anders, partying, studying kung fu, and basically plotting our combined take-over of the planet Earth.

When we had all saved up sufficient funds, we would travel out into the world together and find the kind of adventures we knew were waiting for us.

Partnered with the pair of them, I felt unstoppable. I also felt sure that, in their inestimable company, and given enough time and sufficient quantities of alcohol, I would finally find a girl who was willing to… well. Y'know.

Give meaning to my whole existence. Sort of thing.

I've heard it said that Fate is capricious. I don't know what that means, but I've always wanted to write it. *Capricious!* Great word. Sounds like a Greek island. What I think it means is that, one day Fate can smile on you, wink at you, give you a cheery wave perhaps, or a solid thumbs up. And then the next day, when you're totally not expecting it, she can cop a squat on the kitchen table and piss all over your Corn flakes.

The following things happened in quick succession:

I passed my A-level exams, and was offered a place at Glamorgan University. I asked to defer it for a year, and was granted permission to start my studies the year-after-next.

Pete failed his exams, and was offered a place at Glamorgan on the condition that he attended immediately. Deferment was in fashion; I guess they were running low on students.

Thus, Pete left home for university straight away, and was gone for the entire year. Just like we'd planned, he made friends, had adventures, and met beautiful women – only, I wasn't there for any of it.

Shortly after Pete left, I got fired from Games Workshop, after a witch-hunt that I still don't quite understand. By the time it was over, they'd been forced to offer me my job back, but the magic had kind of gone out of it, so I refused.

Then Anders got fired from Games Workshop, and returned to Denmark.

Suddenly, for no reason I could understand, every plan I'd made was in tatters.

My two best friends – my only friends – were gone.

As was my job, and my only real reason for getting out of bed in the morning.

All I had was one day per fortnight on Coronation Street, the odd spot on Brookside or Emmerdale, and frigging Hollyoaks.

Consequently, on my gap year from education, I did absolutely nothing.

Start How You
Mean To Go On

When it came my turn to head off to university, I was a welter of confusing emotions.

Fear of loneliness warred with excitement within me.

The whole family would be driving down to Cardiff, to see this place where I'd be spending the next three years, and to help me settle in.

Then they were going to abandon me there and bugger off home again.

And I would be alone.

Endless possibilities welled up, an infinite number of paths that spread out from this moment, gleaming with potential.

Unfortunately, ninety-nine percent of them ended with me curled up on my bed crying for the next three weeks straight.

Where the hell was Pete when I needed him?

Oh, that's right – he'd already done this. Been there, passed the test, got the t-shirt. As second years didn't start for another two weeks, he was staying home with the new girlfriend he'd acquired – an effortless act, after all his conquests in our year apart.

But he'd given me some crucial advice, drawn from his own experience of First Night Alone Syndrome. "As soon as your folks leave," he told me, "get yourself straight down to the Student Union bar. You won't want to go – ever fibre of your being will scream at you to stay in your room and hide. I nearly read a book."

Pete sounded disgusted. He wasn't a big fan of books.

"Fight that urge," he continued, "and force yourself out the door, no matter what. On that night, everyone there is feeling the same, and they'll all end up in the Union. That's where you'll make the friends that will stay with you all year."

Anyone who's been to Wales will not be surprised to learn that the university campus was built on a steep hillside. Most of Wales is steep hillside; the only real exceptions are the sheer cliffs along the coast, and the mountains.

The Halls of Residence, where my folks had rented me a room, clung to the summit, whilst the brick building housing the Student Union was at the bottom. Surely that was a mistake! If they'd done it the other way around, you'd be able to drink yourself insensible in the bar and simply roll down the hill straight into bed. Instead, every time I returned to my room I would be hiking up a forty-five degree incline. I'd have legs like tree trunks by the end of the year.

Two U-shaped accommodation blocks stepped up to the brink of the hill. Each arm was given a designation; UA, UB, UC and UD. I never found out what the U stood for. My room was on the second floor of UD, the highest and furthest hall; I'd have had a great view over the entire campus if I'd been on the front. Sadly, I was at the back, and my window faced a car park. The room itself was tiny, a sliver of space just wide enough for a single bed on one wall and a desk on the other. Sitting at the desk meant pulling the chair out until its back rested against the wooden bed frame. I had a shelf, and a notice board, and… well. That was it. When Mum, Dad and Gill wanted to examine the place, they had to do it one at a time. 'Cosy' was the polite word for it.

A communal kitchen sat at the end of the hall, along with the bathroom. Somewhere in the three-storey link which connected this hall with UC, further down the hill, there was supposed to be a TV room.

I surveyed my domain, and I was satisfied. I couldn't wait to customise it – I had enough blank wall space to get at least three posters up. This place was *mine!* And mine...

Alone.

As my family disappeared, heading back to the world I'd grown up in, I took another look around and realised that this was it; I was on my own from here. I missed my parents already – the longest I'd been away from them was that four day school trip to Paris, and then I ended up getting tear-gassed. It would be months before I'd see them again...

Tears threatened.

But Pete had prepared me for that. His advice had brooked no argument. "Trust me," he'd said.

Yeah, right!

I snuck out to the bathroom, managing to avoid being seen by anyone. I checked out my hair (it was still attached) and my outfit (baggy t-shirt and jeans – the stealth-mode of my generation). I stared at myself in the mirror and created a manta: "I am STRONG! I can do this!"

It earned me a funny look from the lad who emerged seconds later from the corner toilet cubicle. I looked down and pretended to be washing my hands until he left.

"Next time, I will make sure I'm alone before I start talking to myself," I chastised my reflection.

At which point I heard another toilet flush, and decided to leg it.

Back in my room I was assailed by doubt. It was now or never; if I didn't go out immediately, I'd collapse onto the bed and spend the next three days peeing into a bottle for fear of meeting someone in the corridor. So I shook the anxiety from my limbs and reminded myself that what Pete had told me made perfect sense.

I will say that this was quite a leap of faith. I'd taken Pete's advice a few times in the past, and the results had varied from extreme embarrassment, to excruciating pain, to nearly being arrested. Under normal circumstances I'd consider it safer to douse myself in petrol and go swimming in an active volcano.

But.

He'd been serious this time.

And if not, I had two weeks to figure out how to bury the bastard when he arrived.

So I set off down the hill towards the Student Union building at the bottom of it.

*   *   *

The evening did not go as planned.

What Pete had failed to consider was that he was a naturally gregarious person. He'd always been popular. He even *liked sports*, for crying out loud! Whereas I'd spent most of the last decade as a pariah. People my own age scared the crap out of me; I instinctively expected them to loathe me on sight, and felt that no matter how normal I tried to be, it was only a matter of time before they saw through my façade. There was only one thing I could do in this situation – one thing I'd had considerably more practice at than most people my age. I could drink! So that is what I did.

The bar was rammed. As the night wore on, I exchanged a few words with people – mostly mumbled apologies for getting in their way when they were trying to get served – and precious little else. There was one brief ray of sunshine, when an incandescently hot girl started talking to me for no apparent reason. I was awe-struck, and tongue-tied, and managed about ten minutes of babbled conversation before she slid gracefully away in search of a more articulate partner. *Emily!* She'd been my one shot, I thought. By the time last orders was called and the Union began to empty, I'd convinced myself that Emily had been my potential soul-mate; the Universe had offered me one chance at happiness, and I'd screwed it up.

As I began my solitary trudge back up the hill, knots of people in front of and behind me chattered merrily to each other, cementing new friendships with drunken laughter.

It's going to be the same as school, I thought. *Maybe not as cruel, maybe not on purpose, but every bit as lonely. If I can't make one friend in a bar full of people…*

I arrived, breathless, outside UD Halls. Loads of people were there already, milling around aimlessly like extras in a zombie movie. Then I spotted Emily. She'd gathered a small group of girls, all of them attractive, and a thrill went through me when she called my name. "Tony! We're locked out! Do you know how to get in?"

The crowd was growing by the minute, and Emily was in the centre of it. I drew upon several pints of liquid courage and waded through the press of bodies. "What happened?" I asked. "Don't your room keys work?"

"No! It's a different kind of lock. There must be a way in, but there's no other doors here…"

Maybe it was the drink talking, but something within me responded to the cry of a damsel in distress. "I'll get us in," I said.

I gave the double doors a vicious shake; it was a fire escape, and could only be opened from the inside. "This isn't meant to be a way in," I thought out loud, "the doors only open outwards, and there's no handles on this side."

I wondered if I could force it. Dozens of people now surrounded the locked entrance, most of them more than a little drunk. I'd probably get away with it…

But the doors were tempered glass. Strong and secure.

As I cast around for another option, I couldn't help but notice that most of the crowd had turned to watch me. I now had the attention of an ever-growing audience…

And then, not twenty metres away, I saw my salvation.

A tiny window, open just a crack.

It was frosted glass, a bathroom window set well over two metres above the ground. I don't think it had occurred to anyone else that they could even reach that window, much less fit through it…

I stood below the narrow opening, leapt up and caught the bottom edge of the frame. I hardly needed to pull myself up, as hands came from everywhere, shoving and thrusting me upwards, sparing no thought for propriety. It was the most intimate contact I'd ever had with a stranger, let alone fifteen of them simultaneously. By the time the last overly-enthusiastic palm had un-wedged itself from between my buttocks, I was halfway through the window. It was a tight squeeze; the crotch of my jeans caught on the latch, tearing an unfortunately-placed hole. This seems to have started a life-long tradition, as almost every pair of jeans I've owned since have ended up with the balls torn out of them.

For now, all my attention was on trying to breathe with two panes of glass pressing into me. Reaching out, I took hold of the top of the toilet stall and dragged myself along it, rapidly reaching the point of no return... At which point, with both feet still outside the building, I fell face-first into the toilet.

My injuries were minor. I had the alcohol to thank for that. I hauled myself up to find that no-one had attempted to follow me in; the unmanly scream I gave as I plunged bogwards probably put them off.

I limped out of the bathroom at top speed, down the corridor and around the corner to the fire doors. With a swift push down on the bar, the doors sprang open, and the press of bodies swept in like a tidal wave.

The rest of the evening went comparatively well.

The first twenty or so people through the door picked me up, cheering, and for the next half an hour I was body-surfed along the corridors, and up and down at least two different stairwells.

When the celebration finally abated I found myself, drink-in-hand, on the third floor, in the kitchen above my own. Everyone knew my name now, including the residents of any houses within half a mile; at least fifty people had been chanting, "TONY, TONY!" at top volume ever since the break-in.

I was standing there in a daze, reflecting on this bizarre turn of events, when one of the attractive girls I'd noticed with Emily came up to me. And I mean, she came *right* up to me, pressing her body against me. Then she drew back, looking into my eyes, and said, "You're my hero!"

And she kissed me. It was a long, lingering kiss – my first, as it happens – and I think it lasted for about a century. Then, with a mischievous smile, she was gone. And another girl took her place. "You're my hero too!" the newcomer exclaimed… and she bestowed upon me the second romantic kiss of my life.

My head span and my spirit soared.

It was around that time that I had the thought; *you know what? University life might not be so bad after all…*

Drinking Responsibubbly

I woke up naked, in my own bed.

How I'd gotten back there I wasn't sure. The whole end of the evening seemed to be missing from my internal database. This was a familiar condition, and was usually followed by a surge of fear and a phone call to Pete, whereupon he would explain just how badly I'd embarrassed myself.

This time though, things were different. Instead of dread, my hangover was tinged with triumph. Not only had I done well last night, I may have done *very* well. In fact, for the next six months I firmly believed I had lost my virginity that night, having vague recollections of much kissing and writhing. The truth, later revealed to me by one of Emily's friends, was less heroic; I'd got stoned and passed out, and they'd had to carry me back to my room.

Had I undressed myself? Or had someone else done the honours?

I never found out.

That morning there was an assembly for everyone on arts-based courses, and I made it in plenty of time. Ravenous, sleep-deprived, with a raging hangover and dozens of minor injuries I couldn't explain, I was the happiest man alive. And that's what I felt like, for the first time ever: *a man*. I had glimpsed what it was like to be popular, and it was a feeling I would cherish.

There's a lot to be said for the hero lifestyle.

Or at least, for being the one who does things that other people don't.

From that moment on, whenever an opportunity presented itself, I became the one who did the crazy stuff.

It didn't always work out well.

But that morning passed in a haze of happy daydreams. I felt relaxed enough to chat to the other kids on my course, and made my first friend there; James, a short, cheeky Welsh chap who turned out to be one of the hairiest individuals on the planet.

Within minutes of the course director's final motivational speech, the huge crowd vanished like smoke. James and I were left in the middle of a small knot of guys, none of whom seemed to have been paying much attention.

"Um… what next?" one asked.

The previous night's shenanigans were starting to take their toll, and my stomach churned noisily. "Anyone hungry?"

We were crossing the road towards the Student Union when I head a shriek.

"*TONY!*"

I looked uphill, and there was Emily, about fifty metres away, with a gaggle of girlfriends. A second later they all started yelling and waving at me, then took up chanting, "TONY! TONY!" until they reached a staircase they were aiming for, and disappeared down it.

The other guys just stood in the middle of the road, staring at me incredulously.

James came up and clapped his arm around me. "Tony, what the *hell* did you do last night?"

Lunch consisted of chips and bacon sandwiches from a café on the bottom floor of the Union building. Then we drifted back outside, at a bit of a loss.

Only to notice the line of students snaking out of the sports hall, and halfway around it.

"Oh shit!" said James. "That must be the queue for enrolment."

"So this is where everyone else went. It'd be nice if someone had told us."

"I think it was mentioned at the assembly," James pointed out.

"Ah..." I'd spent the entire speech re-living the night before. "Bugger."

"Reckon we just join the end, like?"

"Hang on." Emboldened by recent events, I strolled casually past the queue, eventually gaining the dim interior of the sports hall. It was worse than I could have imagined. The line formed a spiral five tennis courts square. In the centre of the hall stood a row of desks, where official-looking people were handing out the all-important student ID cards. Dotted around the edges were stands from the likes of Barclay's Bank and other illustrious organisations. I did a quick estimation of the time it would take to queue in through the door and at least eight times around the interior of the sports hall. Allowing for margin of error, I figured roughly a decade.

Back outside, I reported my findings. A few stragglers joined the queue right in front of us, without even thinking to look inside. Poor bastards. My little group stood to one side, on the verge of joining but not willing to commit.

Then a word popped into my head unbidden; three beautiful letters that solved our predicament perfectly.

I looked at James. "Pub?" I asked him.

He glanced back at the endless shuffle of humanity wending its way towards the sports hall.

"Yeah! Tidy."

(Apparently, to the Welsh this means 'good'.)

So at 1pm on my first full day at university, I led a small posse off campus in search of alcohol.

About three hours later, significantly more lubricated, we ventured back to the sports hall. The plan had worked to perfection; only a handful of latecomers were still awaiting their turn. Or quite possibly they were the same people we'd seen joining the tail-end of the queue three hours ago, which could explain the looks on their faces. Then again, that could have been in response to my next tactic. I found a trio of oversized arm chairs behind the long-deserted Barclay's stand, and together we dragged them into the line, inching our way forwards whilst reclining in style.

The tail end of the queue glared daggers at us, as we lounged around sharing helium from an abandoned Barclay's balloon. People often hate it when you challenge the status quo, I've noticed; as though they're hard-wired to resent behaviour that doesn't conform to their expectations. Had I broken a law? Probably not. They were just pissed off that it hadn't occurred to them.

"Don't queue hard, queue *smart*," I suggested to anyone who was listening.

That evening, with enrolment safely behind us, I arranged to meet the boys in the Student Union nightclub – called 'Shafts', for no immediately apparent reason. The cramped little club was heaving. A sea of eager faces crowded the bar, a veritable ocean of potential. Any of these people could become friends; more importantly, at least half of them were women. And they could become something infinitely preferable…

Sad to say, I'd never had a girlfriend.

I was nineteen, and had been the least popular kid in both my home neighbourhood *and* my school. It was a double whammy that had pretty much defined my social life to that point. Now, suddenly, I was free and clear of all that. I could reinvent myself, be anyone I chose to be. I could even be *me!*

Well, perhaps not too much.

This vast array of beautiful young women – all my own age, almost all single – was more exciting to me than anything I had yet encountered. Surely, with this many girls available, at least one of them would be interested? It occurred to me that I could just start asking, one by one – sheer statistics alone told me I'd find a partner before the night was out.

There was only one problem.

I was bloody awful at talking to girls.

Especially in night clubs.

If you asked Pete, he'd undoubtedly say, "Tony couldn't score from ten yards away if the goalie was a crippled blind boy with his hands tied together." (Or something similar – he had a sizeable repertoire of insults about my pulling power).

But there was something in the air that night. Or possibly in the cider I'd been drinking almost continuously since lunchtime. Whatever it was, it soon had me on the postage-stamp-sized dance floor, busting out my best moves.

Now, my boogying has always had more, ah, *enthusiasm*, than style.

If you asked Pete, he'd undoubtedly say, "Tony dances like he's got his fingers stuck in a plug socket." (Or something similar – he also had a sizeable repertoire of insults about my dancing ability).

But I didn't have to worry about any of that right now. I was here, in the heart of all this happy chaos, surrounded by hundreds of people in exactly the same situation. None of us knew what to expect; most likely we were all a bit nervous about what the next three years would have in store. This was culture shock and sensory overload and sudden unbridled freedom all at once; it's inevitable, really, that a melting pot such as this produces a rather unique environment for hedonism.

So I flailed my limbs in nothing even remotely resembling time to the music, swigging from whatever drink I had in my hand at the time…

And would you know it – before long, I was dancing with a girl. And then I was kissing her. And then she seemed to vanish, and I was kissing someone else.

A tipsy blur later, I was walking past the bar when a random girl grabbed me, stuck her tongue down my throat for a couple of minutes, then turned back to her drink as though nothing had happened. I carried on my way, wondering absently if she'd stolen my wallet. This was far too good to be true! I had a sudden horrible premonition that I'd fallen asleep in the car on the way to uni, and was about to have the rudest awakening of my life.

In fact, that night *was* something special. I spent most of the next three years partying in Shafts nightclub, but I never quite recaptured that vibe.

I had a hell of a lot of fun trying, though.

I was aided in my endeavours by the ridiculous cheapness of the booze; a pint of cider, my tipple of choice, set me back less than £1.50.

Although I should probably point out that this was 1997. The cost of being a student has risen rather dramatically since then. As an aside, I'd been lucky enough to enrol in the last year before tuition fees were established. Up until that point, every young person in the UK was entitled to a free university place, providing they could make the grades and get in. My sister wasn't so lucky; starting her course in Bournemouth three years later, she had to pay several thousand pounds more for her degree than I did for mine. Or rather, our parents had to! Poor buggers. Gill studied Screen Writing and I did Acting... and now here I am, bashing out dodgy memoirs based on a lifetime of extreme irresponsibility, whilst Gill's become a professional ski bum. I'll admit to feeling a bit guilty about how much Mum and Dad spent on us, and how little either of us have achieved to show for it.

I can't bring myself to regret it, though.

That money provided me with some truly *epic* piss-ups.

Oh, and in case you're interested, the same course I studied is currently open for enrolments. And the price? Only £9,000 *per year*.

Which makes £27,000 (US$35,000) – *just in fees* – for the standard three-year degree programme.

Now that's inflation!

Teacher's Pet?

Only a few days in, University was already shaping up to be the best three years of my life.

There was only one real disappointment: the acting classes.

They weren't at the Welsh College of Music and Drama.

Affiliation with this noble and much-lauded institution (where Sir Anthony Hopkins had once studied) had been my second most important reason for choosing Glamorgan University. The first reason, of course, was that no-one else would take me, but I was sort of glossing over this fact.

As far as I was concerned, Fate had been on my side when choosing where to study. She couldn't make me pass my auditions – even Fate isn't *that* powerful – but she'd managed to sneak me in the back way.

Or so I'd thought. But as it turned out, we wouldn't get to visit the WCMD until second year. And in the meantime, what we had to put up with was... Hm. How to put this delicately?

It was bollocks.

One of our first classes was given the delightfully pretentious label of 'exploring a space through movement'. Now, you could be forgiven for thinking this is just a fancy way of saying, 'walk around a bit' – but no! For an actor, to simply *be* in a space is, apparently, quite a profound experience. This was ably demonstrated by highly technical examples, such as sitting still on a chair whilst the rest of the class watched you. As for the movement itself, well, why walk… when you can *buzz?*

"You are all hungry mosquitos!" the tutor announced. "I want you to buzz around the space, feeling that energy and urgency that comes with the need to feed!"

It was one of those moments where I had to look behind me, to check I wasn't being pranked.

And so, with few other options, we buzzed.

A class of thirty-something twenty-somethings, arms either outstretched or tucked up funky-chicken style (your choice) – scurried around the studio, trying to avoid bashing into one another, hoping that if they moved fast enough, they might outrun the crippling embarrassment.

"Okay, you can stop," said the tutor.

Thank fuck for that, I thought.

"Now, you are full! Happy, tired mosquitos, who have fed! How do you explore the space now?"

I wondered if I could get away with taking a nap, and blaming it on art? Or possibly buzzing off down the pub. It was spectacularly demoralising to watch the entire class slouch around the room, each attempting to channel the spirit of a well-fed airborne parasite. Even more demoralising was the realisation that we had another year of this shit. If this was the calibre of lessons we had to look forward to…

The most convincing performance I managed in that class was acting like I gave a shit.

We had one lesson which involved closing our eyes and touching each other all over. The girls loved that one.

At one point, ordered to come up with some sort of partner-based movement exercise, James and I loosely choreographed a slow-motion kung fu battle. It was the kind of thing I might have done in the school playground, aged ten, whilst pretending to be Optimus Prime.

Our textbook was 'An Actor Prepares' by Konstantin Stanislavski – published in 1936! Staggeringly, it's STILL the primary resource for acting tuition, even now. I mean, I know it's an old profession, but we've been to the friggin' *moon* since then! Almost everyone else in the class had already read it, so I bought a copy from the university book shop and struggled through the first few chapters. It was deathly boring – not least because it was a translation from Russian of a seventy-year-old textbook. It was written as the diary of a hopelessly inept actor bitching about how hard it was to impress his director.

The book spawned two sequels, though I must confess, I never even made it through the first one. It hardly seemed to matter; at no point in class was it ever suggested that we put some of these time-honoured exercises into practice. I have a vague notion that we were meant to be studying Stanislavski's 'method' – but I went to every single acting class, and all I know about his method is it still hadn't been revealed when I gave up around page 233.

I couldn't help but wonder what the students at the Welsh College were doing in their acting classes that year.

Somehow, I didn't think impersonating a mosquito was high on their agenda.

I fared better in other classes. Our syllabus was basically the Choose-Your-Own-Adventure of education. We got to select modules from a list, some of which were compulsory, and thus could build a course that most exactly suited our intentions. Universities are full of these courses, I was to discover; my favourite example being the ability, at many institutions around the country, to complete a full-time Bachelors degree in 'Combined Studies'. Catering perfectly to the ADD generation, you could simple pick n' mix random modules from almost any course – perhaps spending a semester taking one class each from Astronomy, Philosophy, Drama and Woodwork. Which sounds like a fun year, but I can't see it translating very well into the job market.

It'd be a *little* awkward when you apply for the career of your choice, and the interviewer asks what you studied at university. Replying, "Uhhh... *stuff?*" probably wouldn't give the best impression.

Regardless. In addition to Acting I picked Technical Studies, which was a blast. This was based in the uni's own tiny theatre, a well-equipped space painted entirely in black. It had a tiny control booth overlooking the stage area with anti-distraction red lighting, which made me want to shout, 'ROXANNE!" whenever it was turned on. This cramped room contained the control systems for a variety of professional stage lights mounted on a steel grid just below the ceiling. We were to learn about all those lights, how to focus and adapt them, and how to program the giant control desk to make them perform on cue. There was also the least state-of-the-art sound-effects system imaginable. The 'Revox' machine was one step up from a bloke tapping shoes on a plank and waving a tambourine at the microphone. It consisted of two reels of tape and a reading head, all mounted on a wooden board like an easel. The reels could be manipulated by hand, giving us hours of fun playing recordings of our voices at super slow speeds. It's hard to believe, but in the late 1990s, this technology was still *de rigour* in theatres around the world. This is because a theatre sound effect has to be instant; a peal of thunder, for example, has to occur at *precisely* the same instant as the corresponding flash from the strobe lights. CDs have a spin-up time, an unquantifiable delay between pressing play and the start of the track. For special effects, this rendered them next to useless. They were still the primary medium through which sound effects were distributed – it just meant that before every show we'd have to search the effects library for all the sounds we wanted, find the CD in the index – and then painstakingly record all the sounds off the CD onto old-school reel-to-reel tape. Bizarre!

We got plenty of practice at cutting and splicing the tape, to get all our effects onto one reel. Then, as the moment approached, we would wind the tape forward by hand, looking for our pencil marks on the tape. Aligning a mark with the tape head meant the sound it indicated would play instantly on pressing the button. Man, it was a lot of work!

Oddly satisfying, though. And infinitely preferable to being a mosquito.

I also chose classes in Directing and Improvisation. Unfortunately, alongside these genuinely interesting modules that I hoped would one day lead me to a successful acting career, there was yet more bollocks.

I mean, how does this grab you as a course title: 'Realism and Naturalism'?

I know, right? *Scintillating.*

Yet there were a whole bunch of them, like 'Expressionism and Epic,' 'Elizabethan and Jacobean Drama,' and 'Surrealism and the Absurd'. What's worse is these modules were compulsory, meaning that while we were forced to choose between the fun and potentially useful stuff, like Acting or Directing, the utterly pointless drivel would be force-fed to us regardless. These classroom-based lectures were apparently aimed at teaching us about historical movements in the performing arts – the knowledge of which was bound to come in useful on the set of the next Avengers movie.

As far as I can tell, they'd added this crap to make our course easier to grade. With most of our modules being performance-based, we faced the 'modern art' problem; what one person thinks is rubbish, another person wants to spend a million dollars on. So to add something more quantifiable to the otherwise highly subjective subjects, we ended up with hours of the most boring work since The Encyclopaedia of Stamp Collecting was last revised.

Worse still; these modules, being essay-based, required *homework.*

Now, my version of library research tended to involve taking out large numbers of books, reading none of them, and then writing the essay off the top of my head. I'd long since developed two skills which could have carried me to the glittering pinnacle of academia; the ability to retain large amounts of information for short periods, and the ability to bullshit. So long as I'd sat through a handful of lectures I could generally regurgitate my notes, but wrapped in such elaborate language that they seemed far more compelling than they really were.

This had allowed me to pass every exam since primary school with flying colours, despite doing little or no actual studying. Well, except for Geography; I can't tell my left from my right, so I mixed up East and West on the compass, scored 32%, and was asked to take History from then on.

I'd never heard of Expressionist Theatre. And I couldn't for the life of me think of anything remotely interesting to say about Jacobean Drama. I still can't, actually, and I doubt I could have done while I was actually studying the stuff, but what can you do? I had no choice. Not only did I have to *go* to the lectures, I also had to *read* some of the dozen or so books I borrowed from the library for each course.

Curses! Surely I didn't sign up for this?

The textbooks were so dry they sucked all the moisture from my room, putting me in desperate need of a pint. But my haphazard and half-drunken skim-reading occasionally produced some gems.

One of my favourites was a single sentence in a dusty book on Realism, that I pounced on and talked up into a full-blown theory. The essay I wrote on the subject was really a gigantic basket of waffle built around one bizarre point: that reality, in this day and age of artificial intelligence, suicide bombings and TV evangelism, is *too unrealistic* to be truly represented realistically.

My essay wasn't returned to me with all the others. I waited, not sure if my work had been lost, or if the teacher had completely forgotten I existed. Eventually I dared to make an appointment with him to discuss it.

He wasn't in the best of moods when I showed up in his office.

"How dare you!" he said, stomping around behind his desk. "Where the hell did you find this theory?" He picked up my essay and threw it back at me. "Do you realize what you've done? I've had to completely re-structure the course to address this! I haven't slept all week!"

It was the kind of existential problem that only happens to people who teach made-up subjects. But it felt a bit like divine justice; you lay that Realism crap on me, and just see where it gets ya.

I passed, though.

Bad Romance

Pete's triumphant return to university called for an immediate party.

He'd met another girl back in Lancashire, and had stayed home as long as possible to be with her. I'll admit to being a bit jealous; I'd been at uni for two full weeks when he arrived, and despite the initial flurry of interest, I still hadn't managed to acquire a girlfriend.

Damn things were more elusive than Donald Trump's tax returns.

So with this in mind, I convinced Pete to head to a popular venue off campus for our reunion.

Bootleggers was a dive bar. But it was a big dive bar, at least by local standards, and was the venue of choice whenever the Student Union was full, or closed, or 'hosting local DJs'. No matter what time of the day or night you went in there, it was crammed with students. It was oddly-shaped, with an upstairs balcony that I *may* have jumped off a few times, and one long bar (which I *may* have danced on a few times). Honestly, I think I was thrown out of Bootleggers way more often than was fair.

Eventually it got bought out and rebranded as the 'Knot Inn', allowing an enterprising group of students to steal the 'B' from the 'Bridge' pub down the road and replace the 'T', leaving us for two glorious days with 'The ridge' – and the 'KnoB Inn'.

But I digress. In case you haven't noticed.

Bootleggers had become a firm favourite with several of the girls I hung out with – largely because they sold a new Alcopop that was bright pillar-box red, and tasted like an alcoholic version of raspberry Fanta. (It also had the distinction of making your vomit bright red, which was quite alarming the first few times it happened.)

On this particular night I knew that Emily would be there, along with her regular gang. I was besotted with Emily. I didn't see her a lot around campus because our courses couldn't be more different; she was being sponsored through uni by the Royal Air Force, and was studying something complicated in the science labs, whilst I spent my days in the art blocks fannying around in a leotard. We still lived in the same hall of residence though, her on the floor above me, so we often bumped into each other when coming or going. On these occasions she was all smiles and delight.

She always made time to stop and say hello.

And she always said hello with a kiss.

That evening, as the cheerfully-coloured beverages flowed, we sat together and chatted about all manner of things. Emily was beautiful of course, but more importantly, I really felt like I could *talk* to her. She was interested, and interesting; mysterious and alluring; flirtatious to the point of being almost attainable, whilst simultaneously being so far out of my league she was in a different time zone.

And somewhere between topics of life, death, God, the universe and the future – we finally broached the topic of sexual attraction.

And she was.

Sexually attracted.

To me!

To say that the feeling was mutual... well, I *did* say the feeling was mutual. I think I may have yodelled it.

As Bootleggers closed and the various groups milled around in search of their missing members, Emily gave me a kiss that was laced with promise.

And then she gave me an actual promise; "Come up to my room tonight," she told me, "and we can get to know each other *properly.*"

I think I stared at her for about five seconds, as my addled brain checked that sentence for hidden traps.

"Just to be sure," I said, "we're going to have sex tonight, right?"

Emily rolled her eyes – those perfect, almond eyes – and said, "Yes, of course!"

I was quite excited, to be honest.

Even Pete was impressed – he told me so, as we sat on my bed, one floor below where my Goddess was waiting for me.

"OHMYGODOHMYGOD! I'm going up there *right now!*"

"NO!" Pete stood, blocking my path to the door. He's not a big bloke, but then, neither was the path to the door; there was less than two feet between my bed and the desk that ran along the opposite wall.

"What? Are you mad? I'm not missing this. No way."

"Just listen to me." He gestured at the bed, and I sat, warily. This had all the hallmarks of one of Pete's advice sessions.

"You can't seem too desperate," he explained. "Chicks don't react well to that. If you show up five seconds after she invited you, looking like you're fit to burst, she'll lose interest."

"Okay, I see what you mean…"

"Exactly! You've got to play it cool, at least give her a little while before you go up there. Make it look like you nearly didn't come. Like you chilled out for a bit, then thought it over, and decided, what the hell?"

"Okaaay… so, what do we do now?"

Pete glanced around the room, his gaze coming to rest on my solitary shelf. He grinned. "Now, we play chess."

"CH– *Chess?* Are you out of your fucking mind? There's a gorgeous girl up there, sitting alone in her room, waiting for me. *She's told me she wants to have sex with me!*"

"Yup, that's right, mate. This could be a good one for you. All the more reason not to rush it. Here," he took the glass chess set, a going-away pressie from my parents, down off the shelf, setting it on the bed between us.

"You cannot be serious."

"Deadly serious, mate. Nothing worse than being too eager. Trust me – one game is all it'll take. By the time you get up there, she'll be begging for it."

I eyed the chess set dubiously, as Pete blew a thin cost of dust off it.

"I can't believe I'm doing this," I told him.

"You'll thank me later."

I did not, in fact, thank him later.

Because Pete had overlooked three crucial facts in this equation. One; that he was way too drunk to be giving any sort of advice, and I was way too drunk to be taking it. Two; both of us were way too drunk to play chess – our first and only match of the night lasted well over an hour. And three; Emily was way too drunk to wait for me. When I knocked on her door an hour later, there was no response. I tried the handle, finding it unlocked, and stepped inside. Emily was passed out on the bed, fully clothed, the blankets knotted beneath her and a teddy bear tucked under one arm.

I considered trying to wake her, but it didn't seem right. Plus, of all the possible outcomes from her being rudely awakened by a sozzled stranger in her bedroom at 3am, sex didn't seem terribly likely.

I looked at that bear, staring vacantly into space, and wanted to poke its eye out.

That could have been me…

Bastard.

It was the first time, but not the last, that I've been mortally envious of a teddy bear.

A week later, I met Michelle. I'd seen her around, as she was friends with the girls from the floor above me, but I'd never really spoken to her. To be honest, I didn't really fancy her, and as she was generally surrounded by girls I did fancy, I hadn't made much effort. But Emily was now beyond my reach; she was dating someone so cool he had a *goatee,* for crying out loud! I couldn't compete with that.

So when a friend of Emily's introduced me to Michelle, I decided to pay attention.

"We're all starting to pair off," she explained, "and Michelle hasn't found anyone yet. I know she likes you, so... what do you think?"

I was stunned. To be told that someone I didn't even know found me attractive – and enough that she'd mentioned it to someone else – was a revelation.

"Sure," I said, "I'd love to go out with her!"

Michelle was tall; bigger-boned than the girls I usually went for, but pretty, with shoulder-length blonde hair. She was every bit as excited as I'd been led to believe; when we met up again the following night, she spent the entire evening kissing me, and after we left the pub, my arm wrapped possessively around her shoulders, she invited me up to her room.

She lived in Glamorgan Court – a new and considerably more expensive halls of residence. Rather than one huge building, these halls were like separate apartment blocks, each four storeys high with five individual rooms per level. Each floor was like a self-contained flat, with its own kitchen and intercom-controlled access – and every room had an en-suite shower!

Paradise.

Especially as I helped Michelle out of her clothes and slipped under the covers with her...

We didn't make love that night.

The phases of the moon, shall we say, were incompatible with our desires.

But we spent the whole night talking, getting to know each other, swapping stories of our childhood and comparing our hopes for the future.

The next day, I was floating on air. All I could think of was that I'd finally found my soul mate, and she'd been hidden in plain sight. I couldn't believe I'd overlooked her before, and was incredibly grateful to Emily's friend for introducing us. What she had created, by bringing us together, was something only sung about in ballads. There was a word for it: only one word, and it was bursting from within me.

I decided to tell Michelle that I was in love with her.

I even wrote her a poem.

She wasn't in when I called around to visit, so I left a message with one of her housemates via the fancy intercom system.

An hour later, I hadn't heard back from her, so I nipped round again, just in case.

I continued to nip round, every hour on the hour, for the rest of the day.

When Michelle did get back, she was happy to see me – if a little concerned about my attentiveness. "The thing is," she said, "I'm not sure we should be getting this close, this fast. It's still early days, and we're here in this amazing place, full of all these new people..."

"Yes, exactly!" I agreed. I was on a natural high, and would have agreed if she'd said it was full of giraffes.

"What I mean is, it's great spending time with you, but you don't need to come by here looking for me six times in one day."

"Oh, of course not! I just *really* wanted to see you."

"Yes... it would seem so."

"And I wrote you this!" I produced the poem, and stood nervously by as she read it.

"That's lovely," she told me, when she'd finished. "But it's very... I mean, I'm not sure we... What I mean is..."

And that was the end of that.

Michelle decided that we were better off as friends, and of course I agreed.

I wrote her a poem about that, too.

Apparently I was going through a phase of it.

A few nights later I met Nik, under less than ideal circumstances.

For starters, it was 3am. I was hammered, which wasn't terribly unusual for me; she was sitting on a table in the kitchen above mine, leaning back against the wall, knees drawn up under her chin, wearing red plaid pyjamas.

She was unhappy about life in general and men in particular, and in need of a good rant. Whereas I just wanted to chat up a pretty girl in her pyjamas.

And Nik was *very* pretty. Tiny and skinny, her pale face was dominated by huge eyes, which I appreciate makes her sound more like a fish, or possibly Gollum from Lord of the Rings, but that's because I suck at writing descriptions of people. Take it from me, Nik was cute – when fully dolled up in her best punk attire, she looked like she'd stepped straight out of a Manga cartoon.

She was thrilled to have found a willing audience, and I was smitten. We spent most of the next few weeks holed up in Nik's bedroom, playing computer games whilst drunkenly comparing tales of our previous sexual conquests.

Funny; I'd known Nik for about ten years before I dared admit to her that all those elaborate stories were lies.

But she admitted that most of hers were, too, so it's all good.

In those weeks, the most intimate thing we did together was watch Jerry Springer on her portable TV. That didn't keep me from dreaming though, and in my state of perpetual hopefulness, I was delighted when Nik decided we were officially a couple.

I already felt like no-one else could understand me as well as she did; both introverts, though we'd handled it in different ways, and both secretly quite terrified of other people. Together, we stood alone against the world – or more accurately, we hid from it in her bedroom, emerging only to re-supply ourselves with vodka.

The was only one word which could possibly sum up what I was starting to feel.

So I decided to tell Nik that I was in love with her.

I didn't write a poem, because there's only so many times a person can make that mistake. Plus, Nik was a cynic of the highest order; whilst I knew she was fond of me, I also knew I'd face an uphill struggle getting her to reveal any more tender emotions she might be harbouring.

The venue I chose was, somewhat predictably, the nearest pub. Nik only dared venture outside when fortified by alcohol, so she hadn't met many of my other friends. This time I introduced her to Pete, and used him to help gauge her feelings for me. The results of the analysis weren't great.

"She's not in love with you, mate," Pete informed me, obviously deciding on the direct approach.

"What makes you say that?"

"Easy. I asked her."

"You WHAT?"

"Yeah. She likes you and all that. She's just not ready for that level of commitment."

"But... but... how am I... what the *hell* am I going to say to her now?"

"I dunno, mate. You were gonna tell her you love her, right?"

I sighed. "Yeah."

"You want my advice?"

I sighed again. "Yeah."

"Don't."

Street Smarts

Dorothy of Pan Artists had flipped her lid when I admitted I was buggering off to university in South Wales. She'd worked hard to get me accepted for the regular gig on Coronation Street, only to find I was leaving the country a few months later. I'd had to promise her that nothing would change; I'd still be available whenever the show needed me. For that, I had to be reachable, and that meant doing something which, at the time, was completely outrageous: buying a mobile phone.

My parents bankrolled this investment as a combined birthday/going away present; partially because they're awesome, amazing people, and partially because they'd heard Pete say there were only two pay-phones in the entire university Halls of Residence, and that he'd often had to queue for an hour just to call home.

I was inordinately proud of my phone.

I was the first person I knew to have one.

It was a dark blue chunk of moulded plastic with an extendable antenna, made by Telital – it was the first pay-as-you-go phone released in the UK. Before Vodafone came up with this idea, the only way to own a mobile was to sign a blisteringly expensive contract and sacrifice your first-born.

Within two years, the legendary Nokia 3310 came out, unleashing *Snake* on the world. Most people in my generation fondly remember this as their first phone. I had one too, but it was my third.

In those early days, before mobile phone ownership was widespread, no-one had thought to make rules about turning the things off. So I didn't – and inevitably, when the calls came through, I was in the middle of a class.

"I'm sorry, I have to answer it," I explained, as eight different tones of piercing electronic bleep approximated *Ride of the Valkyries*. "It's my agent!"

A collective groan would issue from the class.

But that didn't stop me saying it.

Every.

Single.

Time.

Because you know what? Fuck them! It *was* my agent, and that ringtone meant I was getting work. They groaned because they were jealous – of the experience I was getting on film and TV sets all over the country, and of the phone itself.

No-one else had one.

And I knew it was my agent, because apart from my parents – who would never dream of calling me during school hours – Pan Artists were the only ones who had my number.

Typically, the call from Dorothy would instigate a journey which I became heartily sick of over the next few years.

As soon as I was free of lectures, I'd pack a bag and walk a mile to Trefforest station, jumping on the next train to Cardiff.

I generally caught the last train to Manchester, leaving Cardiff Central at 7pm, and arriving around 11pm. Then it was a decent hike to the bus station, carrying a bag bulging with books for studying, books for reading, and three complete changes of clothes (I was ruthlessly professional in this regard, bringing multiple outfits including shoes).

The bus took me to a stop in Chorlton-cum-Hardy, a down-at-heel suburb which has since been gentrified, and deposited me right outside a takeaway. I'd nip in there and buy a whole pizza to myself – justifying it by reminding myself I'd be earning money the following day. The pizza would put a spring in my step as I rushed through the streets towards my Uncle Paul's house. Uncle Paul, Aunty Margaret, and everyone in their household would be long abed by this time; in their wisdom, they'd posted me a key. I'd let myself in as quietly as possible, and tiptoe into the lounge. Without fail there'd be a huge sleeping bag sitting ready for me, and after devouring the pizza I'd snuggle up on the sofa and doze off.

Mornings came all too quickly on those days, but I didn't mind. After all, there was a good chance my work day would mostly involve sitting around reading a book. I'd tidy away my plate and pizza box, roll the sleeping bag up, and leave everything exactly as I'd found it. Having arrived when everyone was already asleep, I was leaving well before anyone else would be up and about – no-one would ever know I'd been there, were it not for the thank-you note I left. The first time I realised this, I signed the note 'Caspar', and became known to that household as 'the friendly ghost' ever afterwards.

It was often still dark when I caught the bus back into the city; my on-set call time was usually 6am. No combination of public transport would get me there in time though, so 5:45am would find me jogging the last mile through the backstreets of Manchester, spanked every step by a rucksack with three pairs of shoes in it, panting my way past the production office, taking the stairs three at a time to the third floor, barging into the Green Room and collapsing in a puddle of sweat.

All to be there when the 3rd AD popped in with his call-sheet.

After which, his advice would usually run something like, "We're a bit behind schedule this morning, so we probably won't need you till after lunch. Just relax for now, and I'll come get you if something changes."

That was my cue to nip downstairs to the bathroom and dry myself off with bog-roll.

Of course, there were plenty of times when we were used all day.

This typically meant standing around in the Rovers Return set for hour after agonising hour, unable to mitigate the crippling boredom with a books or homework. Conversation consisted of:

"Getting much work lately?"

"Yeah, a bit. You?"

"Yeah, same."

And that was about it.

Still nine hours and fifty-seven minutes to fill…

The irony wasn't lost on me. I was studying acting, but had already developed a bad habit of skiving lectures to spend time in the pub. Yet the majority of my acting career so far had been spent in this damn pub, and I couldn't get out of there fast enough!

Some days we'd fire through scene after scene, being sent back to the Green Room to change clothes each time. But the worst days featured long, complex scenes that required dozens and dozens of takes. There was too much that could go wrong, starting with the actors forgetting their lines, the cameras messing their moves up, and stray noises coming from the crew or their equipment. But no small number of outtakes were caused by the set itself – most commonly the beer taps on the bar.

Beer pouring is usually filmed in a separate close-up, because those taps are bloody unpredictable. That's why TV bartenders are always cleaning glasses, and why far more people in films order whisky or wine compared with beer. I saw those taps explode a couple of times, or stutter and dribble; more often than not the pints would be ready-poured, and sitting on a shelf behind the bar waiting to be handed over. I think part of the problem was that it wasn't real beer. Legend had it that back in the golden days of television, it was. Apparently a few of the cast members cottoned onto the trick of blowing their lines repeatedly, as the continuity department would make sure their drink was replenished to exactly the same level for each new take. For this reason, the beer pumps had long since been wired up to dispense a universally-despised, weak, warm shandy. It looked like beer, but didn't taste like it – for which I was grateful, as I hate beer, and over the course of the seven years I worked on Corrie, I must have drunk gallons of the stuff.

Most of the time it came out of the taps reluctantly. The barmaid varied with the era, but she usually spent quite a bit of time coaxing out shandy, half-filling glasses for everyone on set – and then pre-pouring any pints she would be serving during the take.

One particular day, the mix coming out of the taps was ninety-percent foam – I swear they'd been mixing it with dish-washing liquid – and every drink she poured had to sit and calm down for a good five minutes before it looked anything like beer. It had been a long and frustrating day, but I was trying to keep the mood upbeat. As we were handed our glasses for about the fiftieth time, my conversation partner eyed his suspiciously. Fully three quarters of the glass was filled with foam, slowly settling into the brown liquid at the bottom.

He sighed.

Then the cameras started rolling, the actors struck up their dialogue, and my partner lifted his pint to take a swig. Just as he brought the glass to his lips and titled it, I leant forward and stage-whispered, "I know a girl who gives head like that!"

To say he choked on his drink would be the grossest of understatements.

He exploded it, coughing a great gout of suds halfway across the studio.

"CUT!" the director bellowed. Followed immediately by, "Can we have a *little less* animation from the background artists, please!"

I caused loads of outtakes on Coronation Street.

Not all of them were on purpose; the principle cast might get away with that sort of behaviour, but not us.

I'm just a clumsy bugger, and film sets are possibly the worst place in the world to be clumsy. You can't lean on anything, because even things that appear solid tend to make of cardboard, and the floor – which is rarely in shot – tends to feature an elaborate spider's web of leads and cables snaking off in all directions to pieces of equipment you'd swear have never been used. But spend too long looking at the ground and you're bound to walk into something dangling where it shouldn't be – a boom-mike, if you're lucky; a red hot lighting rig if you're not.

Definitely not the kind of pub you'd want to get drunk in.

I'll never forget the day I was asked to play darts.

A tremor of trepidation ran through me.

People did play darts occasionally, in the Rovers – I'd just never been selected for that particular duty before. And interestingly enough, I never was again.

You see, most English blokes can actually *play* darts.

Not me.

I'm crap at darts, because I've never seen the point of it, and because I have the hand-eye coordination of a jellyfish.

It's also very difficult to *mime* playing darts, as unless you throw one you generally still have it in your hand. Perhaps I was overthinking it, but I'd much rather have reclaimed my usual place by the jukebox.

When the first take began, the atmosphere on set became taut. Into the pub walked the two young cast members, deep in debate. When they reached their marks and turned to face each other, I could feel the camera on me. I was right between their heads, and just far enough away that I was fully visible from the waist up. I posed with my darts as though lining up a shot, hoping they'd get through their dialogue quickly. But this was a tense scene; they delivered their lines slowly, with gravitas. Words dripping malice, they faced off against each other... and all the while I stood behind them, awkwardly brandishing a dart.

I'd waited too long, I knew; I was going to have to throw the dart in my hand soon, or it would look ridiculous.

The scene dragged on, another venomous pause, with me feeling more self-conscious by the second.

There was nothing else for it.

I toyed with the dart for a few more seconds, resettling my stance. Then I closed my eyes and threw it.

The couple had reached a stand-off, and were glaring at each other in silent hatred when my dart missed the board completely, slammed into the plywood wall hard enough to make it wobble, and then skittered off across the floor.

There was an audible outpouring of tension, like someone let go of a balloon nozzle, followed by a few seconds when every single person in the place turned to look at me. Between extras and crew, there must have been at least forty pairs of eyes on me.

"Ah… sorry," I whimpered.

The next take went much more smoothly. I still threw the dart – I had to, really – but this time I let fly a fraction earlier, during the couple's final, heated exchange. The dart arced gracefully through the air and sunk into the board – dead centre, a perfect Bull's-eye.

YEEEESSSSS!

They used that take, and a few weeks later I noticed that particular storyline was due to be aired. It was rare for an extra to be so prominently featured on Corrie, and rarer still that you could identify the episode. So I actually bothered to watch it, for the first time since I'd started working on the show. The argument between the young couple was every bit as tense as I remembered, almost to the point where I could ignore myself – until right at the end, as the climax of the scene approached. And there, right between the heads of the lead actors, just as they began their glaring match was me – giving a triumphant and utterly unavoidable fist-pump.

Paperchase

For the budding, wannabe actor in the UK, there are very few resources available to help you in your quest.

In the days when I was studying, there was precisely one: *The Stage,* which billed itself as a specialist newspaper for actors. No real actor would ever bother to read the thing, because it was less interesting than reading whatever the paper had been before it was recycled to become The Stage; bog-roll, most likely. Ninety percent of it was filled with waffle about budget cuts to Arts Councils, and politically correct pieces celebrating the contribution of disabled women's theatre groups. I can't remember ever finding an interesting article in it.

But when I was looking for a job – which was always – the Auditions section of the paper was the only place to look.

The Stage came out on a Thursday.

I'd been buying it for years – or at least, I'd been trying to buy it.

It was supposed to be on sale from WH Smith – the biggest newspaper chain in the UK – but it was still borderline impossible to get hold of.

I'd be in the Cardiff branch looking for it every single week, and every week the same ridiculous farce would unfold.

I'd approach the counter, after ten minutes of fruitlessly searching the shelves.

"Hi there! Me again. I'm looking for a copy of The Stage."

"I'm sorry? What was that?"

"The Stage, please."

"What? Sorry, what do you want?"

"The Stage. Again."

"The *Stooge*?"

"Really? I have to go through this again? The Stage. It's the newspaper for actors."

The woman looked at me like I'd just asked for a fetish journal on fisting penguins.

"Newspaper for *actors*?"

"Yes! I bought it from here last week."

"Janice? Have you ever heard of this… newspaper for actors?"

"Ah! Janice! It was you I bought it from. Remember, last week? The Stage? You found it underneath that pile of flyers for the Pontypridd car boot sale!"

Janice peered over her bifocals at me. "A newspaper, you say? For actors?"

"Oh. My. God."

Due entirely to my dedication and tenacity, I was successful roughly half the time – but to be honest, I don't know why I bothered. I tore through the paper straight to the classifieds, and I replied to every single advert that had even the remotest relevance to my situation.

Over the last two years, I think there'd been six of them.

The vast majority of adverts were from porn companies, requiring female 'actresses' with broad minds. Most of the rest were for strippers. Then there were the regular scams that appeared every week: 'Want a Career on a Cruise Ship?' one teased. Predictably, when I gave in to the temptation and replied to it, it became, 'Buy Our 80-page Report on How to Get a Career on a Cruise Ship!'.

The 'Auditions' section was always full of ads for sales companies, with headlines like; "NOW AUDITIONING for the Role Of Your Life! We need rock stars and film stars, to find fame and recognition on the phones, contacting potential customers about our unique brand of life insurance…"

Pretty much every ad in that section started out with the words 'Become A Star!' and ended with me moaning, "Telesales *again*, the bastards!"

But the real, genuine auditions? Those cattle call ordeals, where thousands of people show up for a handful of jobs, like you see on the first few episodes of *X-Factor*? They don't exist. Not for the readers of The Stage, at any rate.

My apologies to The Stage's publishers, by the way, if it's improved in the intervening years. These days, where every other program on telly is a reality show, there might be a microscopic chance for someone reading those ads to end up on TV as a result. I mean, *The Only Way Is Essex* had to find its ~~sluts~~ cast members somewhere. But back in my day, The Stage wasn't worth wiping my bum on.

Agents advertised in there, too.

Now, there's a rule of thumb about agents, whether they be for acting, modelling, or of the literary variety. It's this: if they're advertising, then you don't want them. Genuine agents are extremely difficult to track down, yet they are still constantly inundated with applications. They could recruit every scrap of talent they'd ever need ten times over – and from people with sufficient determination to seek them out. The last thing they'd want to do is open the floodgates to every desperate oik who buys a newspaper.

So. Adverts from agents were (and are) scams – exclusively, without exception, to the last one.

Seriously!

There's a lot of pirates out there. And not in a charming, Johnny Depp, 'why is all the rum gone?' kind of way.

Of course, it took me a while to figure that out.

They used to say that single females should never go to an audition alone. I guess these days they'd have to say the same for blokes too (what with equality and all that). The warning signs to look for are either in the advert itself, or in the response you get when you reply to the advert. The main give-aways are; any mention of up-front fees (NEVER pay for an audition), and the place where the audition is to be held.

More semi-legitimate fakers will usually have an office or studio to operate out of. These are the guys who are just trying to scam you out of cash, usually for photos or joining fees. If you're asked to: a) meet the agent at his home, or b) 'on location' or 'on set', in a warehouse in some dodgy-looking industrial area – then you're going to get a) coerced into having sex to land the (none-existent) role, or b) raped.

But that almost never happened to me. Mostly, I would end up in the kind of place that, at first glance, seemed to be the real deal. There'd be a waiting room full of people like myself – that is, people with no real skill or experience that desperately want to become world famous actors – and an office beyond, with phones, and whiteboards and stuff. They'd have a video camera set up on a tripod to record the audition speech, and a white-ish-blue square on the wall to stand in front of when you get your headshots taken. And a smiling agent, who simply *loves* your audition technique. You're in luck – their books are open right now, they have a Gold Membership Package that is just perfect for someone with your potential – someone who is really expecting to go places. And the best thing is, they're prepared to waive the joining fee, and it only costs £100 per month more than the Silver Membership (which isn't really worth bothering with, as that would be a waste of your talent).

And then, you're on easy street! They have the professional photos you paid them to take, later that day, which they undertake to deliver to every contact they have in the industry. And they have your audition tape, to bedazzle clients with your amazing acting ability.

All you have to do is sit around and wait for the jobs to roll in (whilst still paying of course) – and all they have to do, is sit around and wait for the monthly payments to roll in. From you, and from everyone else they've conned. It's a brilliant business model, because anytime you get concerned that they're robbing you, and call them up to complain that you haven't heard anything since you joined up, all they have to do is give you the 'It's a tough world out there, not many jobs in acting, that's why you need us!' speech. And if that doesn't satisfy you, there's always the fall back position: tell you that they are more likely to give work to the people who don't keep ringing them up and complaining... and there you go. Instant checkmate.

The ultimate kicker comes when you finally decide you've had enough. You're starting to suspect they've blocked your phone number, your daily emails are going unanswered, so you take the extreme step of calling them on a payphone – just to inform them that, as you've spent over a thousand pounds with them for absolutely no result, you've decided to quit. And that's when they really turn the heat up.

"We've actually been trying to contact you for a week now! Has your number changed, because the one you're calling from isn't on our file? We think we might have some work for you."

"No, I'm using a different phone because... well, never mind that. I'm calling to quit your agency."

"Oh, you're calling to quit, are you? Well, that's no problem. Some people just aren't meant to work in this industry. It can be tough, acting."

"I'm quitting because I haven't done any acting! You haven't found me a single job since I joined a year ago!"

"That's why I've been trying to call you for a week, because we have a job you might be interested in right now."

"What is it?"

"Oh, I can't tell you that. You're quitting, remember? But don't worry, we'll find someone for it."

And this is when your resolve wavers. When you start to question yourself; *Have I pestered them too much? Calling every week asking if they've found work? Have they finally decided to give me something? Are they actually legit? Were all those missed calls on my phone when I was getting hammered on Friday, really from them? AM I MAKING A HUGE MISTAKE???*

Then you remember that it doesn't matter – if you make one more payment to these assholes, then you can't afford to eat for the rest of the month.

Unless you get this job, and you get paid for it…

No. No more! You can't take another day of this, let alone a month.

"Yes, I'd like to quit, please."

"Okay, that's fine. *You can always find yourself another agent.*"

And that's when you realise it: this really *was* your big shot. You had *an agent*, for Chrissakes! The Holy Grail of the aspiring actor – a real, *bone fide* agent – and you're about to throw all that away for something as petty as money? Craziness! After all, your bank loan still has some leeway. Dad can always sub you some cash. And James still owes you £20 from Friday… That's enough to keep you in beans and Cornflakes for at least two weeks.

Long enough to rock that job, and earn your way into the big leagues…

"Okay, forget about all that. I'm in. Again."

"Oh, I don't know about that, I mean, we can't have people on our books who aren't 100% committed…"

"I said, I'm in! I'll do anything you want. Just tell me about that job."

"Okay, okay. I'll get Sheila to call you with the details next week. Meanwhile, seeing as how you're so enthusiastic all of a sudden, I should probably mention that we're introducing a new 'Platinum' level of representation…"

Casualty

I've been blown up a lot.

It's an occupational hazard, being an extra.

They say that drama equals conflict, but proper conflict, of the hand-to-hand variety, lies within the realm of the professional stuntman. Extras make perfect cannon fodder though, so when a really dramatic scene is called for, out come the fireworks and the buckets of fake blood.

I should probably point out that the actual explosions are done under very controlled circumstances, and no mere extra would be anywhere in the vicinity. But we get to show up looking like hell on stretchers, in body bags, or laid out on the floor quite a lot.

Honestly though, I wouldn't have pegged *Brookside* as my first major explosion. A distant cousin of Hollyoaks, it was a fairly dull show about the residents of a fictional street in Liverpool. Now, if I walked the streets of Liverpool on my own, I'd pretty much expect to lose a few limbs – but that's a socio-economic problem, and a bit deep for a daytime soap. No, this was a dastardly, if unrealistic plan, hatched by a departing member of the cast. His character had placed a bomb inside another cast member's night club, and I got to be one of the lucky revellers that attended it.

I'd taken my secret weapon with me; a smart shirt in a shade of burgundy that directors just couldn't get enough of.

Bright colours are frowned upon for supporting artists, whose entire job is not to draw attention to themselves. To help the cast to stand out, we're meant to blend into the background – hard to do if you're dressed head to toe in electric banana. Strong patterns were also to be avoided, as they can create a strobing effect when the camera pans or moves past them. Black and white are the worst... and of course, you can't have obvious logos or brand-names on anything.

Taken all together, it made for quite a restrictive wardrobe.

I'd built up plenty of suitable outfits, and made sure I always showed up with two or three different options. This made the ADs very happy, and never so much as when I pulled out that shirt.

I've no idea why. Maybe they spent so much of their lives obsessing over muted colours that burgundy looked exciting to them? Regardless, it became my lucky shirt, and I was always quick to pull it out when there was a chance of being featured.

This time it worked like a charm. I was coaxed forwards, and made to stand right in front of the camera. A few moments later I was joined by Alex Fletcher, a stunning blonde girl who played one of the lead characters. My job was to stand there, pretending to chat her up, until the bomb-threat came in and we were rudely interrupted by her girlfriend.

There certainly were worse ways of earning money.

A few weeks later, on the set of *Servants,* I learnt that I have an old-fashioned face.

Which is always nice to know.

Apparently some people have a more modern shape to their features. Who knew? I'm not sure what this says about my level of evolution – perhaps I'm a few million years behind everyone else. Or maybe it was because I was too damn lazy and too broke to get my hair cut? Whatever the case, it was to crop up again and again during my long and varied career as an extra. Casting directors often picked me out of a wall of head shots when doing period pieces. You may or may not have heard of the phenomenon of 'resting bitch face.' It seems I have 'resting medieval face.'

But I wasn't complaining.

Servants was one of those shows bursting with promise; in the post Colin Firth Pride and Prejudice world, period dramas were all the rage. In order to give Servants its own niche, the creative types behind it had decided to inject some sex appeal into the genre. Thus, the cast consisted mainly of attractive young actors, and the background artists were similarly chosen. I was a footman, got to wear humongous glued-on sideburns and a ridiculous wig, and spent most of my time on the show trying to chat up the girls. They were all pretty, skinny little things, who split their time between complaining that their corsets had been done up too tight, and fainting for the same reason. The basic premise of the show was to chronicle all the naughtiness that the staff of a great Victorian house got up to behind the scenes…

See what I mean? Heaps of promise. And I did the entire series.

Sadly, it sank without a trace.

When I started writing this chapter, I spent an hour trawling the interwebs, looking for references. All I could find of it is a single Wikipedia entry, about ten words long. IMBD (the Internet Movie Database) doesn't even have a photo!

Servants had been the result of some research. It had occurred to me that, although Pan Artists reigned supreme in the north of England, they were a long way from Cardiff. There were bound to be other agencies in this area that would find me work a bit closer to home. I went back to that precious, and by now much-distributed, BBC list. Supporting Artist Agencies from Edinburgh to London were listed, and it was easy to convince *Southwest Casting* to put me on their books. After all, they were used to applications from armchair enthusiasts – whereas I had my shiny new Student Equity Card! It was card, too – a shitty green rectangle that looked like it had been clipped from the back of a Corn flake box.

The folks at Southwest Casting had never seen one before. I couldn't figure out why, but most wannabe actors showed no interest whatsoever in doing extra work. That's why my performance classmates rolled their eyes at me whenever I told them I was off to work on Coronation Street; they considered what I was doing firmly beneath them. Which is really weird, as the TV industry is notoriously difficult to get any kind of experience in. Even on the crew side, the only way in is to start as a volunteer runner – unpaid. I was gaining valuable on-set experience, and making pretty good money at it. I liked to think I was also getting my name and my face out there a little, although that was putting a *very* positive spin on things.

Still.

When Southwest offered me a day on the UK's favourite hospital drama, *Casualty*, I jumped at the chance.

Filmed in a modest warehouse in an industrial estate in Bristol, Casualty is the ultimate in stealth operations. The first time I made the trip there, following an old-fashioned paper map, I stood right outside the place for twenty minutes screaming frustration at whatever God had seen fit to get me so horribly lost on my first day. I'd done three laps around the estate and ended up in front of a car park. Behind me were a handful of cars and a graffiti'd steel roller door; this couldn't possibly be the place I was supposed to be. Which meant I'd be losing this job, along with any further chance of working on the show.

Until a battered fire door opened and a bloke wearing headphones came out. Edging closer, in case some pissed-off warehouse manager emerged to accuse me of trespassing, I caught a glimpse into the interior.

It was chaos. Running figures, trailing wires, hammering and sawing, a hint of smoke... this was a TV studio alright! But one so inconspicuous that the kids spray-painting the outside of the building probably thought it was a tuna cannery.

Casualty was one of my favourite extra gigs.

I did odd days on it for several months, before Southwest put me forward as a regular. Not long after that, Mum applied to them, and ended up working on the same episode! She's a nurse, you see, and she actually *watched* Casualty, so she was thrilled to be on it. I have a horrible feeling that somewhere she's got a tape of all the episodes we were in…

In my scriptwriting lectures, I'd learned why hospital dramas and police shows are so common on TV. In both cases, plotlines literally walk in through the doors, making life a whole lot easier on the writing team. Theories abound as to why a murder occurs everywhere Jessica Fletcher visits, but no-one ever wonders why the cast of *CSI: Miami* have the same problem.

To round out my roster of agents, I joined Robert Smith (who was in direct competition with Southwest – I had to do some fast talking on this one) – and Kim Astone, who sourced work in and around Cardiff itself.

Kim found me one of my strangest gigs: *Pobol Y Cwm.*

Filmed in BBC Wales' HQ, Broadcasting House, for S4C, I was quite chuffed when I found out I'd been selected as a regular on the show. Kim made sure I was aware of what an honour it was. Much like Coronation Street in Manchester, *Pobol* was considered the gold standard; they didn't take just anyone, and required a high degree of professionalism from their supporting artists.

It was a great show to be on – and also a bit weird.

Great because it always paid really well; shoots inevitably ran on, required an outfit change or two, and paid a similar bonus for being featured in multiple episodes on the same filming day.

And weird, because it was filmed entirely in Welsh.

Now, you'll have to forgive me for stating the obvious there. I mean, the name of the show is a bit of a giveaway. It's a Welsh language show on a Welsh language channel. But for some reason, it never occurred to me that they would actually *film it* in Welsh. As in, the crew all spoke Welsh; the director's commands, the signs pointing to the toilets, and the pay-cheque – all in Welsh!

It made for a fairly confusing work day.

I had no idea what was happening around me. Occasionally some crew member would have to physically position me and point me in the direction I was meant to be facing, but other than that it was like any other day of extra work. Sit around for a bit, get beckoned out into a street-set, hang around until gestured to stand in a certain place, then stand there trying to look natural until gestured to leave again. All around me this phlegm-laced whirlwind of jaw-breaking dialogue raged; laughter, shouting, anger, soothing, apologies, commands, more arguments, and eventually that deathly quiet that falls before the director shouted whatever the hell passed for 'ACTION!' in Welsh.

And I stood amidst it, completely oblivious. Sometimes people spoke to me, and I shot them a vaguely panicked glance; they usually guessed what this meant, gave me a commiserating pat on the shoulder, and turned to find someone else to talk to. A handful of times per day, some crew member – usually a runner – would deign to speak to me in English. Usually to tell me it was time for lunch, or time to go home.

And that was that!

I never knew which episodes I'd been in, and didn't see much point in sitting through an unintelligible show looking for myself. So I've no idea how often I was featured, or how prominently. But it paid well enough – I must have done at least fifty filming days on Pobol Y Cwm.

I still haven't got a clue what it's about.

Friends, Roommates, Countrymen

Pete left university half way through my first year.

The seeds of it were sewn early; this girl he was dating back home must have been very compelling. He couldn't go a week without... whatever she was offering. He took more trips back to Lancashire than I did, and each time he went home, he stayed longer.

When he went home for a week and didn't come back, I had an inkling of what had kept him.

Or so I thought.

I'd assumed a missed train, due to an overly passionate goodbye romp, but when Pete failed to materialise the next day, and then the next, I got worried and called his mum.

"Oh, Pete's injured himself," she explained.

"Oh no! Is he okay? What happened?"

"He's fine now," she said, "but he had to have a little operation. He ruptured some of the muscles in his tummy."

"His abdominal muscles? He's given himself a hernia?"

"Yes, that's right."

"Oh!" Then it dawned on me. *Holy shit!* Apparently, he really had missed that girl.

"*Oh.*" I said.

"He did it lifting weights, in the gym." Her tone brooked no argument.

"Riiight... okay then. The gym. Well, I hope he's feeling better."

"Yes, he's much better now. He's round at Nicky's house at the moment, or you could talk to him."

Round at Nicky's house, eh?

"Okay, well, I hope he doesn't burst his stitches in her... gym."

"I'll tell him you called."

When Pete returned, it was to find a poem I'd written about his exploits plastered all over every noticeboard on campus.

I like to think that wasn't a factor in his decision to leave university for good.

In fact, he'd just achieved something that, like me, he'd been searching for for a long time: a stable relationship. With someone who felt for him what he felt for her.

And someone vigorous enough to let him herniate himself in the process...

I wished him every happiness.

But it left a bit of a hole in my social life.

Performance lessons had graduated from 'exploring the space' to 'inhabiting the space', and the class had split into those that lapped this pretentious shit up, and those that, like me, treated it with a healthy dose of scepticism. Excluded from the popular crowd on account of my weirdness, I naturally gravitated towards the alternative.

And they didn't come much more alternative than Chris.

Slightly older, with a straggling goatee, Chris dressed all in black and had an encyclopaedic knowledge of all forms of music. He also had a delightfully odd sense of humour, and remains by far the silliest man I've ever met. We got on famously.

Hanging out with Chris also brought me into contact with his best friend – a tiny, quiet, pixie of a girl called Sally. Sally's straight black hair perfectly matched her attire; only once did I see her wearing a blue denim skirt, and I nearly had a heart-attack.

Sally and Chris were both Welsh, and had been firm friends from the first days of our course. They were inseparable; Chris the charismatic goofball, Sally his delighted muse. They accepted me into their micro-clique without hesitation. It was well-known that I was a bit strange – therefore, I was one of them.

For the rest of the year, we hung out exclusively – almost incestuously. Rumours abounded, and we were in no hurry to squash them. It was too much fun to imagine the scandal and gossip we'd inadvertently created... so much so that we couldn't resist stoking the fires. Habitually late for lectures, we started arriving together, out of breath, re-fastening our clothes as we slipped into class. How we laughed afterwards at the shocked glances we'd received.

I experienced a brief resurgence of popularity towards the end of first year, when everyone who'd taken the Directing course module needed actors for the scenes they had to direct. It was a mad scramble as everyone dashed to recruit their friends, only to find they'd already agreed to be in someone else's piece. Never one to turn down experience, I said yes to everyone who asked me. Most people in my class ended up in at least one production; some of them were in two, and I knew one brave lad who did three.

I was in six.

I was also directing my own scene, as I'd taken Directing myself – I chose a chunk from House of Frankenstein, and Chris obliged me with a delightfully manic rendition of the Baron. Was my direction any better than my acting? I don't know. I didn't feel like I'd learnt much of either, to be honest, but at least I was getting some practice.

I continued to enjoy Technical Studies, even being invited by a more experienced classmate to operate the lights for a play she was stage managing.

Shakespeare Through The Ages was a modern and somewhat abstract show about the great playwright, and his devotion to his shadowy Dark Lady. My friend convinced our Tech Studies tutor, a short, fuzzy Welshman called Iolo, to design the plan for the lights, and recruited me to operate them during the week of the performance.

The show was playing in Cardiff's prestigious Sherman Theatre, so this was a rare chance to be part of a professional crew. The lighting desk looked like something from the bridge of the *Enterprise*, and took me hours of experimentation to understand it all.

This was also my first introduction to 'cans' – the headset communication system used backstage in theatres. As opposed to most similar devices, cans transmit constantly, and can be muted at the push of a button. This allows for easy communication between people with their hands full of props and scenery, but to the untrained idiot, can be a minefield.

In a cast and crew of more than twenty, there was one young lady that stood out. She played the role of Shakespeare's mysterious Dark Lady, and without ever speaking, she captivated me.

Gods, she was gorgeous – tall and slender, with straight, coffee-coloured hair down to her bum. I'd only really seen her from the vantage of the lighting booth, but swishing gracefully across the stage in a succession of slinky dresses, she quickly became the embodiment of feminine perfection to me.

The play had a motif where, to mark the transition between scenes, her character would ring a bell mounted on the wall.

In the final dress rehearsal, as the Dark Lady moved towards her exit, the director called out to her, "Don't forget to ding the donger!"

Safe up in the lighting box, I nudged my friend. "She can ding my donger anytime," I quipped.

I heard a gasp, and realised my friend was staring at me, eyes wide.

I'd forgotten to mute my headset.

All around the theatre, stagehands were collapsing in fits of giggles, while the cast stared at them in confusion.

The director roared with laughter, tearing off his headset to shake a finger up at me.

My Dark Lady also stared up at me, bemused, while my face turned hot enough to melt glass.

I never forgot to press my mute button after that.

Drunk at the aftershow party, I explained the joke to her, and against all odds, she reacted favourably. She spent the rest of the evening wrapped around me, kissing me so intensely I barely had time to breathe, let alone drink.

It didn't last, though. A week later, her mum dropped her off for our first date – which also became our last date, when I realised with horror that she had only recently turned sixteen...

Awkward!

Her mum certainly thought so.

Second year rolled around, and with it the end of my stay in halls of residence. I moved into a share house with Nik, my almost-girlfriend from first year. Extreme agoraphobia had gotten the better of her and she'd dropped out of uni towards the end of the first semester. Now she was returning to have another try, and we rented two rooms in a tiny terraced house in Trefforest. I was still spending almost all my time with Sally and Chris, and loving every minute. Together we came up with all sorts of crazy schemes, which we loosely grouped together under the banner of an experimental theatre company called 'Giant I'. We wanted to conduct a guerrilla campaign, perpetrating pranks disguised as art on students and public alike. The name 'Giant I' came from a building we passed on our weekly walk through town to the Welsh College. A vacant multi-storey office building, it had the words 'TO LET' posted in the windows of the top floor, in bright red letters that had to be at least as tall as we were. This gave us the driving mission behind our theatre company: somehow, some day, we vowed to break into that building and add a giant 'I' to the window between the 'TO' and the 'LET'.

It never happened.

We all have regrets, and this is one of mine. On my deathbed, (hopefully) many years from now, I'll sigh heavily, and say to anyone who's listening, "If only I'd put up that Giant I…"

And the people with me will smile and pat my hand, and think I've finally lost my grip on reality.

I never got to know the people Chris had ended up living with, as he spent all his time at Sally's house. Sally had moved in with a bunch of girls from her floor in halls, and one of them – a stunning blonde called Katie – became the fourth member of our little ensemble. Katie wasn't doing an acting course, so I hadn't met her until Sally introduced us. She looked like a Barbie doll come to life, and did nothing to dissuade it with her love of all things bright pink and fluffy. Sally and Katie looked like chalk and cheese – one tall and blonde, usually wearing neon pink miniskirts and bunny ears, the other tiny, dark and shy, clad head to foot in all-concealing black – but they both inhabited a world of shared silliness so profound that, when together, we could lose them in it for hours.

It was an outstanding year for partying and drunken shenanigans. One of our greatest triumphs was the acquisition of a huge wooden picnic table from the pub down the road. We went out in the dead of night to get it, dressed as ninjas, managed to sneak into the beer garden and manhandle it out of the gate in complete silence.

And then, carrying the thing down the alleyway behind our street, we came out onto the road just as a car was passing. "Quick!" Sally shouted, "sit down!"

So we sat on the benches attached to the table, facing each other, and tried to act normal. As though there was meant to be a pub table in the middle of this alleyway…

My housemates were seriously impressed with our new table, when we finally dragged it into the back garden.

All except Nik's new boyfriend, who was in the army.

"We do competitions," he said, "everyone puts in cash, and whoever brings back the best thing wins."

"You got something better than this?" I asked him, jerking a thumb at my new table.

"Yeah. One time I broke into Bristol Zoo and stole a penguin."

"WHAT?"

"Yeah! Kept in my bathtub."

"And… what did you do with it?"

"Next night I broke in again, and put it back."

My Second Year At University...

…was much the same as my first year.
   SURPRISE!
   Oh, except I got naked more often.
   Apparently, that's my thing. Who knew?

Studio Sessions

Most people want three things out of life: to be world famous, to have a hot girlfriend, and to kick ass.

Or maybe that's just me?

Anyway. By age twenty, the first two items on this list were in a perpetual stage of work-in-progress; with every waking breath I sought out acting opportunities and girls, not necessarily in that order.

That left item number three: kicking ass.

Or at least, gaining the ability to kick ass.

To this end, whenever I was back home in Lancashire, I attended as many lessons as possible at the local kung-fu school. It was a rarity, in those days; a dedicated, full-time martial arts studio, owned and run by European Full-Contact Champion Mark Strange.

Mark was a phenomenal martial artist, having devoted himself to the study of kung fu from age nine. He'd travelled to China several times as his career progressed, learning from venerable masters in the arts of *Lau Gar* and *Wing Chun*. He took all this knowledge, bundled it with passion and enthusiasm for sharing, and brought it all back home.

To Leyland. Which is a small industrial town in the middle of Lancashire, famous for the Leyland DAF truck factory, and absolutely sod all else.

It was an odd place to found a school of martial arts. London, perhaps, or even Manchester might have been more lucrative options. But Mark was Leyland born-and-bred, and he saw no reason why the ordinary denizens of an ordinary working-class town wouldn't all secretly yearn to become kung-fu masters.

And in fairness, a handful of them did. I was amongst them, and for the few short weeks in between uni terms I was the keenest of the bunch.

When Mark learned that I was studying acting, he confided in me that, in his desire to take his martial arts career to the next level, he was hoping to get into stunt work. It was a logical progression, but he'd come up against a common problem – the Catch 22 which lies at the heart of the entertainment industry. Before anyone would take him seriously, he needed some acting experience. And in order to get some acting experience, he needed to be taken seriously. He offered me a straight swap – I give him lessons in acting, in exchange for kung fu tuition. There was no way I was turning down that deal – I knew I'd be getting the better end of the bargain. I mean, he could actually *do* kung fu, and to a world-class standard, whereas I could barely act my way out of a paper bag.

I wasn't sure exactly what he could learn from me, but Mark was motivated, excitable and impossible not to like. I figured that if my uni experience was going to count for anything, I might as well trade it in to become a ninja.

All I had to do was work out how to teach him acting.

I knew one thing for sure – he was never going to buzz around the dojo like a hungry mosquito.

Mark had already taken several lessons with Jane Bell, who I'll always remember as the Hunch-front of Notre Dame from House of Frankenstein. Unlike me, she was an excellent actor and teacher – but she was never going to learn kung fu. We spent a few evenings in Mark's gym, him coaching me in high-level staff and sword Forms (sequences of movements, like the Kata in Karate), followed by me critiquing his audition speeches. It was easy to see what he was doing wrong, and it gave me an insight into my own difficulties; acting is all about immersing yourself in the role, about completely tuning out of your immediate surroundings and becoming the character you are portraying. I struggled with this part, as did Mark, but for the life of me I couldn't think of how to fix it.

*   *   *

By the end of my second year at university, I still didn't feel like I was on the cusp of any breakthroughs. No-one had made any attempt to explain what I was doing wrong – or even what I was doing right – and as far as a roadmap to acting success went, what they'd given me looked more like a half-finished game of *Battleship*.

Never mind.

During the long break between the second and third year of uni, I managed to land my dream job.

In the first successful audition of my career, I won the 'speaking role' of… wait for it… tour guide! At a small theme park attached to Granada TV Studios, in Manchester.

Okay, so not my absolute number one dream job. But it turned out to be a pretty decent gig.

The main attraction of the theme park was Coronation Street. When the outdoor set wasn't being used for filming, visitors could wander up and down it, posing for photos outside their favourite characters' houses and marvelling at how *small* everything was. (Fun fact – that 'camera adds five pounds' thing also applies to buildings, so they have to be made smaller to look normal-sized). Given the show's long and iconic history, it has a huge fan base in the UK and abroad; as part of their entrance fee, we took visitors behind-the-scenes, to where the magic really happened.

Or so we led them to believe.

In fact, the various departments we toured – make-up, editing, wardrobe etc – were long disused, carefully staged to appear as though they were still in use. If you think about it, it's obvious that we couldn't troop a constant stream of tourists through a functioning TV studio. Producing Coronation Street was an 80-hour-per-week marathon task that never ended, leaving precious little time to squeeze tour groups in – especially as the Studio Tour was booked solid, all day, every day, often several weeks in advance.

Part of our duty as tour guides was to learn by heart a vast packet of material about the show itself, plus myriad other aspects of Granada Studios. No stranger to learning lines, I was confident of being able to absorb the twenty-page document in record time. Unfortunately, I left one vital factor out of my calculation; I absolutely frigging *hate* Coronation Street!

Seriously. I can't stand soap operas. I can't think of anything more boring than taking the kind of ordinary, pedestrian lives we all live, and watching them on TV. I've never understood how anyone working a crappy job, struggling to pay their bills, fighting with their spouse and spending most of their free time down the pub bitching about it all, would want to watch a TV show about fictional characters doing exactly the same. *Argh!* But I'm clearly in the minority; millions of people tune in to Coronation Street and its ilk every day, and the humble soap opera remains the most popular form of entertainment on the planet.

Faced with a ream of facts about the show's history, including lists of statistics like how many births, deaths and marriages have happened on the Street since it first hit our screens, my mind just sort of switched off. I couldn't force myself to finish the document, and anytime I tried reading it I woke up half an hour later from a daydream about killer robots or alien dinosaurs rampaging through Manchester's dingy suburbs.

So, what to do? I was shortly to become a tour guide, leading groups of ardent fans around the home of one of the most popular shows on the planet. Yet no matter what I did, I couldn't retain even the most basic facts about Coronation Street.

Luckily, I now had two full years of professional acting tuition under my belt.

So I did just like they told me in class; I improvised.

Which is fancy acting terminology for 'I made it up.'

My first tour was a monumental success. Managing to disguise my nervousness, I waxed lyrical about the history of Granada Studios, about the esoteric uses the make-up studio had been put to, and about the relentless filming schedule of my least-favourite show. Whenever my script called for me to unleash some relevant statistic, I simply invented one to fit. As my career progressed, I became more dramatic and creative with my 'knowledge', and whenever I was challenged by some die-hard fan, I would simply cast a mysterious look their way, and ask them, "Are you sure about that?"

Without fail, this stopped them in their tracks. My confident posture, coupled with my perceived position of authority, inspired a sudden doubt in their minds. Did I know something they didn't? Had they miscounted? Could the difference between their death toll and mine hint at a sudden massacre to come? After all, I was surely privy to secrets about the episodes currently being filmed... It was a *fait accompli*.

I loved to mess with people. But I made up for my slight indiscretions with an avalanche of jokes, aiming to keep my tour groups laughing from start to finish. It certainly cut down on the fact-checking. And I justified it to myself by considering it preparation for my future career. After all, what is acting, if not lying for a living?

All I cared about was that my tour groups had a good time. Realistically, no-one was ever going to come back and complain about some fact I'd made up, whereas the more straight-laced guides were in danger of getting bad feedback on account of the tour being boring – which it was, if you stuck to the script – and a rip-off, which at £15 a ticket it was, no matter what we did.

A negative report could see us sent upstairs to man the Fox News-sponsored kids play area – a huge indoor jungle gym filled with slides, foam rollers, climbing walls and rope bridges, all surrounding a massive ball-pool. It sounds awesome, and it was – after hours we took turns racing each other through it. But working there was horrendous. It meant standing behind a desk for eight hours, deafened by shrieks of joy and pain from scores of hyperactive kids, and occasionally getting a bollocking from some parent whose kid got a skinned knee.

Worse still, whoever was manning the desk had to assist the cleaners in the event of an emergency – an all too frequent occurrence in the play area. The top secret code developed by the management for such occasions was far from impenetrable; "Code Red in Fox Kids" was a call for the cleaners to head upstairs and mop some kid's blood off the slide.

A sympathetic shudder ran through every one of us when the words, "Code Yellow in Fox Kids!" came across the PA system.

The tour really did rely on our ability to charm and entertain our audience – and to provide a good bit of misdirection. Because if you came right down to it, the tour itself was rubbish. Being traipsed through a half-dozen rooms, featuring such dramatic showpieces as an editing desk, a bottle of fake blood and a couple of dog-eared sets from shows that were no longer in production... it was all very tired. And DVDs had just begun to proliferate; suddenly, every dedicated film fan had access to unlimited bonus features, behind-the-scenes footage and 'making of' documentaries. The magic of TV was becoming less mysterious by the day, and our feeble prop displays and 'be a TV weatherperson!' simulations were looking seriously dated.

But I was a professional, so I upped my game to compensate.

I played it fast and loose with my script, gauging each crowd and making the rudest jokes I thought I could get away with. I made plenty of outlandish claims about shows and characters that had "been filmed on this very spot," and I took the piss out of the crappier tour elements before anyone thought to complain about them. I soon learned all the spots when I could squeeze a giggle from my group, and I worked them mercilessly.

I became pretty good at it, too.

For which I was eternally grateful.

Anything to save me from a Code Brown in the ball pool.

Closure

I loved working at Granada Studios. My mornings were
spent walking around the park in full costume, posing for
photos as a pirate or a Ninja Turtle. My afternoons were
spent misleading a whole host of Coronation Street fans to
the best of my ability. But the tour I gave wasn't all about
that. I still maintain I gave the most entertaining experience
to my customers, and my customer feedback seemed to
support this. For example, we had a full-scale mock-up of
Downing Street, the famous street in London where the
British Prime Minister lives and works. It had never been
used for anything other than the tour, though our official
script required us to gloss over this fact, suggesting, "anytime
a big-budget Hollywood movie like Independence Day needs
footage of Downing Street, this is the closest they get…"

Permanently stationed on the pavement outside no.10
was our waxwork policeman. Or woman – it changed with
the gender of the tour guide who was playing the role.
They'd stand there, motionless, wearing an old-fashioned
English Bobby's helmet big enough to cover their eyes. Their
job was to wait until customers stood next to them for a
photo, then put an arm around the unsuspecting guest –
scaring the crap out of them in the process. It was a great
trick, and a source of much hilarity. But as usual I had to take

it one step further, starting a trend of trying to make the silent policeman laugh. Of course they had to resist this at all costs...

"Here's PC Caroline, our waxwork policewoman. We couldn't afford a full-sized sculpture, which is why she's only as big as a child. Interesting fact: her head is completely hollow! There's literally nothing inside it."

I'd pause to allow our customers to take a good look.

"In case you're wondering, that blonde hair is a wig made from camel toe fur..."

Another pause, to check my progress.

"If you take a look behind her, you'll notice that her ass is actually twice the size it should be... we think the sculptor had a load of wax spare, so he just stuck it on her thighs and hoped we wouldn't notice."

Eventually I'd see Caroline start quaking, holding her breath to keep in the laughter. Then our customers would pose, she'd drape her arm around one of them, that person would generally shriek and leap about three feet into the air, and the whole group would collapse in hysterics. Job done!

Of course, I had to come up with new stuff every day, or it wouldn't work. Somehow, this was never a problem; I'd lie awake in bed, cackling madly at what I'd dreamt up to say tomorrow.

In fairness, Caroline gave as good as she got. "Here's Tony, our waxwork PC," she'd say as she led her group towards me. "Can anyone guess how much he cost? No? He cost ten *thousand* pounds! And before you ask – no, he's not worth it! We used to rent him out for parties at £100 per night, but we had a lot of complaints. Apparently he's quite... ah... *undeveloped* down there. Sometimes people don't believe he's made of wax, and they try all sorts of things when I'm not looking – like pinching his nipples, kicking him in the balls..." Then she'd pointedly look away while people poked and prodded me all over. I once had a young lad push his finger into my cheek so hard it left a bruise. "Wow!" he exclaimed, "he's not real!"

Man, that kid shit himself when I put my arm around him.

Ah, we had some fun. One day there was a solar eclipse, and Manchester fell right along the Path of Totality, meaning it would go completely dark in the middle of the day for a couple of minutes. The whole city was abuzz with anticipation, and the guides were drawing straws over who got to miss the event by leading a tour at that time. My friend Jonathan eventually volunteered. After all, this was Manchester, not southern California; the sky was seamless battleship grey, and no matter what the sun was doing there was at least a mile of cloud between it and us. But the customers in his tour group were understandably miffed about missing the event. They had no choice, as tours ran on a tight schedule and there was no chance of getting anyone to switch time slots.

But sitting in the break room, we came up with a solution. Jonathan took up his position on the low podium in front of the crowd, and began his speech.

"Ladies and gentlemen! I'm very sorry that you've all had to miss this important event to take part in my tour. So I have prepared something EVEN BETTER for you!"

With a flourish, he produced two circles of paper – pictures of the sun and the moon, that he had torn from the front page of the newspaper.

"Now witness nature's greatest spectacle!" he announced, holding the pictures out to either side. And then he began to sing: "DAAAAAAARN… DAAAAAAARN…. DAAAARN!" – a fine rendition of the theme from *2001, A Space Odyssey*.

As he sang the notes, he moved the two pictures towards each other above his head… and at the exact moment the circles overlapped, I flicked off the lights.

Honestly, it was better than the real thing.

That job was pretty much perfect. I was ever-so-slightly obsessed with Caroline, dating one of the other tour guides, hanging out with new friends and getting paid to joke around all day. It was missing only one thing: *Star Wars*.

Which, in fairness, is missing from most jobs.

But the summer of 1999 was the summer of Star Wars. The day was fast approaching when the movie that was like a religion to me would finally be returning to theatres worldwide. Despite the deep sense of foreboding I felt when the name 'The Phantom Menace' was released, I did what any true fan would do: I went to the nearest cinema and asked how many times it was physically possible to see the film on its opening day. The bloke in the box office didn't even need to check; clearly, I was not the first to ask. Six times was the maximum, by missing out the trailers, so I bought one ticket for each showing.

Man, was that ever a mistake!

I remember thinking, about an hour into the first movie, "Holy *shit!* I've got to sit through this crap *another five times?* Oh my God..."

Still, amidst the boredom, the seed of an idea was formed. The next day I went into work and asked if I'd be allowed to do the costume part of the day dressed as Darth Maul. The plan was enthusiastically approved, and I gleefully set to work on my costume, envisaging days of delighting tourists with spinning kicks and getting paid to flail around with a homemade lightsaber.

It was not to be.

I was close to finishing the costume when there came a dark day at Granada Studios.

There was no warning – I caught the train into work as usual, hiked in from the station, and was met with a bunch of very unhappy supervisors. The park was being shut down. It didn't take a genius to see why; despite the best efforts of its guides, the tour was a shambles. The sets were deteriorating, and whatever cash they'd been making on the exorbitant entrance fees, it certainly hadn't been spent on improving the place. The few actual rides in the park were pretty crap, nothing to compare with proper theme parks like Alton Towers. Our strength had always been Coronation Street, but that was no longer enough to keep the lights on. As tours were still booked for some weeks, a few people would keep their jobs, but no-one knew who. For now, tours had to continue, and I set out on my first of the day with a heavy heart.

We were nothing if not professionals, though. Showmen to the finish, we led tour after tour, and every time we finished one, a few more people had been given their marching orders. One by one we were called upstairs and told we had to leave – the only trouble being, we were being made redundant too fast for the queue of tourists, all of whom had paid for a tour which now had almost no-one left to guide it. I got back from my fourth tour of the day – we usually only did three each – to find I was next to be summoned. One of the girls who'd been working there longer than me was coming down the stairs in tears, so I wasn't under any illusions. I strode into the office, head held high, and took it on the chin. The bosses thanked me for my service, and apologised for the lack of anything resembling notice. Or a final pay packet. I surprised myself by tearing up slightly, but managed to pull off a plausible act of cheerful acceptance.

I walked back down the stairs and received a series of hugs from the girls waiting there. "You too?" Caroline asked. I nodded.

"Shit, we've no-one to lead the next tour! Like, seriously no-one! There's only three guides left, and they're already doing tours.

"I'll do it," I said.

"I… I don't think you're allowed. All the others were marched away by security as soon as they came back downstairs."

"Well, is there anyone else?"

"No."

"Then what other choice is there? I'll do. Don't worry, I'm fine."

And so I gave my last tour at Granada Studios accompanied by a security guard, despite the fact that I was officially no longer an employee. I like to think it was my finest one. I pulled out all the stops, finding a passion for the experience that had previously been ebbing out of me. It's hard to do anything but parrot the spiel when you say the same thing day in and day out, but this time it was like I reconnected with the source.

Honestly, I should get fired more often.

My virtuoso performance received a standing ovation from my customers, and several of them came up to me afterwards to promise a glowing review. How little they knew! As soon as the tour was over, I was escorted from the premises. Outside the gates, a bunch of my fellow jobless loitered – we'd all been made to leave immediately after termination, for fear we'd steal something, or make a scene in front of the public. I was the only one who'd been allowed to remain, as they could hardly evict me from the head of a tour group.

"So. Whadda we do now?" Jonathan asked.

"Dunno," I said.

So we did what any group of sensible people would do in that situation. We found the nearest bar and got horribly drunk.

And that was last time I went to Granada Studios.

Well, until the following week, when I was filming Coronation Street on the other side of the lot.

It was the second 'dream job' that I'd been fired from, for circumstances beyond my control. I was starting to think the Universe was giving me some kind of sign.

Loss of that job hit some people much harder than others; one of the lads I worked with committed suicide shortly afterwards.

But for me, it was a relatively small tragedy, so I tried to keep some perspective.

To get that job in the first place, I'd had to tell Granada that I'd dropped out of university.

Whereas in reality, I was due back there in less than a month.

Turns out I was getting good at lying for a living; I'd been planning on handing in my notice at the end of the week.

Love Changes Everything

As I headed into my third and final year at university, the dynamic changed completely.

From spending most of my lectures in the pub, I suddenly found myself so busy I hardly slept. Many of my courses now actually required me to *do* things – and they were big things, like entire plays and movies. Rehearsals for one production or another dominated my days and nights, leaving precious little time for the social activities I'd come to love.

The group dynamic changed too, in a variety of ways. First, Nik hadn't returned to university, so her room was let to a scrawny blonde lad who had all the charm and charisma of a scrotal infection. Dean, a black guy from London and my closest friend after Sally, still occupied the tiny box room next to him – neither of us were terribly impressed with our new housemate.

Dean loved to smoke weed, and I'd been known to partake on occasion. Perhaps this is a good place to mention that I'm a firm believer in the legalisation of cannabis. I once saw two documentaries in the same night – one on a new, multi-million-dollar anti-marijuana task force established by the police in Texas, and one about vast overcrowding in the

US prison system. Fully two-thirds of the population in the prison they featured were in there for cannabis possession or supply. It occurred to me that legalising weed would save a lot of otherwise fairly harmless people from being interred next to murderers and heroin smugglers. Taxing it would then provide a huge stack of cash to revamp those prisons – most of which would then be half empty anyway. It would also stop honest citizens like myself having to deal with nefarious characters to purchase our recreational supplies, and provide legal employment opportunities to hordes of stoners. I appreciate that opinions are like assholes, in that everyone has them, and this is only mine. But to me, it makes so much sense that only a government could possibly screw it up.

Anyway. Dean's friend and associate, who I only ever knew by the initial 'P', moved in downstairs.

Now, P was *heavily* into weed – on the distribution side, so to speak.

One afternoon, looking for Dean, I knocked on P's door, and was surprised to find it locked. After a few seconds Dean opened the door a crack, and one eye peered out. Seeing it was me he let me in, locking the door behind me. I quickly figured out why; on the bed was a pair of kitchen knives and a chopping board – and a long brown bar of hash. It was the size of a movie-style gold bullion bar, and my jaw dropped open at the sight of it. P was busy carving it into chunks for resale, wrapping the cubes in cling-film.

"I... I've never *seen* so much..." I stammered.

P looked at me, and burst out laughing. He gestured with his free hand, and I looked down at the cardboard box sitting next to him – in it was a stack of brown bars, three across by three deep.

"Holy *shit!*" I gasped.

Still chuckling, P flung back the valance on his bed. "Yo, check dis," he said.

The floor underneath the bed was packed with identical cardboard boxes.

It was only a single bed, though so there couldn't have been more than two dozen.

Like I said, the dynamic was changing.

But never so profoundly as between Sally and me.

You know that proverb, 'While the cat's away, the mice will play…'? It's a bit of cliché, so I created my own version: 'While Chris's away, Sally and Tony get drunk together and a group of friends convince them to kiss.' Admittedly, it's not as appropriate for every situation, but it pretty accurately describes this one.

The friends in question weren't mine; I don't even think Sally knew most of them. They had a delightful game called the 'Saliva Chain', where they compared notes of who had snogged who, and tried to figure out if there was anyone in the immediate vicinity who had yet to exchange some form of bodily fluid.

As newcomers, Sally and I fit into this category, so with considerable encouragement from the crowd, we made a significant effort to establish a position in the chain. It was good, harmless fun – and probably would have remained so, had it stopped there.

However.

Two other factors were in play, and they were about to change everything.

The first was a suspicion I'd formed, growing over previous weeks, that Sally found me attractive. Pieced together from tiny clues and subtle hints, I'd nevertheless convinced myself that she was interested. In return, I'd started to notice just how *cute* she was. I already knew this intellectually, of course, but she was so inextricably linked with Chris that it had simply never occurred to me that she was *available.*

The second factor was the kiss itself. It was incredible.

And it set me on a path from which there was no return.

Scarcely a day later, Chris was due to get back from visiting his parents.

Sally and I walked to his house to welcome him back. We'd said nothing about the kiss, or about our spontaneous urge to kiss again before separating for the night.

But I had a plan. I couldn't leave it alone; romantic as the notion of one perfect moment may be, it still hadn't answered the question that was beating against the inside of my head. Was it just drunken silliness? Or was it something more...? And could someone as attractive and alluring as Sally could possibly, really *fancy me?*

My palms were sweating as we paced down the pavement towards Chris's house.

It was now or never.

I stopped outside his front door, and turned to Sally.

"Hey, before we knock, I'd, err, like to ask a favour..."

"Yeah?" Her interest was piqued.

"It's just that... well, after today, I'll never get chance to do this again."

And, fully sober, I leaned in and kissed her.

And she kissed back.

It was magical.

And it lasted for quite a while.

Finally I disengaged, shot Sally a sheepish grin, turned away, and pressed Chris's doorbell.

As plans go, it would have been perfect.

Except that Chris wasn't in.

Which made the walk home fairly awkward.

I wasn't prepared for this sort of emotional quandary. Sally and I had been the best of friends for over a year; we'd laughed our way through all kinds of embarrassing situations. Chris's crazy, irrepressible presence had acted as a buffer, preventing anything mundane or serious from intruding on our wibbly-wobbly world. But he'd only been gone for a couple of days, and what had I managed to do?

Why, make an idiot of myself, of course.

And yet...

Two weeks later, under strict rules of confidentiality, Sally and I revealed our feelings to each other. And after a final week of confusion and soul-searching, we gave in and became a couple.

We agreed to keep our relationship a secret at first, to see if we had something that was worth turning our whole world upside-down for. Because that's what would happen, once

Chris found out; to protect him from unnecessary pain, we decided not to tell a single living soul. Apart from Katie, who apparently knew we were together even before we did. Keeping our love clandestine, at least for a short while, seemed like a suitably noble sacrifice. Plus, it was cooler that way.

I could hardly believe it.

Sally was the first girlfriend I'd had since…

Since…

…?

She was the first girlfriend I'd had.

Holy shit! I quickly decided against letting her know that.

I mean, I was already a hot mess of nerves and insecurities. A relationship based on *honesty?* That was never going to work.

At first, our affair was a furtive thing of stolen kisses and knowing glances. We grew braver though, finding time in our increasingly busy schedules when we could be alone together. Poor Katie, as the only person who knew about us, was probably witness to more illicit behaviour than she'd bargained for. But she was our best advocate and supporter, often helping to convey messages and straighten out the inevitable misunderstandings between us.

For Valentine's Day, Sally bought me a gorgeous folding lock-knife. I was blown away; I'd never been given *anything* for Valentine's Day before, and this present was perfect. It was almost scary how well she knew me! And equally, how well I knew her – I gave her a short, curved, Japanese *wakizashi* sword, in a green lacquered wooden scabbard.

We were a perfectly-matched pair of weirdos, and more than anything I wanted to tell the whole world about it.

But we couldn't.

Because, four months after that first intoxicating kiss, Chris still didn't know about us.

And whilst both Sally and I were starting to realise that we had something special, there was always the chance that it would implode. As it turns out, we were both fairly insecure people, and neither of us had much experience in matters of the heart. Alcohol lay behind most of our intimacy, and also fuelled regular rows about nothing. Mostly because, when you came right down to it, we were both quite scared.

Scared that this could really be something.

Scared that we could mess it up.

Scared perhaps even more that we might *not* mess it up… and what would happen then?

But mostly, just scared that this could quite easily become the most painful experience of our lives.

And so, we waited.

I told my parents, though.

I was so proud to have an official girlfriend, and I think they'd heard me talk about Sally so much they already felt they knew her. I took the knife Sally had given me home to show them. I'm not really sure what that made them think of the relationship.

But it mattered a huge deal to me.

I carried that knife with me everywhere for the next few weeks. It was a constant symbol of my deliciously non-single status, always there in my pocket when I needed a reminder.

And it was still there in my pocket the next time I accompanied Sally, Chris and Katie to Shafts nightclub.

The bouncers on the door always checked our student IDs, and several times I'd been forced to walk back home and get mine. Not so this time – when asked, I dipped into my pocket and proudly brandished my ID.

Along with the knife, which had come out in the same handful.

Ohhh… shit.

Hugh, a stocky, bald bouncer who knew our little group well, was quick to step in.

"Let me see that," he said, and I reluctantly handed it over.

He whistled as he opened it up. "Nice. But you can't have that in here."

"No! Of course not! I'm so sorry, it's…" I glanced at Sally and Chris, who stood together looking horrified.

"It's… well, I collect them, you see. I brought this one back from my parents' house, and I totally forgot I had it on me."

"Yeah, I still can't let you in with it," Hugh said.

"Don't worry, I'll take it home right now," I promised him.

"Actually, you'd better leave that with me," said a newcomer. I didn't know the man, but he was wearing a suit, so it didn't look good. "And your ID," he said, as Hugh passed him the knife.

"I'll have to suspend you from the Union, I'm afraid," the smart-looking man told me. "And this will have to go to the police."

My jaw dropped. It was all happening too fast. I thought I'd gotten away with it when Hugh intervened, but now...

"You'll have to leave the premises, and you won't be allowed to return until your suspension is lifted. If it's lifted. I'll arrange a hearing, and send you a letter."

That's when I recognised him – this bloke was the head of the Student Union.

And I was in real trouble.

Still, it was impossible to get too down about it.

Not when I had Sally to console me.

A few days later, sitting on the sofa in her lounge, I got a text message. From her. Which was odd, as she was sitting on the other end of the same sofa. But Chris was sitting in between us, and the rest of the lounge was filled with her housemates.

"Do you want to stay over tonight?" the text message said.

Does the pope shit in the woods?

I replied to the text, and Sally sent another one with instructions: "Leave with everyone else, wait a bit, then come back. I'll let you in."

At this point Chris declared that, since he was the only one without a phone, he was going to send messages of his own via the TV remote.

Needless to say, I followed Sally's instructions, shivering in the frigid darkness around the corner from her house for ten minutes before staging my furtive return. Unfortunately, one of her housemates answered the door to me, and I had to pretend I'd forgotten a half-eaten bag of crisps (because that was the only thing I could find in their lounge). Sally hid upstairs, sending me apologetic text messages from her bedroom as we waited another half an hour for her housemate to go to bed.

I thought I was going to die of pneumonia, but it was nice and warm in Sally's bed, when I finally got there.

And definitely worth the wait.

House of Horrors

Choosing subjects for third year had been tough. No longer saddled with crap like *Expressionism,* I'd wanted to take everything. Acting and Directing modules were mutually exclusive, sadly. But Scriptwriting was available, so I'd taken that – there were only a handful of lectures for it, with most of the semester devoted to working on one full movie-length script. Similarly, Video Production featured only a handful of lessons, building on previous years' experience with video cameras and editing suites, and then we were left to our own devices. The goal: write, direct, film and edit a short movie, from start to finish.

Awesome!

I don't think anyone on that course, myself included, had any concept of just how much work that entailed.

One of the overriding problems with student films – other than them being filmed by students – is that they are all filmed in student houses. Or, on occasion, a student bar. It may come as no surprise to find they also star students – with the occasional cameo from someone's mum.

There are good, honest reasons for these factors; firstly, the average student film has a budget of less than £10, which barely covers a thank-you pint for the lead actors. Using a house – usually your own – allows you to control the environment, something that is impossible in most other locations without a series of permits and approvals, a huge staff and a colossal budget. Using classmates as the acting talent is often a quid-pro-quo arrangement; for every student film-maker eager to demonstrate his directorial talent, there are at least fifty student actors desperate for any kind of exposure they can get.

So it all dovetails nicely, turning the decision into a no-brainer for most Spielberg wannabes.

But I had a plan that would break the mould.

Because I love a challenge, I had decided to shoot a special-effects-laden monster movie...

In my house.

Using my friends as the cast.

Okay, look – my budget was £10, right? What was I supposed to do?

But to change things up a bit, I was planning on shooting in the loft – an unfinished space that would hopefully add much-needed creep-factor to the film.

I auditioned a bunch of first and second year actors for the lead role, and a slim, likeable lad called Kev was easily the pick of the bunch. Kev had it all going for him; he was good looking, intelligent, and (as far as I was concerned), a great actor. He even had a gorgeous girlfriend – but inevitably, one critical chink in his armour. You see, Kev was a raging alcoholic. In a world where everyone drank to excess pretty much all the time, Kev had perfected the art.

"I just lose all control," he explained to me once. "I start off so happy, then I don't know what happens. Suddenly I'm saying the meanest, most hurtful things, really turning into a complete arsehole."

I knew what happened – it involved finishing an entire bottle of vodka between the two states. But who was I to judge? Most of my recent mistakes had alcohol as the root cause, and my preferred solution was simply a larger application of the same.

Come to think of it, that's still the case.

Due entirely to his drinking, Kev's relationship was on a

permanent crisis-point, always teetering between flaming ruin and emotional reconciliation. I think part of the reason he agreed to act in my film was because he thought I could help him. And I did – I became an expert at calling his girlfriend and apologising to her that Kev was too busy filming to come shopping with her. "Cheers for that, Tony, old mate," he said, sitting on the bed next to me. "I just don't trust myself around her right now."

"Good choice," I said, giving him a thumbs-up. "You just need to separate your drinking time from your 'Emma' time. It's combining the two that is causing the problem."

"You're so right," he agreed. "How did you get to be so *wise?*"

I shrugged, swigging from the bottle of vodka before handing it to him. "Sometimes you just need someone else's eyes on the situation. Another point of view, like."

Kev took a long pull on the bottle, screwing up his face when he was done. "Christ! That's awful. It's like paint stripper!"

"Yeah. It was on special in the SPAR for a fiver."

"Five quid? Really? Were there any bottles left?"

My monster movie revolved around a very simple concept. Kev played a student (didn't see that coming, did you?) – who was moving into a new house. My house, as it happened. During the process he had some disturbing dreams, and heard scratching at his door in the middle of the night. Cautiously investigating, he narrowly missed confronting the beast, which had vanished back into its lair in the loft space only moments earlier. Eventually Kev's character felt compelled to check out the loft, and as he pulled himself into it, flashlight in hand, the monster attacked – causing him to plummet two storeys to his death at the bottom of the stairwell. The monster then retreated to its lair, awaiting its next victim…

The 'monster' was mostly done as a point-of-view shot, with a red filter over the camera lens to represent its demonic vision, and a soundtrack of beastly heavy breathing recorded by yours truly. It was a winning combination; no-one else I knew was trying anything remotely ambitious, relying instead on the standard love-triangle-between-housemates type scenario, which required nothing they didn't already have in terms of props or effects.

But I was determined that this would be my opus.

In hindsight, it was doomed from the start – for a variety of reasons, not all of which were my fault. Of course it didn't help that, of the two people most intimately involved in the production – Kevin and myself – two of them were usually drunk at any given time. The available camera technology was rather poor, and its availability was also rather poor; we were competing for a handful of ageing S-VHS rigs with a whole host of other students, most of whom were taking Video Production as their major, and thus had priority.

But what was really against us was something that should have been painfully obvious from the beginning: as always, my ambition dramatically outstripped my ability to do anything about it. For example, the only special effect I had access to was a dab of Vaseline on the camera lens – which was definitely frowned upon by the library staff who rented the things out. "I don't want to know what you're doing with our cameras," one lady said to me, "but you've got to *wipe them clean* before you bring them back."

My monster, which would only be visible for a fraction of a second, was a store-bought Halloween mask on a broom handle, that I customised with fur fabric and superglue. I had to hope that careful lighting and super-slick editing would compensate for my lack of million-dollar CGI.

I like to think I did rather well.

I didn't, but I still like to think that.

After several weeks of late-night filming sessions (that was the only time the cameras were available), we had some workable footage. My perfectionist streak had seen me plan every shot with a storyboard sequence, prepare daily call sheets like I'd seen on TV sets, and burn through miles of videotape to capture the perfect scene. I'd emotionally blackmailed Sally into emotionally blackmailing her housemates to pose as witches for the opening sequence; Mum had produced three gauzy white robes for them to wear, as they knelt on the floor in a ritual designed to bind the demon-beast. They chanted a few lines of nonsense as they brandished assorted items from my personal collection – a silver chalice, an ornate dagger and an impressive candelabra – and screamed beautifully as the ritual failed, and they were torn apart in a flurry of red-tinged POV rampages.

I had to promise the girls that they would appear unrecognisable and out-of-focus, due to the flimsy nature of the gowns I had them wear. I had no problem with this, and as an added bonus I got to spend an evening with them while they acted their scene, wearing said gowns the entire time. My eyes, alas, had no out-of-focus button.

Finally, we were done. Kev and I shared a last bottle of exceptionally cheap vodka, and he staggered off, somewhat inadvisably, to his girlfriend's house. And I headed to the edit suite, where I would be spending a rather depressing amount of time from now on.

And then, less than a day after filming wrapped, I had an unexpected house call.

From the police.

I'd almost forgotten my recent transgression. I'd attended a hearing with the head of the Student Union, and after showing up wearing a *Greenpeace* 'Save the Whales' t-shirt and apologising profusely, I'd been allowed back in. I'd thought that was the end of it.

Not so.

My housemate Dean answered the door.

It was quite by accident; he was on his way out to a lecture, carrying (as was his habit) a gigantic spliff, ready to smoke on the walk in. He'd knocked on my door to say he was off, then scurried down the stairs and along the hallway. Tucking his homework folder under his spliff-carrying arm, he'd reached up and unfastened the latch with his free hand. He opened the door – and there was Officer Bertram, framed perfectly in the doorway, one arm raised to knock.

I heard Dean call me – practically scream for me – so I ducked out onto the landing to see what was happening.

"Tony, a… *man* here for you!" he shouted up at me, as the copper squeezed past him.

Poor bloke! His face was white – quite an impressive feat, considering it was black before he went downstairs. I'd never seen him move so fast; he sprang out of the door, letting it close itself behind him as he sprinted off down the street.

I stared down at the policeman in the hallway below me, more than a little shocked myself. And then I realised I knew him. Trefforest only had a couple of officers, and I'd been to the two-room police station a few times. Once I'd broken up a fight, and half-carried the battered victim there. Another time I'd handed in a wallet, and I'd also volunteered at their Neighbourhood Watch open day.

"Hi Mr Bertram," I said.

"Hello there," he replied. "Ah, it's you! I thought the name sounded familiar. Can I come up?"

"Of course!"

PC Bertram was here about my knife collection. Being a complete idiot, I'd mentioned having one to Hugh, the bouncer at the Student Union, and he'd been obligated to repeat this conversation when interviewed about the incident.

For a change, luck was on my side. I showed the officer into my bedroom – which was completely bare. A pair of huge cardboard boxes dominated the floor space, containing almost everything I owned.

"Oh! Moving out, are you?"

"No, no! I'm just making a film, as part of my degree. It's a monster movie, about this student who is just moving into a house…"

I could see his eyes glaze over at this. Poor bloke – pretty much everything he dealt with must have been student-related. Constable Bertram was in his 60s, and looked thoroughly unprepared for this modern world, where kids drank too much and had no respect for their elders.

"I'm sorry to bother you," he said, "but I've got to inspect these knives of yours."

"Oh yeah, I did mention that," I admitted. "They're in here, somewhere…" I indicated the pair of enormous boxes.

"Oh." PC Bertram looked crestfallen.

"I can find them, though," I said, and began to rummage.

"That's okay… what kind of knives are they?"

"Oh, you know, just like the one they confiscated." I straightened up. "You've seen that one, haven't you?" I went over to my desk and took the offending item out of my drawer. "It's really beautiful. A Valentine's Day pressie from my girlfriend."

Mr Bertram examined the knife briefly. "Oh yes. So the others, they're all like this?"

"Yeah. I've got…" I drew upon my acting talent, pausing as though to search my memory. "Three… no, four of them, I think, including this one. But this one is the biggest."

"Oh, right!" He seemed to relax straight away. "So they're only small, then. That's not a problem."

"Great! I was a bit worried. I'd hate to lose this knife. My girlfriend would go mad!"

"I'm sorry I had to come and look," he explained, "it's standard procedure. When someone mentions having a knife collection, we've no idea what to expect. But knowing it's you, I'm happy enough not to worry."

"Oh, thank-you!"

"Honestly though, you never know what you'll find. Last month in Cardiff, two officers were visiting a student house, and some bloke came at them with a samurai sword!"

I feigned shock. "A *samurai sword*? Really? Wow, that's nuts!"

"Yes, precisely! Anyway, I don't need to take up any more of your time. I'll show myself out."

"Okay then. Thanks for the visit!"

"Not a problem."

And with that, he was gone.

I let out a long, quiet breath when I heard the front door pull closed.

Then I walked to my cupboard and opened the doors. Resting inside, leaning very obviously against one side, was my sword collection; one medieval style broadsword, one gigantic Scottish claymore, and two curved Japanese katanas – and the last three of a job lot of cheap 'ninja swords' I'd bought for £5 each on eBay to give to friends. I mean, at that price, who could resist?

I closed the cupboard again, and sank back against it. Relief flooded through me, and as the tension drained away it left my legs feeling decidedly wobbly. I stared at the closed door, thanking every God that PC Bertram had come around now – when the film meant everything in my room had been heaped invisibly into the cardboard boxes. Imagine if he'd arrived when my dartboard was hanging on the wall, bristling with illegal throwing knives! When all my swords were proudly on display in the corner by the window. When hunting knives and daggers adorned every surface. To say nothing of explaining the tent-size package at the bottom of one of the crates, which contained a crossbow. Whichever way you cut it, I'd had a lucky escape.

I lay against that cupboard, contemplating its contents, for a good few heartbeats.

It was only then, from this angle, that I noticed something else.

From here I could see the narrow bookcase positioned directly behind the door. On it – at a shelf roughly equivalent with eye-level – sat a loose assortment of *shuriken* throwing stars.

And they *were* illegal.

Like, *very*.

Officer Bertram had been standing right in front of them the entire time. With the door closed, as it had been once he'd entered the room, they had been sitting exposed on the shelf right behind his head. When he'd turned to leave, he'd spun to the left – encountering the door first, and opening it to block the bookcase from view. If he'd turned the other way… Well.

I'd have been screwed.

And quite possibly screwed *in prison*.

Not the kind of ending I'd had in mind for the movie of my life.

And don't get me started on the drug lab downstairs…

Party In My Pants

Sally Katie, Chris and I had some truly epic nights out in our glorious uni career.

I made a conscious decision not to write too much about them, because no-one wants to read a memoir where all the stories start with, "I was really hammered one night…" But a few are worthy of recall.

Mostly, the ones in fancy dress – something we all loved, and did as often as we could. It didn't matter if the club we were going to had a fancy dress party on or not. I was already a big believer in non-conformity; life's too damn short to waste time fitting in. I very much doubt that anyone, on their death-bed, wishes they'd been more like everyone else. Well, apart from *Michael Jackson.*

On Cops n' Robbers night in Shafts, I made black card epaulets for my white shirt, and ended up with a fairly convincing costume. So convincing that a group of Katie's friends we visited on our way to the Union flushed their entire stash of weed down the toilet when they saw me outside their front door. Of course, they could have been slightly paranoid… having a giant stash of weed is a double-edged sword.

The Union's Pyjama Party wasn't nearly as popular as we'd expected – the four of us were the only ones who showed up. That didn't stop us, though, and when they closed Shafts, we carried on partying in the pub next door. We got a few odd looks, which was weird considering there was a 'Pyjama Party Tonight!' banner within ten metres of the pub's front door. No wonder Shafts had been empty – no other bugger even knew it was on.

We did a vicars and tarts night – mostly because Sally and Katie wanted to dress like hookers, and there really wasn't a good male equivalent. To me, it was blatantly obvious I was in fancy dress; I'd simply dressed in black, made myself a tiny collar from white card, and turned the crucifix I'd had since a kid into a necklace. But it had a profound effect on the inebriated student population. Every time I went to the bathroom (and I pee *a lot*), I had guys coming up to me and wanting to confess their sins. And the truly weird thing is, most of them weren't taking the piss – which is what they should have been doing, in the bathroom. I even had one lad cry in front of me as he admitted to cheating on his girlfriend back home. A queue started to form in front of me, and I had the awkward realisation that if I admitted to being a fraud, the last five guys who'd confessed to me would be a mite unimpressed…

On Superhero night I went as a character from the Mortal Combat arcade game, dressed only in a pair of red tracksuit trousers. There was a battle of wills between the bouncers, half of whom wanted to throw me out for indecency, and half who must have found the sight of my scrawny, pasty body hilarious. But when the DJ called on us all to dance like our characters, I Chuck-Norris'd my way to victory, winning a bottle of Champagne and the chance to showcase my best moves in a solo victory dance to 'Kung fu Fighting'.

Ahhh, happy days!

Following an impromptu Cowboys and Indians night, I loved my outfit so much – and had no clean clothes available – that I decided to wear it into Cardiff the next day. I was strolling casually down the main shopping street when I got a phone call from Chris (even he had one by third year!).

"Tony, are you walking through town dressed as a cowboy?" he asked.

"Yes! Of course I am! But… how did you know?"

"I'm sitting in Burger King, and someone just walked past dressed as a cowboy. I figured it had to be you…"

Chris outdid himself on Halloween, buying £10's worth of bandages from the pharmacy and wrapping his head and hands in them. Fingerless gloves, a leather jacket and sunglasses, and he was the perfect Invisible Man. I went as a slasher victim, in a costume so easy I've reproduced it pretty much every Halloween since; take a pair of scissors to a cheap white t-shirt, squirt a tonne of fake blood on it, and voila!

And then of course, there was the celebration to end them all: the eve of the new Millennium. It's said that everyone remembers where they were that night; sure as shit-balls I do.

There'd been a fair amount of speculation about what would happen on that night. But contrary to all expectations, come midnight, the world was still there.

Planes hadn't fallen from the skies; nuclear power stations hadn't spontaneously melted down; and at least as far as we knew, Jesus hadn't shown up with a seven-horned, ten-crowned, bear-footed leopard on a leash.

So we humans did what we do best – we partied.

Sally, Chris and I were determined to party too. It had been a good year for all of us – even better for me, not that anyone else knew about it. For the first time in my life, I had someone to kiss at midnight.

We had to hide behind a bus stop to do it, but that only added to the thrill. I could hardly believe that I was involved in a clandestine relationship with my best friend. The veil of secrecy, though frustrating at times, added an extra layer of excitement to the mix. It turns out, I was a fan of danger. Who knew?

But whilst the year had been a triumph in terms of friendships made, and friendships slightly undermined by illicit sexual liaisons… it was a bit of a bust in several other areas.

Specifically, I was poor.

And all my friends were poor.

We were students. What else is new?

But the parties to mark the Millennium weren't cheap. Every pub that could open was charging admission. Bouncers on every door ensured that no cheap vodka from the SPAR would be getting into any of these places; ironically the outrageous price-hike on drinks was justified by the cost of extra staffing. Ah well! Even bouncers have to eat, I guess. Entire cows, judging by the size of them.

So instead of attending some epic bash, and waltzing the night away in style, we decided to go renegade. We would drink on the run, ricocheting between the few bars we knew where the entry price was reasonable, and the top-secret locations around the city where we'd pre-stashed our booze.

The plan worked well. We were literally running through the night – and it felt good! Freezing air whipped past my face, filling my lungs with icicles. In perfect formation, like a pack of drunken ninjas, we veered into an alleyway.

At which point all notions of being a ninja vanished and I ran smack into a pole.

It was black, that was the trouble. Black, against the darkness of an unlit alleyway at midnight – it's like they did it on purpose. The pole was also hard to spot because it was only three feet high – one of those damned anti-car barriers that crop up all over city centres. To stop cars, ostensibly, though I'm sure they stop the odd pedestrian in their tracks too. I'd run into a bunch of them in my time, because I'm clumsy, not very observant, and my mind is normally occupied with weighty matters, like looking for a suitable bus stop to hide behind for a sneaky snog.

But this was different. There was pain – quite serious pain, and in the one place no bloke ever wants to feel pain. There was also a slight but spreading wetness in the same area. Which meant either I'd peed myself, or…

Worse.

Actually, speaking as someone who *has* peed myself in public, and didn't live it down for several years afterwards, perhaps that *would* have been worse.

But this was… definitely worrying.

Very cautiously, I slid my hand down my pants. Which I don't generally recommend doing in public, but I was in a darkened alleyway, remember.

Your honour.

When my hand came up, there was blood on my fingertips.

Which at least meant I wasn't soaked in wee, which is always a plus.

None of the others had noticed my indiscretion; they'd all carried on, sprinting away into the night. Leaving me alone, in the darkness.

Bleeding from my penis.

Hobbling along in the direction my friends had gone, I tried my best to follow the great tradition of men with medical concerns, and ignore it. But the pain throbbed with every step, and the chafing of my balls was unbearable.

Why, *oh why,* did I have to wear such tight trousers?

As an aside, apparently tight trousers was my thing. I had no idea, until Sally told me, years later. Not only was it a common topic of discussion amongst my classmates, but even Sally's mum had once commented that my jeans didn't leave much to the imagination. I'd like to blame fashion, but fashion, for me, is like UFO abduction: I'm pretty sure it exists, but I've never experienced it myself.

All I can say is, I honestly thought my ass was smaller.

Anyway. I eventually caught up to the others, most of whom simply assumed I'd stopped to have a crafty pee in the alleyway. Which was nearly true, if involuntarily so.

The group moved out onto the wide swathe of grass in front of City Hall. A temporary fun-fair had been set up, and was in full swing. The bright lights and screams of delight were distinctly at odds with the throbbing in my penis.

I staggered along at the back, trying to hide my winces, but Sally soon noticed my discomfort.

"Ran into a post," I explained to her.

This didn't surprise her at all.

"It was black," I pointed out, "and it's dark."

"But you're okay?"

"The thing is, I kind of cut myself."

"Oh?"

"Yeah. But I don't know how badly."

"Shit! Show me."

"I   can't!"

"Why not? What's wrong?"

"Sally, look… I've… I think I've cut my willy."

Her eyes went wide – and then she burst out laughing. "I'm so sorry," she said, when she regained control of herself, "I didn't mean that. It's just so…"

I could see another guffaw building up inside her.

So I did the only thing I could, under the circumstances.

I put my hand down my pants again.

"Shit!" The sight of blood showed Sally I was serious. "If it's that bad, maybe you should go over there." She pointed to the centre of the fun fair, where a trio of ambulances sat surrounded by green-jacketed paramedics.

"I am NOT going into one of those ambulances and getting my cock out! Bloody hell, I'm pissed as a fart. They'll probably arrest me for sexual assault!"

Sally chewed on that for a minute.

"Okay, look – my sister is here, in this park, somewhere. I can text her and find her. She's done loads of first aid courses… Maybe she can help?"

And so it came to pass that, on the eve of this shiny new Millennium, I found myself hiding in the dubious cover of a small shrubbery, while my secret girlfriend's older sister poked my penis with a hairclip.

"I think you've been lucky," she said, which I thought was a strange thing to say to someone who's bleeding from their genitals.

She pointed with the hairclip. "Three cuts down here, and one up there."

I winced as the clip came a little too close for comfort.

The four wounds perfectly matched the four buttons that fastened my jeans. The impact had driven them all into my flesh – one into the bit of my belly just above my willy, and the other three right into the old fella himself. To me they looked horrendous, but then most things are when examined by the flame of a cigarette lighter, after midnight, in the middle of a hedge.

Sally's sister took a deep breath, and imparted the bad news. "I think you might need stitches."

"*Stitches?* Are you fucking kidding me?

"I'm just sayin'…"

"There is *no frigging way* anyone is putting a needle and thread anywhere *near* this thing!"

"Fair enough. I don't think you'll bleed to death or anything. But I don't have any plasters with me, I'm afraid." She dug through her purse for a tiny packet of tissues. "Here," she said, handing me one. "Keep pressure on it. That should stop the bleeding."

"So, I stand here, in this hedge, with my cock wrapped in a tissue, squeezing it."

"Yes."

"I am *so* getting arrested tonight."

She shrugged. "On the upside, it'll make a great story to tell your grandkids."

"Huh. If kids of any kind are still a possibility."

"Speaking of which –" I swear her eyes caught a glimmer of light from one of the nearby rides, and twinkled as she parted with her last piece of advice, "– you should probably avoid getting an erection. I'm thinking you'd squirt blood like a hose with a hole in it."

She left me there, hiding in a bush with my cock in my hand.

It was a weird end to a weird century.

On the upside, I was doing well at uni, and I finally had a decent, albeit complicated, relationship. On the downside, I hadn't made much progress in my acting career, and I was bleeding out of my penis.

It didn't look like I was going to become famous anytime soon.

But at least I was holding my own.

Life's A Ball

I was no stranger to performance anxiety.

As the end of university groaned into sight, there was one enormous hurdle to overcome: the final acting piece.

Our course was heavily dominated by women; there were only six guys in my class, myself included. Our tutor had a tricky task, finding a combination of plays that could accommodate such a skewed demographic, and when he announced his decision, I was both thrilled and appalled.

Because he'd chosen to split the class into just two groups.

One of them had a fairly even mix of both genders; Chris, James, and every other lad on our course would be in this one.

Which left me, in a play on my own... with the nine remaining girls.

And the name of my character was *Don Juan*.

Now, opinions on our tutor varied amongst the girls on my course. Some found him creepy, whilst some openly admitted to fancying him. But there was no doubt in my mind that he was a misogynist of the highest order.

In the world of drama, I'm sure there are plenty of plays with female-heavy casts. To have chosen one that successfully relegated an entire class full of women to mere sex objects took balls.

Still, it could have been worse; as scripted, the opening scene of *Don Juan Returns From The War* had my character, and half the girls, all naked together in a bath.

There were sighs of relief all round when he mentioned he was changing that bit.

I was now in a slightly awkward predicament.

The tutor, who will remain nameless in case he is still pretending to be an acting teacher somewhere, was strangely fond of me.

Which was nice, but I didn't really like him.

And he *really* didn't like Sally.

Sally absolutely frikkin' *hated* him.

So though I was pleased and intimidated in equal measure to be awarded the lead role in our production, it came as no surprise when Sally was given the worst. She had almost no lines, and whilst she'd be on stage throughout the entire play, she spent the entire time confined to a rocking chair in the corner.

From that thankless and frustrating vantage point, my new girlfriend and potential soul-mate got to watch as the drama unfolded – and I seduced every single member of the cast, one after another.

Most of them, twice.

Sally had the dubious honour of playing an elderly lady; the spirit of the one that got away. She was Don Juan's true love, and the only girl in the entire production that I didn't have to kiss even once.

Talk about awkward!

We got through it, though.

We were professionals, or trying our very best to be. And the show went well; James was so enthusiastic after watching our dress rehearsal that he bought me a pint and sat in the bar at the Welsh College, praising my performance. Shit, for a few minutes, I actually thought I was good.

Sally, on the other hand, had a shitty experience from start to finish.

Hamstrung by her role, she'd been given virtually nothing to do, yet several times our tutor's unfairly harsh critique reduced her to tears. She'd been forced to swallow that embarrassment and return to class for more of the same; there wasn't any other option, if she wanted to graduate.

When it came time to give our own feedback, I wrote in my performance journal that, whilst I felt he'd been fair with me, if he'd treated me the way he'd treated Sally, I'd have stabbed the motherfucker.

It was important to me that this complaint be taken very seriously, and the journal had to be handed in as part of my evaluation.

My protectiveness towards Sally had cranked into overdrive, and I don't think I really considered the ramifications of making a death-threat towards my tutor in a document he was going to grade.

Still. You've got to have your priorities, right?

Being separated from Chris for countless hours of performance lectures and rehearsals had given Sally and me plenty of opportunities to sneak off together.

We'd become closer than ever, supporting each other through an emotional and stressful period, and my heart was starting to whisper to me.

When the time came to tell Chris about us, Sally decided that she should be the one to do it. I fully supported her choice in this matter, because I was far too chicken-shit to do it myself.

It can't have been easy, for either of them. For Sally, it must have felt like admitting to betrayal; for Chris, it was the sum of all his fears.

And for me, well… I hid.

But I did it *for them*.

When the deed was done, Sally was drained.

I never dared ask what she'd said, and just thinking about it made my guts clench.

Chris didn't speak to me for weeks.

Funny, it never turns out this way in soaps. There's arguments and tears, yelling and recriminations… and then three episodes later it's all back to normal, and all anyone cares about is the long-lost brother who's come back from the dead.

Sadly, real life is considerably more awkward.

Just as we feared, the revelation of mine and Sally's relationship completely destroyed our happy little group dynamic. It was never the same again.

As the end-of-year ball loomed large, Sally threw Chris an olive branch, and arranged for us all to go together. Although privately gutted, I had to acknowledge that it was the right thing to do. It was vital to Sally that she be reconciled with Chris; having a boyfriend was all well and good, but not if it came at the expense of her closest friendship.

Thus, we attended the ball as we'd done almost everything in university; as a trio. Chris and Sally wore top hats and tailcoats, honouring a pact they'd made long before I came on the scene. I wore a tux I'd had to buy for extra work, and swallowed my disappointment that Sally wouldn't be smouldering on my arm in a dress that made my classmates' eyes pop out.

Most of the people in our year still didn't know about us, and I'd fantasised about surprising them.

Think you're hot stuff, do you? Well, the hottest couple of the year came from this bunch of weirdoes, and we've been right under your noses the whole time!

Mind you, half of them thought Sally, Chris and I had been involved in some kind of incestuous threesome for the last two years.

Still, I vowed to myself, I'll get my moment alone with her.

There would be crazy dancing, and there would be crazy drinking...

And then there would be the end of the night.

There would be the last dance...

And no matter what else happened, that one was *mine.*

A minibus brought us all to Cardiff Convention Centre, and dispensed us outside.

The act was balding rock duo *Right Said Fred*. Both guys were enormous, muscle-bound powerhouses, and we all went mental when they sang their signature hit *I'm Too Sexy For My Shirt*. Still not quite the coup we'd had at the end of first year, when our ball had been headlined by a little-known singer from defunct boy band *Take That*. He'd obviously been booked for peanuts, at a time when he was desperately trying to launch a solo career, but by the time Robbie Williams took to the stage to serenade us with his debut single *Angels*, his star was well and truly on the rise.

As the evening drew to a close, I focused myself. This was it; the moment I had been waiting for. My palms were sweating. All of me was sweating! I was drunk after all, and had been dancing like a maniac for the last three hours. But now, as the music softened and the rings of friends on the dance floor gave way to couples, I prepared to make my move.

Each song was progressively slower. As a veteran of countless school discos, where the boys stood on one side of the room shuffling nervously from foot to foot all night, and the girls hung out on the opposite side, giggling at us, I knew that the most romantic song of all would be saved until last. This was the time that youthful ideals of true love overcame awkwardness. Here and there, solitary boys would cross the diminished gulf, brazenly talking to the girl they had chosen, before leading her into the middle of the floor and wrapping his arms around her. And then he'd carry on doing the nervous shuffle, because that was what passed as dance moves amongst teenagers.

But that was as far as it went.

Hell, I'd never even got to the dancing stage.

But this time it would be different.

This time, I had a girlfriend.

She didn't know it yet, but I was in love with her.

And tonight, I was going to tell her.

Just as soon as the music was right...

I glanced at my watch. The band was cutting it awfully fine. With less than ten minutes to go, they'd played several slow-ish songs, but nothing slow enough to drive the friendship zone from the dance floor.

There couldn't be more than two songs left. Sally and Chris were still two-stepping in comedic fashion to Cyndi Lauper's *Twue Colouws*.

I sighed out a breath. This was it: the last song. It was time. I stepped up to Sally, prepared to take her hand and whisper in her ear. I still hadn't figured out what to say, but I would start by begging her for the last dance. She wouldn't refuse me that. I'd draw her off a bit, give us a little space, fold her tightly in my arms, and do the shuffle dance for the remainder of the song.

Because that was still the only move in my romantic dancing arsenal.

Then, assuming I hadn't stood on her feet too much, as the music wound down, I would gaze lovingly into her eyes, and kiss her.

And then I would whisper in her ear, those three little words that carried a whole universe of significance; *I love you.*

I waited, what seemed like an eternity, as the penultimate song slid past. I'd stopped dancing, stopped moving at all. I was transfixed by the magnitude of my endeavour, by the immense importance of what was about to happen. In a few short minutes, my life was about to change.

The song finished.

I stepped close to Sally as the next song began.

And it was *Celebration,* by Madonna.

What the FUCK?!?!?!

The DJ kicked the volume up, and the dance floor flooded, people surging on to shriek and flail their legs around with drunken abandon.

"SELL-uh-BRAY-shun time, COME ON!" they wailed in unison.

That cornerstone of disco tradition, the last slow dance – *my* dance – was not to be.

Sally and I split up that night.

It was just too hard. Having Chris there, seeing him chatting, joking, having fun. And all the while wanting nothing more than to push him away from Sally, so that I could have some alone time with her. My best friend, and the girl I was in love with – how's that for an impossible choice?

And it would all have worked out so well, because they got on like a house on fire – without me. I was the spanner in their works; Chris had loved Sally for longer than I'd known either of them, and although he'd accepted they would never be together romantically, he was happy enough. So long as his best friend wasn't dating her...

Yep – I'd single-handedly managed to create a situation so awkward, so emotionally confusing, it could have been a plot line on *Home and Away*.

That night, frustrated beyond belief by the string of events that had yet again robbed me of my perfect moment, I solved the problem in one fell stroke. I took out my frustration on Sally, ranting about everything that was wrong with the situation and painting myself as the victim of it all. Needless to say, she took offence at this, and when the smoke cleared in the morning we were no longer a couple.

For the next few weeks, I led a double life.

It was kind of like being Spiderman, only much, much crapper. And with considerably less spandex.

By day, I was an ordinary university student, attending to the one chore that just wouldn't die – editing the monster movie I'd made with Kev. By night, I was the same student, only passed out in a haze of alcoholic regret. Usually on the toilet.

Splitting up with Sally had left me hollow; I tried to fill the void with the demon drink. I was doing pretty well at it, except the booze kept coming out the other end of me almost as fast as I put it in. Hence my venue of choice for the ensuing unconsciousness. Eventually, Dean gave me an ultimatum; stop moping, or start wearing underpants. Apparently he was sick of spending 4am dragging my naked ass out of the bathroom and up two flights of stairs just so he could go for a pee.

As more and more people drifted away from university, their coursework handed in and their exams completed, I decided to focus on the one thing I still had going for me: my career.

Because university was over. My studies were done.

I was now officially an actor.

It was time to join the ranks of Britain's young and talented new performers.

In unemployment.

The Things You Do
For Money

I moaned about The Stage newspaper – endlessly, and to anyone who would listen – and yet, my first break, when it came, sprang directly from those much-maligned pages. I'd applied for every halfway decent sounding job in there for years, with nothing good to show for it. But then, within days of finishing my university course, I finally got a bite. I had so many irons in so many fires that I showed up for the audition knowing only that the company who'd contacted me was called 'Thunder Wolf'. It sounded pretty cool, so I had high hopes. I'd send out half a rainforest of CVs lately; if I kept it up I'd have Greenpeace protesters chaining themselves to my printer.

Thunder Wolf was owned and run by a very large Welsh woman with fabulous make-up. Her name was Janice, and as she explained the nature of the company, I couldn't help but think she'd been a tad dramatic with the name. Rather than spewing out action movies or science fiction, Thunder Wolf fulfilled possibly the least exciting niche in the whole entertainment industry; Theatre-in–Education.

Basically, T-I-E is where a group of performers take a show with educational content around a bunch of schools.

Performing to audiences ranging from 5 to 11, there isn't much call for swearing, blood splatters or graphic nudity. Which is a real shame, as if there was, the kids might actually give a shit about what was happening on stage. Instead, TIE shows are cheesier and hammier than a pizza chef's trousers, and so politically correct they usually only hire disabled black lesbians.

I'm not really sure why they picked me. Unless 'idiot' counts as a minority?

Suffice to say, it was not my dream gig. But it was a step up from extra work. It was real, professional acting – only just, but it definitely qualified. Audition speeches not being my forte, I was majorly relieved to discover the owner of the company wanted a bunch of us to 'workshop' a piece. This is awesome for me, as it mostly involves making shit up. Knowing she was looking for TIE actors, I gave her totally over the top enthusiasm mixed with plenty of clowning and silly faces. As one of the silliest people alive in the world today, I felt like I'd done okay – until she asked me to sing.

I refused, figuring it was better to leave her respecting my honesty than to traumatise the poor woman. I'd flunked the audition anyway; if singing was part of the performance, there was no point convincing her to hire me.

So I was secretly thrilled when, two days later, I got a call from her.

I was in!

I gave a triumphant cry and punched the empty air of my bedroom. Why oh why couldn't I have taken *this* call in the middle of Performance class?

I'd love to have seen the look on the tutor's face when I apologised; "I'm *so* sorry, but

that was Thunder Wolf Productions, offering me a role. But it's full-time for two months and I'd miss graduation, so I've told them I'll think about it."

Eat. That!

There's just something about scorn that brings out the petty in me.

In reality, there was no way I was passing this up. I explained to Janice that I still had some video editing work to complete for uni, and she promised it wouldn't be a problem. It gave me quite a buzz to think that I was starting my first gig of professional acting work even before my degree was even graded.

Success! Well, kind of.

During the three-day rehearsal period, I was partnered with a two girls; Vicky, a bubbly brunette the same age as me, and Kerry, who was slim, wiry, and maybe five years older. Both girls were veterans of the Theatre In Education trenches, although neither had worked for Thunder Wolf before. Together, for the next eight weeks, we would be travelling the country with a show about stranger-danger, called, "Where Have You Gone, Freddy Fogg?"

The audition had given me an idea of what to expect, but the full concept of the show took my breath away. Not with its innovative design, clever writing or inspiring message (because it had none of those things) – but instead with its staggering cheapness.

It was based around a game show, with me as the host – 'Les... Miserables!'

I know! Argh! A pun almost as painful to me as it was lost on the ten-year-old kids we performed to. The show began with a cringe-worthy introduction (which I performed off-stage, doing my best imitation the voice over dude from Blind Date) – and went downhill from there.

"Ladeeeeeeeeez and gentlemen, it's time for, 'Saaaaaay NO! Or saaaaay nothing!' And heeeeere's your host – Leeeees, Miserables!"

I jogged into the middle of the set, waving to my imaginary fans, grinning at their complete lack of thunderous applause. From there I explained the show, and introduced the contestants – the two girls, playing a pair of school-aged kids. According to the script, they had been friends with a fictional character called Freddy Fogg, who had gone missing. Reading between the lines, it was quite clear that little Freddy had been skin-suited, but this was never specifically mentioned.

I asked the contestants questions about how to respond to 'Stranger Danger' – like, not getting into a stranger's car, not taking sweets from them, and not agreeing to give a blow job for less than market value.

For each question, there was a predictable wrong answer from Kerry (who was wearing her baseball cap backwards, in the universal sign of a dunce) and an equally predictable right answer from pig-tailed Vicky. At the end I tallied the scores – not difficult, as I only had to ask three questions – and we dragged a 'volunteer' up from the audience to help me present the winning medal. It was simplistic to the point where a trained monkey could have taken over without any appreciable difference in quality. Hell, any one of the kids watching us could have done my job – it required nothing more than remembering a handful of lines, reading the questions from the cards in my hand, and doing all of it in a ridiculously over-the-top impression of Bruce Forsythe.

The set consisted of two painted plywood screens, and a lectern for me. The girls sat on stools, in clothes they'd mostly provided themselves, and… that was it! With the possible exception of the white van hired to transport the set from school to school, the entire show could have been created from scratch for about £10.50. Given a biro and the back of a Cornflake packet to doodle on, I reckon I could come up with a more compelling concept in about half an hour.

It was the kids I felt bad for; their expectations on being told they'd be watching a show in school must have been sorely let down. I tried to make it more amusing for them, doing a progressively more ridiculous caricature for Les, but after a while I had to admit the truth: they didn't care. I mean, it was a lame-assed show on a lame-assed topic, shown to a generation of kids who considered everything to be lame-assed by default. I didn't watch horror films until I was fifteen, as Mum was afraid they would turn me into a psychopath; these days we were up against *Grand Theft Auto.* It seemed laughable to be warning kids that, if they were approached by a stranger, they should run away and tell an adult. Most of them thought the answer to Stranger Danger was, as one nine-year-old boy proudly told me, "Tell 'im to fuck off, then knife the cunt."

Professional pride kept me trying, and I scored the occasional chuckle from my audience by scattering little jokes throughout my lines. I even tried to recruit the teachers with puns and suggestive glances. When we were done, and the kids were filing out, inevitably one of the teachers would approach us and thank us profusely, saying, "they just adored it!"

Which I knew to be a lie. But that's what teachers say, standard issue, to anyone good enough to donate their time to the kids under their care.

Except we weren't donating anything. We were being paid – and pretty well, too, given the hours. And the company we worked for… well. They were getting *very* well paid. There were all kinds of government grants floating around to fund exactly this sort of extra-curricular activity, and some schools were simply paying for us out of their own pockets. I don't know any of the figures concerned, and I don't want to get sued, but I'm sure you can imagine – hiring a theatre company to bring their educational show across the country to your school, doesn't come cheap. Someone was making a *killing* out of this – and I don't mean whoever abducted Little Freddy Fogg.

I couldn't help feeling a bit guilty about it. At the end of every show, I busied myself pulling the set apart, and let one of the girls take our feedback forms to the staff. I was too embarrassed to look them in the eye; if *I'd* spent a thousand pounds on what we'd just offered, I'd be ready to slap someone. Luckily, Kerry was made of sterner stuff than me. Either that, or she honestly believed in what we were doing… in which case she was also a lot stupider than me.

Which is saying something.

But if you ignored the blatant con we were perpetrating on the nations' education system, life was good.

My bank account certainly thought so. I was finally making a living wage. And it was easy. *Like taking candy from a room full of small children…*

And to some degree, I didn't care that I was working for a cheapskate pirate and flailing around like a dickhead in front of rooms full of people who couldn't care less.

Because in spite of my private reservations, one vital prediction had come true.

I'd always believed wholeheartedly, against all the odds, that it would happen.

And it had.

I was now a professional actor.

Well… kind of.

The Blackening

The next few weeks were a kind of bliss.

When I think about the jobs some people do just to keep food on the table, I have to admit that Theatre-In-Education, at least my half-assed version of it, was pretty damn easy.

Accommodation was booked for us in a different county each week, usually in a self-catering cottage somewhere in the countryside. We dragged ourselves out of bed around 8am, just in time to battle through whatever passed for local rush-hour traffic to reach our first school of the day. After making ourselves known to the teachers there, we arranged our two bits of plywood and performed. The show lasted half an hour, but that was only with relentless padding out – most of which was my job. If we'd been in the mood to rush, I reckon we could have knocked out the entire gig, from set-up to dismantling, in about eight minutes flat. Adding in time to liaise with the school staff and wait for the kids to file in and out, our presence in each location totalled about an hour and a half. Very occasionally a school would have stumped up the cash for two shows, so we'd repeat the whole nightmare for a slightly younger (or older) audience, before being on our way. The longest days we did involved two schools with two shows apiece; these were few and far between though, with most days featuring either two or three performances.

No matter what happened, we would generally find ourselves back at our accommodation by 3pm, with the rest of the afternoon to do with as we pleased.

We seemed to spend a lot of time shopping.

I also decided to take up running.

It occurred to me that I wasn't in the best of shape. Drinking had been my hobby of choice for the last three years, and I'd long since abandoned any pretence of being in the university Karate club. I tried to squeeze in the odd Kung fu session whenever I was back up north, but other than that my primary form of exercise was drunken dancing. And since my break-up with Sally, I'd been doing the drunken part all by itself.

Now I found myself in gorgeous countryside, on a farm which incorporated a lake and several horse paddocks. Unable to carry on drinking at the rate I had been for fear of alarming the girls, I found myself waking up with time to spare before setting off to our first school. I tried running a lap of the fields, and a few days later I upgraded my route to two laps. The girls couldn't believe I'd survived the last three years on a diet almost exclusively of Corn flakes and toast, so together they vowed to teach me healthier eating habits.

They failed. Unless you count eating an apple once. But it was a nice thought.

Anytime I got a day off, I jumped on the nearest train back to Trefforest. There were only two things left to do there. First, I had to say a tearful farewell to Dean – who was pretty much the only friend I had left at this point – and second, I had to finish editing that bastard monster movie.

I'd been working on it forever. It was long, lonely work, and frustrating as all hell because I had no idea how the editing machines worked. We'd had one class on the subject at the start of the year, with twenty-odd squirming bodies crammed into the windowless, airless room. A handful of my classmates had sat and played with the controls while they were being explained to us, and then a reverential tone had been used to introduce the gleaming plastic box in the corner; our very own AVID Digital Editing Suite.

AVID was just a PC running extremely expensive software, so it didn't look all that special, and it hardly mattered because we couldn't get near it; Glamorgan ran a degree course in 'Video Production', and those students had the machine solidly booked until the next millennium (which at the time of demonstration, was about three months away).

So I'd dutifully taken notes on the workings of the manual editing desk, none of which made the slightest bit of sense to me when the time came to actually use the damn thing. It was a monster; two linked TV screens loomed above a control deck the size of a Cadillac. *How the hell did they get it in here?* I often wondered. It was way bigger than the door. *Did they build the whole library around it?* Just sitting in front of all those and dials and sliders made my jaw go slack. At any minute I expected James Bond to burst in and demand I surrender my satellites. Sadly, the only people who ever came to the edit suite were students on the appropriate section of their course. They were all immediately identifiable by their red eyes, rounded shoulders and inability to converse beyond a grunt. These poor bastards had drawn the short straw in their video production groups; they were doomed to spend an eternity of sleepless nights slumped in front of the edit screens, endlessly rewinding the same shaky clips of an interview in a shopping centre, whilst the 'friends' who had filmed the interview drank and danced and shagged the night away on the other side of campus.

Editing is hell.

On the upside, it pandered to my lack of faith in humanity. I'm not entirely sure that *is* an upside, but whether a product of nature or nurture, I'd always found it impossible to completely trust anyone other than myself. I was a confirmed control freak with a delicate and creative task to complete, and the enforced isolation and antisocial hours helped me focus my scattered brainwaves into a laser. As did the vodka I smuggled in.

I say the hours were antisocial; this is because the only times available this late in the year were between midnight and 6am. So I showed up at the tiny Media Kiosk beneath the library and booked all of them. I can still hear the howls of dismay when the video production people found out.

And so it came to pass that I sat there, night after night, staring into a pair of monitors, twiddling a wheel that allowed me to scan back and forth along my video clips. Meticulously, painstakingly, I spliced them all together, always bearing in mind the golden rule: copy only from the master tape, as copying a copy loses quality every time. *Especially* when you're working with VHS...

For my younger readers, I should probably point out that movies used to come on *tapes* – miles and miles of ribbon wound around a pair of spools, inside a plastic case the size of a paperback book. I know, right? Sounds like I'm making this shit up. Hell, anyone reading this in ten years' time is going to need paperback books explaining to them...

Anyway. I edited the tape. It took a long, *long* time. I had moments of despair, I had urgent re-shoots, and I ate way too many crisps. But with less than a week to go until the submission deadline, I was finally happy. Now, I'm a perfectionist, as I may have mentioned. The irony is not lost on me that I am also one of the clumsiest, most scatter-brained and generally imperfect individuals on the planet – but what is life, if not contradiction?

The movie was perfect. I mean, I'd mastered the art of fade-out. I'd used every bit of camera trickery I could and my extremely limited budget to achieve special effects that, at least on the tiny, grainy edit screens, looked halfway decent. George Lucas I was not, but for a film shot entirely in my bedroom and attic, and edited in a dark cupboard in South Wales, I thought it was pretty good. All I had to do was add the soundtrack of suitably ghostly background music and it was good to go. So I settled in for a last night in front of the infernal machine, popped in my tapes, and pressed go.

I made only one mistake.

Amongst the vast array of controls on the edit suite, there was a lever which controlled the visibility of what you were recording. In the fully-up position, it had no effect at all; in the fully-down position, it faded out the image to nothing, allowing you to record tapes of pure blackness – the pre-digital version of formatting a hard drive.

Guess what I did?

A little over half my movie had played through before I caught the error. By this point in my life I was already well acquainted with that stomach-clench you get when you've just done something monumentally stupid. If I'd been standing, I'd have collapsed; but I was sitting, and I really needed a pee, so I just sat there in shock and quietly wet myself.

Which probably didn't endear me to the person who'd booked that seat next.

But smelling like piss was the least of my worries. In one stroke, I had recorded over half my movie with pure black-screen. Nothing was left of it; none of my beautiful, subtle cuts, my masterful fading work, the painstaking colour-correction, the cleverly-worded opening credits, the perfectly-timed, near-subliminal glimpses of Sally and her friends conducting their ritual.

Gone.

By rough estimate I'd spent close to a hundred hours editing that thing.

Now, with less than a day until the deadline, and the edit suites booked solid by frantic students who'd left it too late, there was almost nothing I could do.

I still had two hours left on my current booking, so I sprinted home for the master tapes and a change of pants. In two hours I edited together a crude, chop-shop version of my previously perfect movie, and handed it in with a hand-written apology. It took me three tries before I could write it without including swear-words.

At this point, I didn't even know if I would pass the course.

Hell, I didn't know if I'd be collecting a degree at all in two month's time.

My Performance grade hung beneath a pall of uncertainty, partially because of the slight death-threat I'd made against the tutor.

My Scriptwriting coursework had been submitted almost ten whole minutes before the final deadline, but I couldn't be entirely sure of its quality as I'd written the entire thing in one long, vodka-fuelled all-nighter.

And then there was this. A poorly-filmed, terribly-edited monster movie, starring no monster and one alcoholic student.

Things weren't looking great, to be honest.

The Wolf Comes Home To Roost

A few weeks later, I had a machine gun pointed at me for the first time in my life.

Janice hadn't bothered to mention that our school for the day was on an army base; we had neither the proper permits, nor any knowledge of the correct procedure.

"You're a traveling theatre company, huh?"

Even to my ears, it sounded fake. Like a Scooby-Doo disguise; all we needed was some bad wigs and clown make-up. Luckily, that was a more trusting era. If this had been post-9/11, they'd probably have shot us on general principle.

Eventually it was all straightened out, and we made a late and rather nervous entrance to the private-run school for the kids who lived on the base.

"We'd better do a good show here," I joked, "or they might not let us leave!"

The TIE tour had gone from strength to strength. I'd found my stride, and discovered all the little points where I could sneak in extra jokes and draw a laugh from the kids. The staff members thanking us after each show had become far more enthusiastic and animated – always a sign of a job well done.

I've never been big-headed, but I was sure the improved reception we were getting was down to me; the girls had so little to work with, and hadn't altered their acts at all. But I didn't mind. I just wanted to leave a place without feeling like I'd ripped them off.

We'd been living in a series of antiquated farmhouses. Janice specialised in finding out of the way places, presumably at a hefty discount, and penning the three of us together in the middle of nowhere. Our lengthy morning drive back to civilization gave us ample time to bitch at each other, and we developed the kind of group dynamic that often emerges when three complete strangers are forced to live and work together; that is, two of us entered into an uneasy alliance, and spent the next two months plotting how to hide the third one's body. My friendship with Vicky was really a bonding in the face of adversity; Kerry turned out to be domineering, dictatorial and opinionated. She had hard-line Christian values; in her late twenties, she was still proudly a virgin, because she went to bed with and woke up with Jesus. Whilst I struggled to avoid swearing on stage in front of the kids, she would actually get upset if one of us accidentally took the Lord's name in vain around the house. As someone who was used to making conversation with a bunch of wasted students, I upset her quite a bit.

Consequently, I avoided mentioning my new hobby, which was breaking into the current farm owners' indoor pool at midnight, and swimming in it naked.

It was a delightfully liberating experience, but one that I felt Jesus – at least, her version of Jesus – might frown on.

We spent the following week incarcerated in a place we named 'Crapstone Villas' – not because it was poor quality, but because the whole farm reeked of shit. And it wasn't just our environment that stank; after careful calculation, we'd noticed a disturbing pattern to our paydays. They'd been getting later and later each week, to the point where, well over a month in, the payments had lapped themselves. Our wages were coming in on Fridays once again, only one entire week's worth had evaporated en route. It was suspiciously subtle. I had to ask myself: was our boss ripping off schools by sending us out, only to rip us off even as we did her dirty-work? How devious a criminal mastermind was she?

Repeated phone calls to Janice were met with confusion, then anger, and then she stopped answering them. There wasn't much else we could do but push on as our schedule dictated, but despite a few weeks in gorgeous country cottages, there was a certain degree of tension in the air.

When the news came in about my degree, it was an anti-climax. I'd passed, and been awarded a second-class grade of 2:2 – what's known in student circles as a 'Desmond' (after the South African Archbishop). It wasn't a great result, but probably what I deserved; it was a rare piece of my work that hadn't been written whilst at least partially inebriated. The blame for this fell squarely on my own shoulders, but I'd reconciled it philosophically. My degree certificate, when it was issued, would not be worth the paper it was printed on. No bigwig Hollywood director would give two cheesy farts about my qualifications, or lack thereof. Whether I made it in this world or not, it would all come down to me. To my confidence, my experience, my skill and my charisma.

Put another way, I was screwed before I even started.

The graduation ceremony fell on the same morning as our last show of the tour. I didn't mind missing it. I'd considered not showing up at all, but the lure of seeing Sally and my friends again proved too strong. Inevitably, they were in the pub when I arrived, so I slotted myself seamlessly into their celebration as though I'd never left. It was strange, how everything had carried on in my absence. Part of me wanted them to acknowledge that I'd been away, and confess to missing me. I felt like I was still a part of their lives, but a removable, even disposable one.

Bittersweet, I think, is the word for this.

The following day, Vicky drove our tour van back to Thunder Wolf's Welsh HQ, where we returned the flimsy bits of set and donated the few costume items we'd acquired during our travels. There was an awkward stand-off with

Janice, as we confronted her about our missing pay, but she assured us it was an honest mistake and would soon be rectified. I'd have believed her if she'd been the slightest bit apologetic, rather than prickly and hostile – she acted like she'd been caught red-handed and forced to pay compensation, so we couldn't help but treat her as such.

We retired to a nearby pub, and spotted a face we recognised. One of three girls from the other Thunder Wolf team, she was sitting by herself and didn't look happy. We chatted to her, half expecting to hear a similar tale of missing pay cheques – but what she had to say was far worse. Her group hadn't gelled – in fact, they'd hated each other. Arguing about every aspect of their trip, from food to room choice to morning routines had made her last two months a living hell. Screaming matches had dominated their evenings and their performances had suffered, with poor feedback and complaints only driving the tension up further. Threats to leave had forced Janice to retaliate with threats of non-payment, and they'd battled on, loathing every minute of it, until going their separate ways an hour ago.

Ouch.

Vicky, Kerry and I exchanged raised eyebrows and retreated to a booth in the corner. Suddenly, our experience didn't seem bad at all. We'd had a few differences, but had enjoyed ourselves on the whole. And as Vicky rather sheepishly produced a bottle of Champagne, and they both congratulated me on getting my degree, I realised that I was actually going to miss them.

*   *   *

The lease had expired on my room in Trefforest, though the landlord agency had allowed me to leave my stuff there for a few weeks. This was amazing, as they'd been absolute bastards while I lived there, even trying to deduct £100 from my security deposit for 'fireproof curtains' which had never existed in the first place. But although my gear was in storage, they'd issued a stern warning against me trying to live there. The house was locked up and empty. Gas and water had been turned off, and any electricity we'd paid for had long since been gobbled up by the meter. So when I arrived there after dark, having caught the train in from Cardiff, I snuck in using spare keys I'd had cut secretly, and explored the place by torchlight. It wasn't until I started filling two large black bags with clothing and possessions that it occurred to me there could be a police escort waiting for me by the time I was done. I hastily removed the handful of knives I'd packed, just in case, and slipped out as quietly as I could. Which, being one of the clumsiest individuals on the planet, plus a bit drunk on Champagne and dangerously over-burdened, wasn't very quiet at all.

If the cops had come investigating, they'd have found me flat on my back in the middle of the street, chuckling at myself from under a pile of luggage.

I wasn't cut out to be a cat-burglar.

A few hours later, I lay on the sofa in James's new flat in Cardiff. He'd offered me a place to crash until I found another room to rent, for which I was extremely grateful. I'd been so preoccupied with the end of the tour that I hadn't really though about what would happen afterwards. My parents were finally moving house; Dad was currently living in a caravan in Somerset, while two-hundred miles away Mum and Gill were frantically cleaning the Lancashire house ready for its new owners. Their lives were a chaos of long-distance commuting, motorway traffic jams, meetings with bank managers and an endless parade of property-viewings.

By contrast, my world had shrunk to this small, cosy space on a good friend's sofa. I lay there, reflecting on the last two months.

They had been a success, I decided. I was still owed two weeks' wages, but I was reasonably sure they would show up at some point. Our feedback had been glowing, and despite the unpleasantness with Janice, my conscience was clear.

Compared to what the other group had gone through, we'd been incredibly lucky. Even Kerry had reconciled with me by the end, and free from the burden of working, travelling and living together, we'd been able to share a few drinks and part as friends.

Personally, I felt I'd changed quite a lot. I was happier, more carefree. I was fitter, and drinking less. Somewhat symbolically, I'd traded my all black ensemble for a more adventurous palette, and discovered new confidence in myself. And why not? I'd survived life on the road with complete strangers, overcoming obstacles, learning from my mistakes, evolving my performance, making kids laugh, and proving to myself that I had what it takes to be an actor.

I felt triumphant.

The only downside was that I was now unemployed, destitute and homeless.

Y'know – like most actors in the country.

A Few Days Extra

There's something about being homeless and unemployed that instilled a sense of urgency in me.

I was in a bit of a quandary. I was in no rush to return to Lancashire – that part of my life was definitely over. Pete was back living there, but he'd made friends and established a life in the years since quitting university. Currently, he was working in the village pub where we used to drink as teenagers. I'd love to have seen the manager's face when he read Pete's application form and realised he'd been serving him beer since he was fifteen. Pete now had a car and a long-term girlfriend, and to my eyes had become thoroughly domesticated.

I still had a bed in my parent's house, and all my books were still there because packing them up would take a week. I'd promised to handle that chore the next time I was up filming for Coronation Street, but moving back in there – even temporarily – would be a mistake.

I had a foothold in Cardiff. Friends there, and contacts. I knew where everything was, and how things worked. And also... Sally was there.

I'd only been back a few hours, I was infatuated all over again.

Faced with creating a permanent encampment on James's sofa, or adopting the folding bunk-bed in Dad's leaky caravan in Somerset, I spent ten hours a day pounding the pavements around Cardiff, determined to find a place to live. And on Richmond Road, only ten minutes' walk from the city centre, I did. A grand old Victorian town house on a street lined with them, it was semi-detached, three stories including the converted roof space, with prominent bay windows and a lovely façade of dressed stone. I wasn't renting the whole thing, of course. A note in the window advertised the building's conversion into student accommodation. I nipped in and met the owner, who was overseeing the work. We came to a fantastic agreement. I admitted that I wasn't a student, and he offered to pretend that I was. Leasing the house exclusively to students would grant him a massive 75% reduction in the building's Council Tax; allowing even one room to go to a non-student, however, reduced the discount to a measly 5%.

"So don't tell anyone," he warned me, "or I'll have to kick you out!"

I was more than happy to comply. The rent was student-cheap, and as I was the first person to enquire, I got my pick of the rooms. Well, except the front one, with the bay window – that was reserved for the landlord's son. I chose the room behind it, which was being converted from a dining room. It had its own private access to the garden, a sink in one corner, and a gorgeous marble fireplace that I begged him to leave.

"It doesn't work," he shrugged. But that, too, was for the best. Even back then, people knew that allowing me access to fire was a bad idea.

I was doomed to make the long trip back to Lancashire, though. When I rang Pan Artists to tell Dorothy I was available for work again, she booked me up for the next two weeks straight. "They've missed you on Corrie," Dorothy told me. Apparently, I'd established some sort of reputation in the industry. All that bollocks I'd been putting on CVs for years had turned out to be true! I was widely considered to be reliable, punctual and professional. Which meant that I actually bothered to show up for jobs I'd been booked for, did so in a timely fashion, and managed to avoid pissing anyone off in the process. Not exactly brain surgery, but it was amazing how few people could achieve it.

I was also known for never turning down work, and for the level of enthusiasm I demonstrated on set. Awesome! Now it was time to cement my reputation. Literally; on my first day back at Coronation Street, repairs were being made to some cracked flagstones outside the corner shop. The camera was pointed in the other direction to avoid accidentally capturing workmen, so I couldn't resist. I sneaked over to the fresh concrete they'd poured, and drew my initials in it with a finger. I wrote 'J.S.' for James Slater, because writing 'T.S' would make it a bit too obvious who to fire for vandalism. Random fact: Coronation Street is one of only two places in the world where I've immortalised myself in concrete – the other being a small patch of footpath near Sukhbaatar Square in Ulaanbaatar, the capital city of Mongolia.

Following an eminently forgettable day on *Brookside,* I spent an interesting afternoon in Goathland, in the North Yorkshire moors, filming a popular police show called *Heartbeat.* Dressed as an old-fashioned country bobby (albeit one that had lost some weight recently – the trousers they gave me could have smuggled two close friends onto set) – I got chatting to a young bloke called Jason. He told me he was a regular, new to the show but really enjoying it. We got on quite well, and it wasn't until the next day, when I was telling Gill about it, that she slapped her forehead in despair at my ignorance, and waved a magazine in my face. Jason was the show's lead actor. He'd been hired to replace departing cast member Nick Berry, and his face was plastered over every newspaper and gossip mag in the land. A fierce debate was raging about his suitability for the role; he was already being measured against his predecessor, though not a single episode featuring him had been shown yet. *Poor bastard,* I thought, feeling sorry for him in spite of his position at the forefront of one of the UK's most beloved TV series. I couldn't even bring myself to be jealous of him.

Someone I had recognised, and had been secretly thrilled to talk to, was veteran actor Bill Maynard, who'd been playing old rogue *Claude Greengrass* since Heartbeat began in 1992. In an amusing disconnect, Bill's off-screen persona was very different from the gibbering, scruffy yokel he played for the show. His cut-glass accent and aristocratic bearing were a wonder to behold; when he went into character his spine seemed to sag in on itself, hunching him over as his eyes fluttered and his hands twitched. It was like watching someone age fifty years in a matter of seconds.

"Bloody hell, he's good," I said to one of the production runners.

"Yeah... he's a pain in the arse, is what he is."

"Oh? How so?"

"He's not allowed to be here. He was 'retired' a few months ago, but he keeps showing up, demanding to be given lines! He's had two strokes, and no-one will insure him, so anytime he comes on set we're supposed to shut it down. It's usually my job to convince him to go and sit in his trailer... But yeah. He's a damn fine actor."

Bill was never on Heartbeat again, but his refusal to quit led to the creation of a spin-off series, called *The Royal.* This was set in a fictional hospital of the same name, allowing Bill to continue playing his beloved Claude Greengrass – in bed!

The following day, I scored an eleven-hour shoot on *Hollyoaks,* which I generally considered a blessing and a curse in equal parts. Because the crew were so disorganised, days on Hollyoaks invariably ran long, resulting in a nice chunk of overtime pay. Filming was characterised by a complete lack of anyone knowing anything about what was going on. On most shows I spent some time gleaning bits of pertinent information about things like lunch, predicted wrap time, number of episodes being filmed and what the rough storyline was. It was considered unprofessional to come right out and ask these questions, on the grounds that we were paid to do whatever we were told, not to worry about when we were going to get fed. Typically I'd spread my enquiries out, slipping questions into casual conversation with various cast and crew members as the chance arose. But on

Hollyoaks, it was impossible. No-one knew the schedule because there was no schedule; lunch would happen whenever they hit a snag, or ran out of film, or the director passed out from shouting too much; wrap time generally occurred when more than half the crew threatened to go on strike.

The storyline was always kind of nebulous because, as a teen drama, Hollyoaks wasn't big on plot. 'This lad fancies that girl, but she fancies this other dude and so there's going to be a fight' pretty much summed up every episode.

On this particular occasion there was a load of new faces milling around the studio. The word was, in addition to the pool of regular extras, the production company had starting hiring 'talent' from a string of modelling agencies. I guess we weren't pretty enough; in a blatant attempt to boost ratings, they'd decided to fill the background with more attractive people.

Which was all well and good, except these new Supporting Artists had never worked in television before. They didn't know how to behave, what was expected of them, and had even less clue about what was going on than the rest of us. Of course, the same could be said of anyone who was new to the job – or to any job – but with these guys and girls, the biggest problem was their attitude.

It was like having a dozen mini-divas on set. Not one of them wanted to be there. They all thought they were better than this – and light-years better than *us.*

They took themselves very seriously, sulked when asked to do anything, and yet would climb over each other's dead bodies to get closer to the camera.

Pretty much the exact opposite of what extra work is about.

They all showed up with a folder full of CVs and headshots, sat clustered together at one table, as though sitting with the rest of us could cause contamination, and spent the whole day complaining, comparing portfolios, and looking bored.

But they were very pretty.

The girls all wore *exceptionally* high heels. Never the most practical of shoes, wearing them on a film set was about the worst thing you could do short of setting yourself on fire. Watching the otherwise graceful girls step awkwardly over every snaking cable on their way across the studio, it was impossible not to take bets on how far they'd get before assplanting into a bed of lighting fixtures. Every trip was an agony of stumbles and near-misses – it was heart-in-the-mouth viewing. It took about half an hour for one of them to go to the toilet. I only wished we'd had some popcorn.

About halfway through the day, I found myself chatting with a stunningly attractive, yet rather vacuous girl; slim, with long, perfectly straight blonde hair, immaculate make-up and fake nails that could take an eye out. She was only seventeen, but I could tell her future wish-list included a rich older boyfriend with a sports car, a walk-in wardrobe and a tiny fluffy lapdog called Foo-foo.

"I don't get why they've hired us, when all they want is for us to sit around, doing nothing all day," she pouted.

"Well," I said, "that's what most of these gigs are like. They never know when they'll need us, so they pay to keep us here, ready and waiting."

"But like, why don't they just let us go *out,* go off and *do stuff,* then, like, call us back when we're needed."

"Ah, I think they'd be afraid we wouldn't come back. Or they'd have to pay someone to go and find us. It's just more convenient to have us hanging around."

"Not for *us* it's not," she pouted.

"Yeah, well, that's the life on an extra."

"I don't *want* the life of an 'extra'. Extra work sucks. My agency should be finding me proper modelling work. I don't know why they'd even hire people like me to do this kind of job."

I bit my tongue on a sarcastic reply, before remembering that, judging by our conversation so far, she wasn't bright enough to take offense.

"Honestly," I told her, "I think they hired you to make the rest of us look good."

The Lynx Effect

Making a living from extra work alone is really tough. Especially for anyone not living in London. Had I not been supported by my parents, I never could have paid my way through uni on the handful of days work I got. To say nothing of travel costs; every time I came back from Cardiff for a job, nearly half of what I earned went on train tickets to get there. So whilst I yearned for more time on set and the pathetic amount of exposure that came with it, I couldn't afford to be choosey. It's funny – more pretentious thespians refer to work they consider beneath them as prostituting themselves. I didn't consider anything beneath me, including actual prostitution, if it came to that.

It nearly did, on a few occasions.

So when offered bits of non-acting work, I didn't turn my nose up at them. Like a photo shoot at Anfield Stadium for Liverpool Football Club Magazine.

Not being a football fan, it was the first time I'd been inside a stadium. It was a massive place, made bigger by being empty. They'd booked fifty of us, and we roamed around echoing internal corridors built to hold thousands. Outside on one of the seating terraces, we gathered into a group to receive our instructions.

The crew handed out various scarves, hats and t-shirts, then got us to sit in an imaginary stripe three seats wide, running from the top of the tier to the bottom. We sat still for a few minutes, staring at a camera on the pitch in front of us. Then they asked us all to get up, swap our Liverpool accessories with someone else, move up or down the pack a bit, and sit in the next stripe over. By the time we'd done this twenty or thirty times, we'd filled every seat in the terrace at least once. They planned to composite all the images together, giving them one clear shot of a stadium bursting with dedicated fans.

It was well organised, and the whole thing only took about four hours. I couldn't help thinking, why on Earth hadn't they asked the magazine's readers to do it? You couldn't make TV shows using fans in the background as they'd be forever gurning at the camera, harassing the stars and holding up notes that said 'Hello Mum!'. But a photo shoot for Liverpool Magazine? What footie fan wouldn't donate an afternoon of their time, for the chance to see inside the empty stadium? Much less be in their club magazine! Shit, offer them a sausage roll and they'd stay all night.

Still, I was glad they'd decided to pay people like me to do it. Too bad the old cynics from Corrie weren't there; they'd have demanded we get paid separately for every shot we were in…

It makes me think, though. The rise of reality TV is based on exactly this economy. Why pay professionals to act, when you can get regular people to do almost anything for free, just for the chance of being on telly? Even better – pick a medium, like cooking, dancing or renovation – and dangle a single lump-sum prize in front of people. Then film twenty episodes of them fighting each other to the death for it. Simples! And *so* much cheaper than filming explosions and car chases.

The flurry of extra work was well-timed, but I didn't let it lull me. Complacency is an actor's worst enemy – along with poverty, other actors, and the acting industry itself of course.

It's definitely not for people who like an easy life.

To stand a chance, I was keeping up my fire-hose tactic of applying for everything I saw advertised. The Stage newspaper, local papers and, increasingly, casting websites and email newsletters, were all sources of potential jobs. None of them offered anything *real,* of course – the only way I was getting into the next Mission: Impossible movie was by finding a proper acting agent. But I was clawing my way slowly up the ladder, and doing anything and everything I could to stay fed on the way to the top.

So, when I got a call from a company called 'ID', asking me to come to London and audition for a promotional campaign they were running, I said yes without knowing or caring what the actual job was.

I mean, I'd applied for so much, it was impossible to keep track. And so little of it ever came to anything – I barely took notice of where I was sending my CVs these days.

Consequently, as I packed a bag for the trip, I was forced to admit that I didn't have a fucking clue what I was going to audition for.

I couldn't help but feel that might harm my chances slightly.

I travelled down to London on the train, sneakily abusing my Student Railcard despite it being technically invalid. In fact, I continued to use the card for a further two years, even managing to renew it without being asked for proof of my student-hood. Which is probably why I didn't learn to drive until I was thirty.

Anyway.

The audition, after I'd battled my way through Central London to find it, was a dream. It was like someone had reached into my head and found the ideal scenario for me, and then decided to run with it.

For starters, it was informal. I met the promotions team in their office, shook hands, and cracked a few jokes. Then we went into a large, sparsely-furnished room, and the two girls and a guy who were interviewing me sprawled on a sofa. Sarah, a pretty blonde girl in her early twenties, seemed to be the group's spokesperson.

"So, as you know, we're looking for someone to help us promote the new line of Lynx razors."

This was news to me, but I gave her the nod-of-all-knowing.

"Okay, great. I'm sure you've seen adverts for Lynx deodorant in the past?"

"Oh yes, for sure." I was on more solid ground with this one. Lynx was (and still is) the BO-basher of choice in high-school locker rooms around the world. In the US, it's known as 'Axe'.

"Great. So you already have an idea about the brand, the sort of image it's trying to project?"

"Yup."

"Okay. You know the guy from the Gillette ads? He's lean and tough, muscular, with a chiselled jaw and sculpted abs... he's a fighter pilot, he drives fast cars... he's a real man's man."

"Yeah!"

"The Lynx guy is *not* that guy."

"Ah..."

"What we're after is pretty much the opposite. The Lynx guy is a bit of an idiot, he's a bit more ordinary... he could be your mate, having a pint in the pub, then doing something crazy to make everyone laugh. He's a normal, down-to-earth young lad. That's why he relies on the Lynx Effect to get girls chasing him."

I grinned at her. "That makes a lot more sense! Honestly, you had me at 'idiot'."

"Okay... So, what we're doing here is sending you out to a whole bunch of places, could be shopping centres, town centres, all over really. And we want you to *become* this Lynx Guy, talking to people, mucking about, and drawing as much attention to the brand as possible."

"Wow. I can *so* handle that."

"Great! Let's see it, then. Show us what you'd be doing as The Lynx Guy."

And so I showed them.

I went mental.

I jumped.

I danced.

I turned cartwheels.

And all the time I span out jokes, silly puns of the kind that made my friends groan and push me away when I told them too loud in supermarket check-out queues. I was sarcastic. I was silly. And above it all, I took the piss.

Seriously – it was like this job had been invented just for me.

When I paused for a breather, the merriment in the eyes of my audience told me I was on the right track.

"Can you sing?" Sarah asked.

"Not at all!" I boasted, then proceeded to bust out a rendition of 'Everything I Do (I Do It Fro You)' by Bryan Adams that was so awful they had tears in their eyes by the first chorus. I hammed it up obscenely, gesturing and winking at my audience, and by the time I was done the trio on the sofa were laughing hysterically.

"Brilliant!" Sarah said, when she could, "Loved it!"

Not one to miss an opportunity, I spun out a few more jokes, clowning around and generally being me – only, a version of me that's had wine for breakfast.

It was a version that I'd had lots of practice at lately.

One by one, the interviewers got up and shook my hand.

"I'll be in touch," said Sarah.

"But I've got the job, right?" I was on a natural high, and couldn't stop performing. "Send the car tomorrow morning, and tell the driver I need the minibar stocked with RED M&M's. He can keep the other colours. Actually, I'm colour-blind, so he can probably leave the green ones in there too."

"Um, I don't think M&Ms come in green…"

"WHAT? You're telling me this NOW? My God, what have I been eating?"

Sarah was still chuckling as she ushered me through the office and into the lift. She came in with me, as the key-card around her neck was needed to operate it.

When we reached the ground floor, she hugged me goodbye. Then, this being a trendy ad agency in central London, and her being a young urban professional, she went to give me a peck on the cheek – on each cheek, presumably, like Europeans do. Only I turned the wrong way, and ended up meeting her lips to lips.

Which surprised her a little.

And was probably not the most professional way to start a new job, but it was done now, so I escaped from the lift, and the huge marble and glass lobby, and went in search of a pub.

On the train home, I wrote a note to myself in my diary (I only know because I'm reading that diary now). In it, I instructed my future to 'Always remember this feeling!' If only I'd actually described the feeling, I'd not only be able to remember it, but could also share it with you. Sadly, I left that bit out.

But I get the impression I was rather happy.

And why not?

Despite not being acting work, this audition had been the biggest opportunity of my life so far. And for once, I was reasonably sure that I hadn't screwed it up.

Except for committing borderline sexual assault on the interviewer.

But I seemed to have gotten away with it, and the vibe I'd felt from the team at ID had been entirely positive.

I really believed I was in with a chance, and that alone was cause for celebration.

Because as far as I could tell, if I got this job, I would become the face of Lynx Razors in the UK.

I dozed off picturing my chin twenty-feet tall on a series of massive billboards. God only knows how big that would make my nose...

Call To Adventure

I waited for two anxious weeks to hear back about the Lynx job.

And then, one relatively innocuous Thursday, there came the call I'd been waiting for.

Sarah from ID confirmed that I'd been successful, and that my mission, should I choose to accept it, was to rendezvous in London the following week for an introductory meeting.

I was over the moon. More than anything I'd done so far, this felt like the big leagues. Okay, it wasn't acting in the strictest sense of the word, but I had to believe I was moving in the right direction. I just needed to get one foot in the door... hell, I'd settle for a toe. And if things went well, the exposure I'd get from a job like this... I could very well end up with my chin in there.

Travelling down to London, I already felt like I'd made it.

For starters, ID were paying for my train fare; they were also putting me up for a night in the kind of hotel I'd only seen in movies. Barring one budget holiday to Ibiza, my typical family holiday was a wet weekend in a Welsh caravan site. To be suddenly catapulted to the dizzying heights of the *Ramada*... well. I belatedly realised I should have worn the jeans without holes in them.

The intro meeting went as well as could be expected. Although I tried to resurrect my clown act from the previous visit, this was far more of a business trip. The ID guys and gals had convinced themselves I could handle the performance part of the job; now they needed to make sure I was adequately prepared for the logistical nightmare of a long-term, one-man road-show.

Because that is what the job entailed.

It's hard to fathom, really, but I hadn't asked many questions that first time around. All my focus on seeming enthusiastic, and charming the pants off my prospective employers. I'd been afraid that asking too much about the nature of the job would sound ungrateful, or make them question my commitment.

Now, the full spectre of the Lynx Job was laid bare.

And to be frank, it was terrifying.

From a line up of hundreds, ID had hired five of us. Five mortal men – boys, really – who were to be sent out into the world, and sacrificed on the altar of advertising. Okay, so that's a tad melodramatic – but only because you don't yet know what we were being asked to do.

And neither did I, until then.

I was being hired to become the face of Lynx Razors.

This meant a photo-shoot, which was scheduled for the following day, and a full-scale advertising campaign with co-ordinated TV and magazine spots, to be arranged at some point in the future.

For now though, myself and my four compatriots formed the 'boots on the ground' portion of this bathroom-brand invasion. We would be travelling the length and breadth of the country (of the entire UK, in fact) – and bringing the Lynx Effect, in razor form, to the masses.

Naked.

Well, mostly.

Our uniforms were provided to us on the day. They consisted of a pair of purple, Lynx-branded boxer shorts… and nothing else.

They said they wanted to attract a lot of attention. And bloody hell, they were going to get it.

I sincerely hoped they wouldn't send me anywhere that sold eggs, or tomatoes...

I was familiar with how promotional campaigns usually unfolded, but this one was a doozy. Each of us would take a van containing a bathroom 'set', and drive to a series of locations, whereupon we would erect the set, and "do our thing". We'd been hired for our spirit of enthusiasm, our irrepressible *joie de vivre* – quite possibly our lack of sound minds – and our balls.

The latter of which were sure to make the odd appearance, owing to our officially-licensed boxer shorts not having any kind of fastening on the fly.

"Oh my God!" said Sarah, as I presented myself in uniform. "That's borderline pornographic!"

"I did warn you that I was a bit hairy," I said, feeling rather more self conscious than usual.

Which is understandable, since I was the only person wearing nothing but underpants in a room full of busy office workers. More than a few of them had ended their phone calls abruptly to watch what was happening, which only added to my paranoia.

Better get used to it, I thought, *this is going to be my life for the next couple of months...*

"Is there any chance you could put a button on here, perhaps...?" I demonstrated the problem by reaching into my shorts through the fly. I decided against flopping out my penis in front of the entire staff just to prove the point, but that decision was going to be taken out of my hands if I wore these things in public.

Which is exactly what I was being asked to do.

"Ah, well, you could always *sew* a button on there," Sarah suggested.

"Yeah, right..."

My sewing ability had been amply demonstrated during the staging of my first year Directing piece. I'd had to make a green sash for the costume of Baron Frankenstein, played with devilish delight by Chris. Making the thing had required one solitary line of stitching; this had taken me close to four hours to accomplish, during which time I had sewn the fabric to my bedspread once, my jeans twice, and to the skin on my legs when I decided to forego the jeans. It wasn't my strongest skill.

The other guys, when they appeared in their own costumes, also felt somewhat exposed. But as none of the ID office-types seemed poised to whip out a needle and thread, the issue became moot.

A few other logistical issues were explained to us. We would be travelling to and from each location in vans, and when the locations were sufficiently far from where we lived, we'd be put up in hotels. We would also have a generous budget for expenses, specifically food and fuel. Our paperwork had to be filled out by a manager or contact in each venue, and the office was to be kept informed of our progress.

It was at this point – still wearing nothing but my boxer shorts – that I felt compelled to poke a small hole in their plans.

"I can't drive."

The ID crew exchanged horrified glances.

"Oh," Sarah said at last. "You're welcome to hire someone to drive you, but it would have to come out of your wages..."

Luckily, I was not alone. Perhaps they should have mentioned it in their advert, because two of the other four guys also didn't have driving licenses. We ranged in age from nineteen to twenty-two; particularly for those who lived in London, driving and owning cars wasn't really an option at that age.

In the end, this problem was solved in a completely fair and reasonable manner.

The other four guys had all been allocated to work in 'London and Home Counties,' – thus, they would be driving relatively short distances, going home most nights, and would be able to allocate most of their expenses budget to paying a friend to chauffer them around.

As opposed to me. Because my area of coverage was a bit different. Whilst those four guys took care of London between them, I would be responsible for *the rest of the fucking country!*

Plus Scotland and Wales.

Because you know how they feel about being left out.

It could have been a major stumbling block for me – could even have made the entire job unfeasible, were it not for one little thing; I had a secret weapon.

I had my baby sister, Gill.

At least, I hoped I did.

Gill was still living at home with our parents. She'd applied to uni, but like me had decided to take a year out before attending. This concept of a 'gap year' was still a relatively new idea, and not one the universities were keen on. That's why Pete had been blackmailed into cancelling his plans for a year out, leaving me high and dry in the process. Luckily, Gill was a model student, and had aced all her exams. She'd been allowed to take a year off in between college and university (though she still had no idea how to spend it) – and right now there was only one exam result that mattered to me.

Her driving test.

I had just over a week before the Lynx tour began in earnest.

And roughly in the middle of that week, Gill was booked in for a double lesson with her driving instructor – the latter half of which would be her test.

"So you see," I explained to her on the phone that night, "it's really an added incentive. If you pass, there's already a driving job waiting for you."

"And what if I don't pass? It takes most people two or three goes you know, and there's a month-long waiting list to book another test..." The poor girl sounded almost hysterical.

"Hey, don't worry about it, dude," I told her. "Honestly, there's no pressure or anything."

"Really?" I could hear the relief in her voice.

"Yeah, really! Just for God's sake, don't fail."

I was jubilant, because the rest of the ID meeting could not possibly have gone better. I'd been flirting with Sarah after the other guys had left, and it wasn't until we were in the lift again, on the way out, that it occurred to me to ask a question. I didn't want to appear rude – a habit which, as an Englishman, is deeply ingrained in me. It generally does more harm than good, as most people are a lot harder to offend than you'd imagine, and the things we English consider impolite to mention cover a fairly broad range of topics.

In this case, *money.*

I'd overheard two of the other guys saying that our wages would be £150.

If so, that was not a bad week's pay. Especially not when the job entailed mostly mucking around in a pair of boxer shorts.

I'd earned slightly more working for Thunder Wolf – £180 per week – but that had been a Monday to Friday job. The Lynx gig had a varying schedule, and the suggestion was that we'd be only working three or four days per week. Added to that was the paid-for hotel accommodation and the expenses budget, which meant I'd essentially be living for free the entire time. *Every penny could be saved.*

For booze, naturally.

"So," I said to Sarah, as the lift dropped towards that immaculate lobby, "I feel a bit cheeky asking this, but I wondered about the pay for this job. Is it true that we're getting £150?"

"Oh, yes," she replied, "I'm sorry, we probably should have gone over that. Yes, it's £150 per day."

The doors opened and I just stood there, trying to speak, but finding it impossible with my jaw resting on the carpet.

"The expense account is only £30 per day, but you'll have to keep all your receipts to claim it."

I nodded.

"Okay, so, have a nice day!" And she hugged me again. And then she kissed me.

I must have made an impression that first time around.

Size Matters

Two days later, Gill passed her driving test with flying colours.

I have to say, I wasn't worried for a microsecond.

With that slight cloud lifted, it was sure to be clear skies and plain sailing from here on. The tour itself would be a breeze.

Of course, my optimism has been known to obscure the facts on occasion.

When the schedules came in from ID, Gill looked at them and her poor eyes popped so far out of her head they knocked her glasses off.

We'd been given our start-date, in the middle of next week.

And we'd been given our first destination: *Aberdeen.*

Now, I appreciate that not everyone reading this has an understanding of UK geography, so here's why this was concerning. Currently, we were hanging out in Somerset, in the southwest of the UK, helping our parents move into a lovely cottage they had just bought near Taunton. Aberdeen is in the northeast of Scotland – a lovely, if rather moist country, that sits above England and is actually a lot bigger than most English people think.

To wit; Taunton to Aberdeen, according to Google Maps, is five-hundred and forty-five miles, and with no traffic, presents an optimistic best journey time of approximately nine hours.

Not that we had Google Maps in those days; we would be doing it all the old-fashioned way, with a crumbling map book borrowed from Dad, and a few handy hints he'd scrawled for us on a piece of paper. 'If you hit Spaghetti Junction,' one note said, 'you've gone too far.'

Which was lovely to know, but I couldn't see how that would help us, were we to find ourselves sucked into the invisible grip of Spaghetti Junction and spat out who knows where.

One thing was for sure: it was going to be one hell of a first trip for Gill, less than a week after passing her driving test.

The other delightful surprise ID had in store was our vehicle.

"It's here," Sarah told me on the phone, "you really need to come and get it."

I broke the news to Gill in our time-honoured fashion.

"Hey, dude!" I said, handing her a glass of cider.

She eyed me suspiciously; possibly because she already had a glass of cider, which I'd offered her to lessen the shock of her imminent departure for Aberdeen.

"What's wrong?" she asked.

"Nothing! Nothing at all." I took a swig of cider myself, for fortification purposes. "So, our chariot awaits."

"Oh! Right."

"Yeah, ID want us to go get it. Tomorrow, ideally."

"Oh, right? Wow. Where is it?"

"It's the same place I went for the auditions. They must have parked it outside their office."

Gill put down her cider, which is rarely a good sign. "Their *office*? Isn't that in central London?"

"Ah... yeah, pretty much. I mean, their postcode is 'W1', like how posh it that?"

"Tony, tomorrow is Friday. What you're saying is, you want me to drive a car *out of central London on a Friday afternoon*?"

"Car? No, of course not! We couldn't fit the set inside a car. No, they've hired you a Transit van."

Gill's eyes widened even further, and she started to foam at the mouth just a little bit. I had a horrible feeling she was about to fall over backwards.

"Here!" I said, "have a glass of cider!"

ID very thoughtfully provided a train ticket again, and I bought Gill's to give her a taste of what it was like to have things magically paid for on expenses. This was a sign of things to come, I promised her. And for once, I was right.

We made our way through London via the Tube, and arrived at ID's offices in possibly the most exclusive business district in the entire city.

Sarah was super-friendly to Gill, and showed us into the lift. This time we went up – to a rooftop parking garage that I had never even suspected was there. It made sense; parking was London's second biggest problem, after the utterly insane traffic situation.

"Here she is!" Sarah beamed.

Our van sat alone in a pool of sunlight. The others had all been collected, leaving only our vehicle dominating the centre of the car park.

It was fucking *huge.*

Enormous; gigantic; vast; the biggest van I had ever laid my eyes on, gleaming white and flawless, as though to taunt us with its very perfection.

The van was over six-and-a-half metres (22ft) long.

It was nearly two-and-a-half metres (8ft) wide.

And not far off three metres tall, but that didn't matter a whole hell of a lot.

Gill stared at it, with a strange look on her face.

Was it fear? Abject terror? Was she about to tear across the rooftop, gibbering madly, and throw herself over the edge? I could hardly blame her. If I'd had any inkling of what I was asking her to do... well, I'd still have asked her. I'm nice like that.

Gill was pacing beside the van, craning her neck to try to look into the driver's window. She couldn't; the van was far too tall, and Gill, at seventeen, was displaying her somewhat gnomic heritage. Compared to her, the size of the van was even more laughable – she'd need to stand on a box just to get into the thing. But, as she completed her first circuit, I could see that it wasn't fear on her face. A healthy dose of trepidation perhaps – after all, she was about to drive this behemoth down a five-storey ramp and into London's Friday afternoon rush hour – but no. What was showing on her face was... anticipation? Lust! Yes, Gill was excited about the prospect of driving this gargantuan vehicle – and I could tell she was already developing a sense of pride about it.

Of course! For now, at least, this thing was *hers*.

She'd never driven anything bigger than a compact Nissan Micra – or anything less than a decade old (barring the instructor's car she took her test in.)

This monster was not just big, it was also brand new; the number plate was this year's issue, meaning this vehicle had to be less than six months old.

Peering through the window, I could just about see the odometer. It had less than 200 miles on it.

No wonder she was excited.

This had to be the single most expensive vehicle that either of us had ever been inside. Including the plane that took us to Ibiza.

Gill hauled herself up into the cab, and spent a few minutes gazing in awe at the sea of buttons and dials that graced the dashboard. This conveniently allowed Sarah to disappear back into her cosy office, leaving Gill and I – and the van – alone on the rooftop.

Which is what we'd been waiting for.

This was the only test-drive Gill was going to get, before she had to negotiate slip roads, roundabouts, junctions and one-way systems, all the way out of London. To say nothing of three hours on the motorway to get home.

I looked between the seats, into the cavernous interior of the van. A great many mysterious bundles, all cocooned in bubble wrap, had to be the components of our set. According to Sarah, the van was fully loaded with everything we needed for the job; bags of boxer shorts, several luxurious black Lynx-branded towels (which I still have to this day), a Polaroid camera (ditto) and boxes of film. This was because part of the promotion gave lucky customers who purchased Lynx products the opportunity to have their photo taken with me… Hm. I couldn't see this getting many takers. We also had a portable stereo on which to play our officially licensed theme music, and stacks of product samples and flyers. They really had thought of everything.

Except the fastening on my boxer shorts, of course.

Surely that wouldn't be a problem?

I mean, it'd be a shame for ID to spend all this money on such an elaborate promotion, only to have the Lynx Man arrested for indecent exposure on day one. On the other hand, that would make for great tabloid headlines, and was probably a far better promotional strategy than sending five idiots prancing around shopping centres. Maybe that was the real plan all along?

After a few laps of the car park, and a few nervous three-point turns when the car park proved to be narrower than the van's turning circle, Gill crossed herself and began to edge down the ramp towards street level.

I couldn't help wincing at every bump and jolt.

"So *big*," Gill breathed, as she inched around a tight bend in the ramp.

Then we reached the exit, and sat looking down the street.

To our left, the way was clear.

To our right, the way was also clear.

"Wow, no traffic," Gill said. "Did we go the right way?"

I pointed to the nearest street sign. "Yup, this is us. Turn *that way*, and go to the next junction."

"Okay…" Gill took a deep breath. A series of them, in fact.

Then she eased the gigantic van out onto the road, swinging a little wide to avoid barking the tyres on the kerb, and just like that we were off.

Into the maze of narrow side streets inherited from London's medieval past.

Gill had the steering wheel in a grip of death, her hands white-knuckled and shaking. Together we scanned the surrounding area, frantically searching for any sign of approaching traffic.

There was none.

"What the hell happened here?" Gill asked. "Did the zombie apocalypse come and go while we were talking to that Sarah chick?"

"Dunno, dude. How long were we in there?"

Gill nudged the speed up, gaining in confidence with every passing minute. Slowly, cautiously, we navigated our way through the district. I was tracing our route with one finger on Dad's ancient A-Z of London, while Gill devoted all her attention to the road in front of her.

She didn't need to spare any attention for the traffic, because there simply wasn't any.

On our whole journey out of the W1 postal code, we didn't see a single car. Until we passed a petrol station, and that was our first clue as to what was going on.

"Shit! Tony, that fuel crisis thing?"

"The what?"

"Fuel crisis! Haven't you heard? It's been on the news all last week, but I can never be arsed watching it. Apparently there's this massive shortage, and all over the country people are running out of petrol."

"Oh, really? No way. I haven't seen TV in ages. I moved mine into the new flat last week, but I haven't got it hooked up yet."

"Yes, I'm forgetting you're homeless."

"No any more I'm not! Dude, you should see this new room. It's huge, and has this awesome marble fireplace."

Gill mumbled agreement, as both our heads swivelled to stare at another petrol station. The queue went past the pumps, along the forecourt and back down the road for about half a mile.

"Holy shit! How lucky are we not to be in the line?"

Gill glanced at the fuel gauge. "Whatserface said they'd had the vans all delivered full of petrol. I wondered why she'd mentioned it. Now I know! Shit, this fuel crisis must be a big deal around here."

"Well, it's the biggest, busiest city in the country. Without petrol, the whole place will grind to a standstill. Looks like it already has."

"Luckily for us!" Gill was grinning. It wasn't hard to see why. She'd taken a huge gamble coming here, accepting this job, and trusting that I would make it all work out. I knew myself, and I had considerably less faith in my ability to resolve situations in a favourable manner. Regardless, Gill had faced her fears and done what she had to do – and done it well. Through some incredible act of kindness (which, to most other citizens of the UK was an act of pure bastard-ness), Fate had intervened once more.

All we had to do now was get home.

And, you know, to Aberdeen afterwards, but I was trying not to think about that part.

The Bigga Picture

Bombing along in the fast lane at 70 miles an hour, the journey home was a triumph.

Or at least, the first half of it was.

The second half was slightly marred by the police pulling us over for speeding.

A very polite young officer cut through Gill's babbled apologies to calm her down, before pointing out our mistake. No-one had thought to mention this to us, but due to the size of the van it was legally restricted to 60mph, and wasn't allowed in the outside (or 'fast') lane of the motorway at all.

I explained our relative new-ness to the scene of high-speed juggernaut driving, and I must have done a pretty good job of convincing him we were complete idiots. He decided not to write us a ticket, for which we thanked him effusively. Armed with this new knowledge of our limitations, we proceeded more cautiously, arriving home to find the van so big it wouldn't fit down our driveway.

The next two days were spent going over the paperwork we'd been given, and alleviating the shock of it all by drinking large quantities of cider. The sheer scale of what we were about to attempt was ludicrous. All we could do was laugh at the absurdity of the situation, and reassure each other that we'd figure it out. Somehow.

Honestly, I think we were both quietly crapping ourselves.

But as departure day loomed closer, we had some chores to take care of.

First and foremost, we had to pull all the bits and pieces of the set out of the van and figure out how they went together. From now on, every day of work would begin with this ritual; Assembling The Bathroom!

It went something like this:

Remove a few dozen components from the van. The largest of these being a pair of ten-foot 'walls' made of particle board, which individually weighed about as much as I did.

Remove three quarters of an acre of plastic and bubble wrap from said components.

Request tools from Dad.

Discover that tools are still packed from the move, and are believed to be somewhere inside Box 17C.

Give up looking for tools and attempt to screw the set components together with butter knives.

Swear copiously.

Realise that the set does not fit together properly.

Realise that the set is upside-down.

Realise that the set will not fit right-side up, as it is taller than the ceiling.

Realise that the set will still not fit together, even outside.

Realise that the set is not waterproof, and is a bastard to carry inside when it starts raining, as most of it is still screwed together.

Realise that the mirror is never going to stay up with Velcro; that the handles will always be wobbly, that floppiness is a permanent characteristic of the glass shelf, and that when dropped onto a foot, the set causes immense pain and a further increase in both the volume and quantity of swearing.

Finally, we had the damn thing built.

Depressingly, the next step was then to pull it all apart again – only, we made sure to leave it in as few sections as possible, to make our job easier when we arrived in Aberdeen.

The set did have its good points.

Most importantly, I hoped that having it positioned prominently in store would add an air of legitimacy to my antics. Otherwise, customers would just think there was some crazed, semi-naked lunatic roaming the aisles; it wouldn't be long before someone called the cops.

The set was also a bit of a safety blanket. What I was being hired to do was, by most people's standards, pretty daunting. I mean, how would you feel about stripping down to your underwear and spending the whole day running around a busy supermarket? Yes, yes, I know, it sounds like great fun. In fact, why don't we all go and do it right now, just for shits and giggles?

No takers?

In all honesty, I was a shy person who did a damn good impression of being an extrovert. I was far from confident about my body – far from confident about most things, actually – and I would be going into battle unarmed and unarmoured, with the meanest bunch of bastards in the known universe: the Great British public.

God help me!

The more I thought about it, the more nervous I got. What the set would allow me to do (so I hoped) was to hide in plain sight. If I found myself facing a tough crowd, being harassed or jeered at, I could retreat to my little bathroom corner and stand there facing the mirror, quietly shaving until whoever was abusing me got bored and wandered off.

The set also looked very professional; battleship grey walls, a gleaming ceramic sink, and the aforementioned floppy glass shelves for displaying the new range of shaving products – all surmounted by an enormous 'LYNX' sign. Anyone seeing it would know that I was operating in an official capacity, and not just some nut-job with a shaving fetish.

The downsides of the set were more obvious. Firstly, it was a titanic pain in the arse. Incredibly heavy, ridiculously cumbersome, and extremely unforgiving of soft appendages like fingers or toes that found themselves trapped beneath it. Carrying it into our designated location each day was going to be the hardest part of the job (or so I thought at the time!). It did provide me with a handy place to store my gear (like the stereo and Polaroid camera, which I was constantly afraid would get nicked), and of course it ably displayed the products I was promoting.

The sink, however, had no plumbing. I was meant to incorporate as much shaving as possible into my routine, but without a source of running water, or any way to dispose of the resulting mess, this rather pivotal aspect of the show was impossible.

But all that lay in the future.

For now all we had to do was return the set to the van (after first lining the cargo bay with an offcut of the carpet we'd bought for Gill's new bedroom), apply Band-Aids to our cuts, and relax with a glass of cider.

In case you're wondering – the new house Mum and Dad had bought was next door to a cider farm. I had to applaud their taste, though I don't think this factor weighed heavily in their decision-making process.

Our early departure the following day was hampered slightly by the packing process. This was hampered in turn by the fact that everything Gill owned was packed in moving boxes, and everything I owned was in Cardiff.

But it has long been a tradition in my family to be late for absolutely everything, and we were both well used to it. Thus, it didn't phase us to be setting off on a minimum nine-hour drive at around 2pm.

We took the motorway for most of the route, blasting past Bristol and Hereford and Crewe, and narrowly avoiding Preston before speeding through the lakes and mountains of Cumbria. This fantastic countryside is amongst the most popular in England, and we drank it in. It would become progressively more beautiful, as well as wilder, the further north we headed. A brief stop in Carlisle gave us chance to prepare ourselves psychologically for the transition into a foreign country. It was a landmark occasion for Gill; the first time she had driven outside England.

Back in those days, before the advent of GPS, not much was known about the roads in Scotland by those of us who lived our lives in England. It was not uncommon to find maps with fanciful drawings of mermaids, and 'Here Be Haggis' filling the blank areas beyond the border. Our route now became considerably more convoluted, as for some reason the Scots weren't as fond of motorways as we were, and only had a few of them.

"There's not enough cars to need them," Gill explained.

I think she was confusing Scotland with Mongolia.

Regardless, we now had to head for Glasgow, before veering sharply to the right towards the Scottish capital, Edinburgh. Shortly before we reached this ancient city, we passed a place that deserves to be equally well-known.

"Hey Tony!" Gill's yell snapped me out of a light doze. "Check out that sign!"

I squinted as we zoomed past. "That place was called Bigga?"

"Yeah!" Gill chortled. "But Bigga than where? That's the question."

"I saw it on the map earlier," I admitted, "but I expected it to be Bigga."

"I bet they've got a Bigga shopping centre," Gill said.

"I bet they serve Bigga burgers," I countered.

I could see the gears turning in Gill's head as she searched for the next pun. "I wonder if the people are bigga? Or are they Biggans? Like, big 'uns? So if one said to you, 'I'm a biggan,' and you could say, 'You're not bloody kidding, you shouldn't eat so many pies!'."

This opened up a whole new avenue of punning. I couldn't resist it. "Imagine you asked them, 'Where are you from?' And they say, 'Bigga.' And you're like, "WHERE ARE YOU FROM?" And they say, "Bigga." And then you're like, "WHERE. ARE. YOU. Oh, forget it."

We joked all the way through Edinburgh and out the other side.

"Edinburgh was a decent size," I noted, "but that other place was definitely Bigga."

From Edinburgh we crossed the Forth Bridge and headed north towards Perth, before zigzagging eastwards again towards the coast.

By the time we hit Dundee, night had well and truly fallen. The road we were on twisted and turned through the foothills and was unlit for most of its length. This made for scary driving, as all the other cars were locals blasting home at top speed. Gill was feeling tired, and I was feeding her Redbull to keep her awake. Lucky girl that she is, Gill inherited an undiagnosed form of narcolepsy from Dad, and when she hits a certain point she can fall asleep with almost no warning. This was definitely something we didn't want to happen when travelling at sixty miles per hour down an unlit laneway, so we cranked up the stereo and bopped our way through the darkness.

The last stretch ran through a hilly no-man's land, then briefly up the coast to Aberdeen. Gill had done a phenomenal job getting us this far, but she was no match for Aberdeen's vicious one-way system which led us round in circles for almost an hour, as we searched in vain for our hotel.

When we finally found the place, the van didn't even come close to fitting into their meagre car park. With narrow streets and severely limited options, we ended up leaving the van at the railway station and hiking back to the hotel.

Where it turned out we'd been allocated a nice big double bed to share.

Great! We left the staff trying to untangle this one, and headed out for a well-deserved pizza.

Tomorrow, the job would start in earnest. Or rather, in Boots, a popular chain of Chemist stores, the local branch of which would be the first store to suffer the onslaught of my pasty, hairy, body.

Our double bed had been replaced with two singles, and we gratefully collapsed. It had been the longest road trip either of us had ever been on; Gill had driven more miles in one day than she had in the whole six months she'd spent learning.

"You know what," Gill said, stifling a yawn, "that pizza was alright, but I could have eaten a Bigga one."

Lifeshaver

And so began one of the strangest, most memorable, and most lucrative periods of my career. I've done a lot of different jobs as I've travelled around – some I'm proud of, others not so much. But for sheer what-the-fuck-am-I-doing-ness, being the Lynx Man will always stay with me.

We began by carting our set into the Aberdeen branch of Boots the Chemist.

It was a huge store, with a warehouse at the back, and we carried my bathroom through it one piece at a time. Which was a pain, because every time we went in or out of the warehouse door, the damn thing locked behind us. As carrying most of the set was a two person job, we just had to knock and wait for five minutes each time we needed to get back in.

Having said that, I wasn't gutted about the delay. I was grateful for anything which gave me a moment's respite before starting to disrobe in a shop full of people.

But all too soon, the time came. I nipped off to the customer toilets, surprising an elderly gentleman when I emerged superhero style, only without a spandex suit beneath my underpants.

Oh yes! The clothes came off, and armed only with a towel and a cheeky smile, I made my first tentative circuit of the store.

And what a journey it was!

People shrieked when they saw me. More than a few tried to run away. I scored disapproving glances from a wide demographic, from housewives to pensioners to kids who were quite blatantly skipping school. It was every bit as terrifying as I'd imagined – and then some. Pant-wettingly so, in fact – only, that was one reaction I absolutely could not afford to have. Using this as my excuse, should anyone care to ask, I spent a healthy portion of that first morning hiding in the toilet.

At least the staff seemed happy to see me.

"They were all talking about you," Gill told me, when we met up for lunch. "When I walked past the staff room, they were saying how much they'd like to see you without your towel." She sounded disgusted; probably because it was her brother they'd been talking about. Personally, I was kind of chuffed. Going professionally near-naked in public is pretty tough on the self-esteem; I'd been on the receiving end of more hostile stares in one morning than in most of my life so far – since high school, anyway. It was quite an ego-boost to know that I hadn't unilaterally revolted everyone in the vicinity.

So as I headed back into the shop, preparing to bare myself to scrutiny once more, I made a conscious decision to have fun with it. Sure, there would be people who didn't approve; the same was true of most things I did. I was here to do a job, and nothing anyone else said or did could change that. I was stuck with it – and so was my audience, whether they liked it or not.

And if I was to stay sane for the next three months, the haters had to be ignored.

And I had to find a way to enjoy myself.

And the best way to achieve both these things was to muck around.

Which, strangely enough, comes quite naturally to me.

I began by stalking people. I'd pick an unsuspecting target, and follow them around the store. When they noticed me and turned to look, I'd freeze – then sidle slowly back around the end of the nearest aisle. I'd peak out very obviously, and resume following them as soon as their back was turned. Before long I had most of the store watching my antics, as I skulked along doing imitations of whoever was in front of me, stopping when they stopped to peruse items from the shelves, and hiding behind the displays as soon as I was spotted. Sometimes I would sneak up and strike a suitably heroic pose right behind a customer, freaking them out when they turned around to find a half-naked stranger in their face. I tried to do it in a way that was silly, rather than creepy, hoping the guffaws from passing customers helped take the sting out of my mockery.

And then, when that particular gambit began to wear thin, I fell back on the one thing I had promised myself never, ever to do in public.

I sang.

I sang into a can of NEW Lynx Shaving Foam, starting on my set – for reasons of crippling insecurity – before taking my tuneless wailing on the road. This time when I ambushed customers, it was by serenading them; they never saw it coming, as I made my way stealthily along the aisles, choosing the most unsuspecting target as my victim. Then, borrowing soulful ballads from the likes of Bryan Adams, Richard Marx and Celine Dion, I gleefully murdered them on bended knee, without warning, from point-blank range.

It was a hit.

Well, I don't know if it sold any NEW Lynx Razors, but it sure as hell put smiles on a few faces.

The staff were in stitches. Especially when, egged on by the manager, I singled one of them out for a song, crooning to her whilst writhing suggestively around on her check-out.

I got a standing ovation for that one.

By the end of the shift I was charging around the store, whirling my towel above my head, stopping to challenge people to impromptu dance-offs. I performed possibly the most faithful recreation of the audition scene from *Flashdance* ever produced by a grown man in a towel. By the time I was done, I was knackered.

"You're bloody nuts, you are!" said the manageress, shaking her head in disbelief as I packed my gear up. Gill had arrived to help pull the set apart, and we even had someone offer to stand and hold the warehouse door open as we carried it all back to the van.

"So, sounds like you had fun," Gill commented, as we set off in search of food.

"Yeah? It went pretty well, I reckon. I mean, they seemed to enjoy it."

"If by 'they' you mean those check-out chicks, they wouldn't shut up about it! If I had to listen to one more lewd scenario about you and a bath full of baby lotion... UGH! I don't think they realised that I'm your sister. God, I hope I don't have to go through *that* every single day."

And that's when it hit me.

Today had been a triumph. A slow start for sure, but over time I had built my confidence, learned how to work the crowd, and spent most of the afternoon galloping around the store on an adrenaline high. By the end, I felt like I was delivering my Academy Award winning performance.

But tomorrow, I had to do it all over again.

Starting cold, with a new bunch of strangers who would almost certainly hate me on sight, as most people do when confronted with something they don't understand. And assuming it all went well, and it ended on another high note... the next day, I'd have to do it again. And again.

Forever...

Well, for the next ten weeks, at any rate.

They say time flies when you're having fun. But staring down the barrel of it from right at the start, that ten weeks looked like a bloody long time.

*   *   *

We got a late start on that night's drive to Glasgow.

Although theoretically only three hours away, recent experience had taught us not to trust these kind of statistics. Thus, setting off after 8pm, with full darkness already cloaking us, was possibly not the wisest of decisions.

Not that we had much choice. It took us two hours to repack the van, find a place to lose it, hike back into town, find food and eat it, then get back to the van and plan our route.

We'd been driving for hours – which is to say, Gill had been driving for hours.

I looked over to see her eyes half-closed, her head nodding, and realised she was about to fall asleep at any moment.

"Shit, Gill, you okay?"

She jerked back awake, and nodded. "Yeah, just… *so tired.*"

"Look, we'd better pull over. There's no traffic. Let's just take five, have a power nap or something, just close our eyes for a bit. We can't be too far away now."

Gill nodded again, too tired to argue, and she pulled the van to a halt on the hard shoulder. We were on one of those rare Scottish motorways, the M9, just past Sterling, as far as I could tell. I hadn't been paying too much attention, as the route was fairly straight forward. The day had been a marathon, emotionally and physically, and I was knackered.

Gill switched off the ignition, and fell instantly asleep.

I stretched, put my head back, and seconds later I was asleep next to her.

In my dreams I was flying, soaring over the landscape below. Then I was bobbing in the wind, or possibly in the ocean, gently bouncing in the current as I was swept out to sea.

I came hazily awake, prickled by some sixth sense, swimming groggily towards consciousness. I was still moving, still bouncing, which added to my disorientation. Was this part of the dream?

Suddenly, I jolted awake. *No.* Something was wrong.

Very wrong.

I *was* moving.

The van was moving.

Backwards.

"SHIT! GILL!"

My yell brought her awake with a start. She blinked rapidly, looking around her for the source of alarm.

"Gill, we're MOVING!"

"Wha..? Oh! Shit!"

She fumbled at the side of her seat, before remembering where the parking brake was. She found it and yanked hard on the handle, bringing us to a violent, lurching stop.

"What...? Where are we? What's going on?"

"I dunno, dude, but start the car, quick."

She groped through the dark beneath the dashboard, locating the keys and twisting them. The van roared to life, the headlights flicking on automatically...

To reveal nothing.

Nothing but darkness. No traffic rushing to meet us, no sound beyond the purring of the engine.

We were alone.

Which was probably for the best, as we were no longer on the hard shoulder.

We'd been too tired to notice, but must have parked on a slight incline. Gill, asleep almost before we'd stopped, had forgotten to apply the handbrake, and gravity had done the rest.

In the few short moments we'd been asleep, the van had rolled backwards down the hill. Silently, with no lights on, it had reversed across all three lanes, and was coasting backwards down the fast lane of the motorway, picking up speed.

Like most of the roads so far, this section of motorway was unlit – and, fortunately, unoccupied. If something *had* chosen that moment to round the bend at the bottom of the hill... well.

"Holy crap!" Gill said. "That was a close one!"

"Ah... yeah, I'd have to agree with that."

"Whew! Shall we carry on then?"

"I think we probably should."

"At least we don't need to worry about falling asleep now," Gill commented, as she eased the van into first gear.

"Yeah," I replied, sarcasm easing its way into my voice. "We should do that more often. A near-death experience is way cheaper than a Red Bull."

"There's bound to be a few of them on this trip," Gill agreed.

"A few of what?"

She snorted. "Near death experiences!"

"Really? Why?"

Gill flashed me a grin. "Tony – it's *us*…"

The more I thought about it, I had to admit – she did have a point.

Accidents Will Happen

FAX Message received from Sarah at ID:

Hi Tony,

We're delighted that your early feedback has been so positive! With regards to your request, it's very creative, but we feel that sticking a fake beard on your cardboard cut out of Mathew Broderick and standing him on your set with a sign that says, "Shave Ferris!", might detract from the message we're trying to convey.

I've never credited Gill with prescience, but something about her prediction of near-death experiences rang disturbingly true.

Partially, it was the pressure we were under.

I was already starting to wonder about the way this trip had been organised. There's a certain disdain shown by Londoners for anything outside of London. Dad, who ran the Manchester office of a large computing company, had famously been asked by his London-based boss to 'drop something off' in Newcastle on his way home. When he baulked at the task, complaining that Newcastle was over 150 miles from Manchester and a six-hour round trip at best, her honest answer had been, "But they're both up North, aren't they?"

You can draw a line across the country, roughly level with Milton Keynes, and predict with a reasonable degree of certainty that 90% of the people who live below that line will never cross it. More than that, they will never *want* to cross it, and will actively avoid crossing it, even to the point of ignoring any information about the mysterious realms that lie beyond.

If you've ever read or watched 'Game of Thrones,' England's north-south divide is what George RR Martin based the politics of Westeros on.

So it wasn't too hard to imagine a scene in the ID offices, where they divided up the list of targets. "Tony's in the North," someone obviously said. "We'll let him sort that bit out." Thereby committing me to cover two thirds of the country by myself, visiting a new city, often several hours away, almost every day. This meant working from 9am until at least 6pm, packing up the set, finding some dinner, and then setting out for our next destination around the time most sensible people were curling up in front of the telly with a glass of wine. We invariably arrived knackered, often in the small hours of the morning, and crawled into bed only to wake up five hours later and do it all again.

It was exhausting.

And expensive, although I didn't fully appreciate that until we were a few weeks into the tour.

You see, our expenses budget had been set at £30 per day, which had seemed extremely generous. I was already treating Gill to posh dinners and drinks out, loving the idea of a rock-star lifestyle. But when Sarah broke the news to me that petrol was also to come out of our expenses, the situation changed dramatically. We were racking up hundreds of miles per week, often stopping to refuel twice in a single trip. Our fuel bill alone came to more than £30 per day for the first two weeks, leaving us nothing at all to spend on non-essentials like food. Other consumables, such as batteries for the every-hungry stereo, film for the Polaroid camera, all-day parking charges for the van, toll-roads etc – all of these came straight out of my pocket, for the entire trip. Which I wouldn't have minded, if they'd actually *paid* me.

The most galling aspect was that the other four guys who'd been hired had divided London and the surrounding counties between them. This meant they'd all be working within a reasonable distance of home. Their travel times would be minimal, their fuel costs a fraction of ours, and the money they saved on their expenses could be used to live it up in their gloriously free evenings. Whilst we frantically scoffed McDonalds burgers in a motorway service station, before heading back out into the rain-slicked darkness to complete our late night driving marathons.

I mean, I really appreciated the job and everything, but Sarah and the ID crew, if you're reading this – you *suck* at division of labour.

*   *   *

Having taken the better part of an hour negotiating another agonizing one-way system, we arrived at our hotel in Glasgow and checked in just shy of 1am. We still had a bit of admin to do, and Gill stayed up to write her diary (for which I am eternally grateful – not only that she was so diligent in keeping it, but also that she is now letting me to read it for 'research' purposes!). It was after 2am when we finally hit the sack. Our alarm was set for 7:30.

It will come as no surprise when I say we got up late. It was only our third day since leaving home, and already the punishing schedule was taking a toll. With barely time to shower and get out, we had to forego the delicious cooked breakfast that came free with our room. I figured that Gill could find something to eat easily enough once she'd dropped me off, and I needed to lose some weight anyway. There's something about having your midriff on display all day that boosts self-consciousness to obscene proportions.

We legged it out of the hotel, jumped in the van and nosed into Glasgow's rush hour. And into that bastard one-way system, which was proving yet again to be our nemesis. I had a pretty good idea of the direction we had to go in, but no matter what we tried, the roads just wouldn't let us. We got pushed further and further off course, as every turn we *had* to make proved impossible, or illegal, or both. I swore and swore again, as we made a third circuit down a series of streets that seemed determined to trap us forever.

"Oh, you have GOT to be KIDDING ME!" Another 'No Right Turn' sign blocked our way, forcing us down an alleyway in the opposite direction.

I was stressed, and poor Gill was getting frantic. It was only my second day of work, and I was terrified of getting a 'Late' mark on my feedback form.

We crawled down a series of narrow side streets while I fumbled with the map, trying to make sense of the spidery lines. The map was completely the wrong scale for this – it was only an exploded diagram of the city centre on one page, and amongst the many features not covered was the one-way system.

"Shit! Look, up ahead, I think that's the main road again."

Gill's fists clenched on the steering wheel.

"I think we've got to turn left, then a quick right."

Gill followed my instructions, re-joining the larger road and cutting across two lanes into a turning pocket. She pulled up at an intersection, eyes fixed on the traffic lights ahead.

"It's got to be down there," I said, pointing across Gill at the side street on our right. "Shit! We can still make it."

The lights went green, and Gill floored it.

Only, the lights hadn't gone green for us.

In her panic, Gill hadn't noticed that the green arrow, indicating it was safe to turn right, hadn't been lit.

The two cars in front of her had gone anyway, burning rubber to cross the junction before the oncoming traffic got started. Gill followed them automatically – but our giant van was an altogether less agile beast.

As she swung the van in a tight curve, a black BMW sped towards us, crossed the junction at top speed, and slammed into our front wing. With a sickening crunch the car bounced off us, ricocheting sideways, and smashed into the side of a shiny grey Toyota Avensis.

It was over in a second.

In fact, I was still screaming as Gill pulled up in the side street we'd been aiming for.

Her face was white, her hands were shaking. She pulled the parking brake on and folded over the steering wheel, head in her hands, sobbing.

"We're okay," I told her. "It'll all be okay. No-one's hurt." I rubbed her back, the seats not being ideally position for a hug. "Don't worry, it's totally fine. I'll sort it out."

Then I checked the wing mirror, and spotted an angry-looking man in a suit advancing down the road towards us. So I left Gill in the van and went to face the music.

Fortunately, I was right; no-one had been hurt.

And to be honest, we'd gotten off quite lightly. When the BMW ploughed into us, our huge plastic bumper had taken the brunt of the impact. It was now sitting in the middle of the junction, having been torn free in the impact. Other than that, we had sustained no obvious damage.

The same could not be said for the other two vehicles.

The BMW, whose irate owner was already on the phone to the police, had come off worst. The front of the car looked like a badly-chewed rubber-tipped pencil, crumpled on both sides from multiple collisions. After striking us, the driver had been violently deflected – straight into the side of the Toyota, which had been t-boned.

Bummer!

Both the BMW and the Toyota displayed 'V' year license plates, confirming that both vehicles were less than a year old.

The drivers took it rather well, considering.

The police arrived quickly. In the meantime I collected our bumper and slung it in the back of the van alongside the set. I convinced Gill to stay in the car and let herself recover; there was no need for her to be involved in a swearing match on top of an accident.

Things calmed down when the police arrived. I'd apologised profusely to both drivers, and swapped the insurance details from a packet of documents ID had supplied with the van.

The accident was blatantly our fault. Mine as much as Gill's, or perhaps more so, as I'd been the one piling on the pressure. My frustration at being late for work and lost in this bloody impenetrable road system had been to blame, causing Gill to make a mistake she normally never would have.

But that didn't matter to the cops. They were friendly as always, and calm, and thorough. It took less than fifteen minutes for all our statements to be taken, at which point we were allowed to go. Gill was still pale-faced and shaky, but she managed to drive us to the nearest car park, where we both lay back in our seats and let the shock wash over us.

It hadn't been the most auspicious start to the day.

I called Sarah at ID, and told her what had happened. She generously offered to let me take the morning off, and I gratefully accepted. I was recovering quicker than expected, possibly due to me being rather familiar with the effects of shock.

It wouldn't have been fair to leave Gill though, as not only was she younger and more fragile than me, she also had the burden of knowing that she'd been behind the wheel during the accident. Whilst I worked hard to cheer her up, I could tell that the moment of collision was replaying over and over in her head.

"Hey, if you're gonna crash, you might as well do it in style! Take out a brand new Beemer! And might as well do it in a giant Transit van. His repair bill has gotta be ten grand. Ours... more like twenty quid!"

But she wasn't buying it.

"Right," I said, coming to a decision, "bollocks to this. Let's go get some breakfast."

"Breakfast?" It was the first thing Gill had said in a few minutes – quite possibly a record for her.

"Yeah. We ran out of time at the hotel. Might as well take advantage now."

"You know, if we'd only stayed to eat breakfast at the hotel, this might not have happened."

"Yeah. Actually, I think it's a lesson for me. About not stressing over timing and delays. And not letting it make me so crazy. It's just not worth it. It reminds me of what Dad always says."

"Better five minutes late in this world, than fifty years too soon in the next," Gill recited.

"Exactly."

And on that sobering note, we locked the van and went in search of breakfast.

Shaving Money

FAX Message received from Sarah at ID:

Hi Tony,

Fantastic report about you from one of our Key Stores, they loved your energy and wished they could have you back again! But I'm afraid you can't walk around stores with a bucket asking people for donations to 'Shave The Children', as this could land us in hot water, legally speaking.

The show must go on.

Although I was starting to think some higher power didn't want it to.

Perhaps whoever is watching from on high had seen enough of my pasty, hairy body?

We eventually made it to the store, and I managed to strut my funky stuff as though I hadn't been involved in a traumatic road traffic accident a couple of hours ago.

And then, on the way out, we got stuck in a lift.

Now, the film industry would have us believe that in every elevator there's a convenient escape hatch in the ceiling, allowing our heroes to evade detection by climbing back up the elevator shaft.

Sadly, this is bollocks.

They just don't exist in the real world – I know, because I've looked.

Every. Single. Time.

If I ever find one of the buggers, I'm going to climb out of it just to see what happens; it's been an ambition of mine ever since watching *Die Hard*. Sadly, I fear they are confined to myth, along with guns that never run out of bullets and timers that take fifteen minutes to countdown ten seconds.

So, no escape hatch. No way out – just a small steel box, in which we were stranded for such a stressful half hour that I actually preferred being in the car crash.

You see, I have lift-phobia. I don't know why – just something about the lack of air, the unyielding surfaces, the small-metal-boxiness of the things – I'm breaking out in a cold sweat even now, just writing about it! It's odd, because I love caving, and tackled the army's confined spaces course with relish.

I think what bothered both Gill and I at that point was that the store was already closing when we left with our gear. We'd taken all the other pieces out to the van, and were making one final run. As far as we could tell, no-one knew we were in here. It was a small freight elevator in the back of the stockroom, not the kind of place some roving security guard would stumble upon us – so we faced the very real prospect of being stuck in there all night.

Fortunately, the manager came by to lock the store room door, and heard us banging away inside. She'd obviously had a similar experience with this lift – not that she'd shared this information with us earlier – and she knew how to reset the system and get it moving again.

So we sat in our van, now bereft of its bumper, a pair of nervous wrecks.

"I need a drink," I said, to no-one in particular.

"Me too," said Gill. Which was slightly amusing, seeing as how she was technically too young to purchase alcohol.

I'd done a fairly thorough job of corrupting her over the years.

But we still had to drive to Edinburgh first, and Gill demonstrated tremendous courage by doing exactly that.

The Universe must have been ashamed of the amount of shit it had shovelled on top of us lately, as it allowed us a comparatively smooth, hour-long trip.

We checked into our hotel to find the electronic door had malfunctioned, locking us out of our room. We left the corridor with a whole team of blokes brandishing screwdrivers, and retired to the bar, where we finally got our drinks – courtesy of the apologetic manager. Who obviously didn't realise Gill was under age, probably because not many underage drinkers show up at an exclusive city-centre hotel, chauffeur-driving a recently-crashed van the size of an Egyptian pyramid and sporting the world-weary stare of someone two decades older than themselves.

Poor girl. She'd had quite a week.

And it was only Tuesday.

*   *   *

As the days wore on, our routine became more established.

I continued to add new bits to my act, some of which went down better than others. One of my favourite tricks, which still makes me chuckle to this day, was to walk around offering free samples. This is something that people see every day, and they tend to develop conditioned responses to it. Most commonly, they either studiously ignore the person making the offer, or take whatever is being held out automatically.

Of course, I was advertising a revolutionary new series of razors.

So when I offered free samples, what I was giving out was shaving foam.

I'd stride briskly around the store, barking "FREE SAMPLE, sir?" at every third or fourth customer. Roughly half of them would raise one hand without thinking – and into it, I would spray a healthy dollop of shaving foam from the can I was carrying. Then I was off around the corner, heading down the next aisle to repeat the process. After a while I'd retire to my little bathroom corner, giggling uncontrollably, and watch as droves of people roamed the store looking confused, each still holding out one hand full of glistening white foam. There was nothing they could do with it; I saw them standing in line at the check-outs, one hand protruding uselessly as they fumbled for their wallets or purses with the other.

I'm sure there were some complaints made about that one, but it cracked me up every time, so I carried on doing it. One of the fringe benefits of moving on to a new place every day: no-one knew in advance what I'd be doing, and by the time anyone decided to stop me, it was generally too late.

Singing into a can of shaving foam continued to be a huge hit. ID had specifically requested that we spend as much time as possible actually shaving – I think they'd created this image of The Lynx Man as a living sculpture, staring into the mirror for eight hours a day whilst shaving continually. Pretty much the opposite of what I was doing, but then, they'd asked me to cause a stir. Perhaps they thought the sight of a man clad only in a towel, calmly shaving in the middle of a supermarket, would cause enough of a stir by itself. And who knows? Maybe they were right. But I couldn't stand still for that long. It was too damn cold! And even without the lack-of-running-water problem, I discovered early on that shaving several times consecutively leads to a face red-raw and enflamed, chapped from constant wetness in air-conditioning and so sensitive that even thinking about shaving hurts. I'm sure the ladies are with me on this one. Imagine shaving your bikini line ten times in one afternoon…

Sensitive? No kidding! Wanna shave it again…? Thought not!

But no-one complained about my lack of shaving. I pulled the blades out of one razor to make a dummy version, and used that whenever I felt like a shaving show was required. It was a great way to hide when swarms of customers were circling the store with huge handfuls of shaving foam, looking for someone to shout at.

At the end of the first week we found ourselves back in Lancashire, camping out in the empty shell of our childhood home, after an epic six-hour drive from northern Scotland. Having worked our way slowly southwards throughout the week, some genius organiser had managed to schedule the last day not far from the first one – back in bloody Aberdeen!

It had been a long and fairly eventful week. I'd been glared at, sworn at and even spat at; I'd been praised, kissed, had my arse pinched, my towel stolen, and some complete dickhead had stolen my razor – not even a real one, but the bladeless dummy I'd been using in shows. Good luck with finding a use for that…

I'd made people laugh, people scream, and at least one person acknowledge homoerotic impulses they'd never even known about.

I'd even managed to keep my cock from flopping out in front of people.

Mostly.

I don't know if I'd sold many razors, but not a single customer had asked to have their photo taken with the Lynx Man.

Miserable bastards.

Gill had spent her days watching movies, shopping, and trying to sleep in the carpeted back of the van. When sleep eluded her, she'd been studying our atlas, pinpointing our destinations for the coming weeks. It was with relish that she revealed her calculations – by the midpoint of the tour, we'd have travelled over 3,000 miles in service of the Lynx campaign. Gill was no longer fazed by the prospect of driving around unfamiliar city centres in terrible weather during rush hour, navigating one-way systems and squeezing the gigantic van into the tightest of parking spots. "I'll be sad when we have to give her back," she commented at one point.

"You never know," I teased, "if you crash it a few more times, they might let you keep what's left!"

The next week was, thankfully, far less eventful.

As was the week after that.

Eventually, the days of the tour began to blend into one another, a blur of increasingly impressive hotels, late night driving, and sour-faced store managers telling me they'd already had the 'Lynx Man' promotion.

They were wrong; they'd had the precursor to my visit, where a relatively normal young lad had stood in the foyer and handed out leaflets. But the confusion resulted in many phone calls back and forth to the ID offices, and several hours sitting in van, or in various staff canteens, waiting for the official verdict.

I have to say, ID had really fumbled the ball on this one. Their communication with the stores had been almost non-existent – a real shame, as I was the one putting in all the effort, yet they couldn't be bothered to make a handful of phone calls.

In Newcastle we spent several days in the Metro Centre, which at that time was the biggest shopping centre in Europe. People there had been overwhelmingly friendly – I'd had at least three offers of jobs, and several more of, ah, intimate companionship. If Gill hadn't been sharing my hotel room, I certainly wouldn't have been lonely.

Then, to keep us on our toes, we spent the following week at the opposite end of the country, in Portsmouth, Plymouth and Southampton. Communication didn't improve dramatically, leading to inevitable mix-ups: it took us an hour to reach Calcot, thirty miles from our hotel in Gloucester, only to find nothing there but a row of dilapidated cottages and a sizeable herd of sheep. A concerned call to ID returned the phrase, "Oh, sorry, it's Calcot in Reading."

To which my stunned reply was, "But... but that's another seventy miles away! That's nearly a hundred miles from the hotel you put us in!"

"Oh, really? Never mind. What time can you get there by?"

I waited till I was off the phone for a monumental session of cursing my employers.

"Just think of the money," Gill reminded me. "ID may be screwing you, but at least they're paying you well for the privilege."

"Great. That does not in any way make me feel like a prostitute."

Gill shrugged, and fired up the van. "Well, if it makes you feel any better, you get to keep your clothes on for another hour..."

Caught In The Act

FAX Message received from Sarah at ID:

Hi Tony, thanks for the feedback forms, glad you're still getting such positive comments. However, we feel that preaching sermons comparing the three blades of a Lynx Razor to the Holy Trinity, under a homemade banner that reads 'Jesus Shaves', is highly inappropriate. Please stop it.

I'd sent a lot of daft requests to ID.

I just couldn't help myself. I think it's a medical condition; whenever anyone asks me to fill out a 'serious' form, I come over all silly. Even last year, I added a note to my tax return explaining that I considered rum a legitimately deductible expense because, "No-one would ever read what I write when I'm sober."

I sent the messages to ID in the comments box of my feedback forms, usually while still giddy from the show, hoping to give them a chuckle. I also did it to remind them I was still alive, as they seemed to keep forgetting.

But amongst requests for a portrait of the Queen with a moustache (so I could sing 'God Shave Our Gracious Queen' to it), and similar suggestions, I made one honest, sincere, even serious, request.

I asked them not to send me to Cardiff.

In fact, I downright *begged* them not to.

After all, there were four other Lynx Men floating around out there – surely one of them could be coaxed north of The Smoke? I mean, they were getting paid the same as I was… right?

No chance.

As the paperwork came through for the second month of the tour, I was more than a little perturbed to find that Cardiff was listed right in the middle.

Bugger!

It was one thing to dance around in a towel for a living far from home, where no-one would ever know about it – quite another to repeat the process in my home city. Where all my friends lived. Where I would not just be exposed, I'd be… *exposed.* You know?

Damn Sarah! It's like she was doing it just to mess with me.

Of course, it did make sense logistically. At least from ID's point of view; they knew I lived in Cardiff, so they hadn't bothered booking a hotel for the two nights we'd be there.

On the upside, this meant that I could finally meet my new housemates. Technically I'd been a resident of Richmond Road for a month already, but I was yet to put a foot through the door. It also meant Gill could see my new place, and I could dig through my long-abandoned university possessions, which my parents had lovingly transplanted. But it would be a hard fall back to the real world; instead of ordering 5-star room service, we'd be cooking fish-finger sandwiches for dinner, and then sharing my rather shabby double bed.

For once, the journey to our destination was easy. Having spent the last few years navigating Cardiff, albeit on foot, I had a fairly good grasp of the place. As for the store I'd be performing in the following morning… why, that was easy. It was another Boots chemist – right in the middle of the main shopping street.

Nothing like hiding in plain sight, right?

Gill and I arrived at the place I'd be calling home for the next year in the middle of what appeared to be a house-warming party. I was later to discover that it was more of a permanent fixture, with dozens of people coming and going at all hours, staggering in, passing out on the sofas, only to vanish with the influx of new visitors a few hours later. Although technically only ten people were living there, the lounge alone was usually occupied by twice that many.

More than a tad curious, I ditched my bag in my room and headed straight for where the noise was coming from. I stepped into a long, narrow lounge, stuffed with mismatched sofas that looked like they'd been rescued from landfill. At least twenty people turned to regard me suspiciously.

"Who are you?" asked a skinny Welsh lad, who turned out to be Ewan, the landlord's son.

"Err…   I   live   here."

"Oh! You're our new housemate?"

"Yes. I'm Tony."

"TONY! Great to meet you! We were wondering when you'd show up. Where've you been all month?"

"Oh, you know, just working."

"Ahhh! So, what do you do for work?"

"Ummm…."

This was going to take some explaining.

Luckily, I had Gill for that.

She bounded out from behind me, introduced herself, and began to regale the room with tales of our exploits.

"…and the van was rolling backwards down the hill…"

"…the BMW was practically a write-off…"

"…she accused Tony of being the Antichrist…"

"…so lost we had to sleep in the van under a pile of towels…"

"…and she screamed, 'Why the hell am I covered in shaving foam?'"

Gill was a one-woman stand-up show, and her audience were spellbound.

By the time she was done, I'd been painted as a half-crazed superstar, blundering around the country like something out of a National Lampoon movie.

My soon-to-be housemates, their mates, and their mates' mates, all stared at me in disbelief.

"So, you really get naked in public for a living?" Ewan asked.

I shrugged. "Only for a few months."

"What do you do for the rest of the time?"

"Oh, mostly I do TV extra work. You know, in the crowd scenes? Real blink-and-you'll-miss-it stuff. On shows like Coronation Street and Hollyoaks."

"Wait a minute – YOU'RE IN CORONATION STREET?!"

And that was the beginning of my reputation in Richmond Road.

I'd worked so hard, all my life, to make friends and get people to like me. When all I really needed was to get Gill to do it for me.

We spent the evening drinking, chatting, and – weirdly – playing Monopoly with my housemates. It was all going so well...

And then I caused Gill the first existential crisis of her life.

Someone in the throng had rolled a joint, and it was being passed around the room. When it reached me, I took it without thinking, smoked a polite half-inch off it, then passed it to my right.

That's when I looked at Gill, and froze. Her eyes had gone as wide as dinner plates, and I belatedly realised that Gill had never seen me smoke. Never seen me do anything illegal at all – unless you count buying her alcohol and feeding it to her until she threw up.

Oh-oh.

Later that night, as we staggered drunkenly back to my room, I 'fessed up to Gill about my occasional use of marijuana. The poor girl was horrified – traumatised, even, by what she had witnessed. I can laugh now, because we've both loosened up a bit. In my case, I was fairly loose to start off with, and I went through periods where I was slacker than a clown's trousers. But for now, for here, Gill had witnessed the falling of an idol. Having been raised strict Catholics by tee-total parents, and never having been nearly cool enough at school to get into any kind of trouble, this revelation disturbed her on an unprecedented scale. She wrote in her diary that night that she was praying for me, as she was terrified that I had lost my way – and that as a consequence, my immortal soul was in peril.

Bless her!

It's quite amusing, because I discovered this particular diary entry quite recently, while staying at Gill's new house in New Zealand. She was hosting a party for a group of new mothers, and I was hiding out in her spare room. With nothing better to do, I picked up her journal of the Lynx trip, which she'd lent to me for research purposes. When I read about her concern for my soul, I laughed so loudly that she thought I was having some kind of fit. She came barrelling in from the next room, and was most embarrassed when I read the passage out to her.

"What's up?" I heard someone ask her, as she re-joined the party. "Is your brother okay?"

"Oh, yeah," she replied, "he's reading my diary, and he just found something funny."

I bet that surprised a few people.

*   *   *

The next day dawned with depressing inevitability.

My house-warming hangover did little to improve my mood, but I still had a job to do. Gill said little as she drove towards Boots, but she was back to herself – at least the cursing part – by the time we'd finished putting the set up.

And so I began my performance, hoping against hope that no-one from my class would discover me.

After all, it was only one day! What were the odds – I mean, *really* – that in a city of almost three-hundred and thirty thousand people, one of my thirty-odd classmates would happen by that particular shop on exactly that afternoon?

Of course, it didn't help that one of them worked there.

A girl I knew only vaguely from my course came in for her shift about an hour after I started mine. It wasn't until I spotted her standing there, stunned, that I realised who she was.

Ohhh... shit!

And she must have put some serious effort into getting the word around, because out of my class of thirty-odd people, the only ones who didn't show up at some point that day were dead. (Or possibly just busy, but dead sounds way more dramatic.)

It seemed like every time I turned around, there was someone standing there, laughing at me.

Admittedly, that was pretty normal for me. Even more so since I'd taken on the Lynx job. But this time, they were people who knew me. People who could put a name to the embarrassingly white and jiggly bits I had on display.

Still. The show must go on!

I gave up trying to hide. It's never really a viable tactic when you're the only undressed person in a shop full of customers dressed for October. Instead, I started milking it – ramping up all my favourite tricks, singling out any classmates that dared approach me for a serenade on bended knee, or a swift chase around the shop squirting a can of shaving foam. I knew I'd be hearing about this for years, so I might as well have some fun with it.

And I did...

But then I turned around, and standing there with a look of incredulity on her face was Sally. Incredulity. It's not something you get to see on people's faces often. Not unless you surprise them on your next shopping trip by stripping down to your underwear in the middle of a busy supermarket. On Sally, it looked like an equal-parts mix of horror and amusement – her eyes were gleaming with mirth, but her jaw was stretched so far open that other customers were having to step around it. Chris, on the other hand, opted for the subtle approach. He merely stared at me, pointed with one outstretched arm, and shouted, "TONY! YOU'RE NEARLY NAKED!"

Of course, it wasn't the first time either of them had seen me in that state – but it was the first time in public. Well okay, the first time in *daylight,* in public. Okay, the first time *sober,* in daylight, in public...

"Look!" said Sally, waving a can of deodorant, "I've bought a Lynx thing. Now I can have a photo!"

I didn't have much choice, really, so out came the Polaroid camera – and between them, Sally and Chris managed to burn through an entire cartridge of film.

I took my revenge on Sally by folding her into a big hug. Never one for public displays of affection, getting an overly enthusiastic squeeze from the Lynx Man put a serious dent in her stealth mode. Chris of course was incorrigible, and hugged me back just as enthusiastically. He wouldn't let go until I threatened to drop my towel.

And that was when Sally, fishing around under my sink for evidence, hit the jackpot.

"Oh my *God*," she gloated, "is this you?"

"Eh?" I turned to see her waving a sheaf of my paperwork at me. "Don't touch those! That's my feedback forms…"

"So this IS you!"

"Well, no, it's just—"

"*This* is your job title!"

"No, no, it's more like—"

"So, you're officially known as—" she brandished the paper as proof – "the *Triple Blade Babe?*"

I developed a sudden interest in my feet. "Um… yes."

"BWAH HA HA HA HA HA HA HA HA HA!"

And that's when I knew – it was going to take me a long time indeed to live this one down.

*Ghost Stories
For Christmas*

It was mid-October, when I found myself in the presence of true greatness.

The Lynx tour was more than halfway done; Gill was already looking forward to a less frantic existence, living with our parents in Somerset, whilst I was trusting once again that Fate would step in and guide me towards my next opportunity.

So far, my luck with this had been a bit hit and miss.

But for once, Fate was early.

Ghost Stories For Christmas was to be a series of four half-hour episodes, based on short stories written in the early 1900s by notable scholar M.R. James. It was being filmed in six days on a shoestring budget, by BBC Scotland – presumably because they were the cheapest branch the BBC had. The shoot was to be entirely on location in Peterborough, roughly in the middle of England, a hundred miles north of London. For this reason, the director had contacted Robert Smith, whose agency handled most of the casting in the midlands, and asked for help finding local talent.

I imagine the conversation went something like this: "Do you have anyone on your books who's trained as an actor, but who is so pathetically desperate that they'll work for an extra's wage?"

"Hmmm…"

I like to think he thought of me straight away.

The offer was far too good to pass up, and by pure chance it coincided with a week in which no stores had been booked for me to visit. The timing was impeccable, which sent shivers running up and down my spine. *Could this be it?* I wondered. *My big break, come at last…*

Because why else would everything line up so perfectly?

It was almost too good to be true.

The part was non-speaking, of course. Robert warned me that filming days would be long, with no special penalty rates for overtime.

"Now here's the good news," he said. "There's only going to be five of you in this thing, so the exposure should be great. I'm sending you, and three other lads…"

"Yup,"

"And the fifth member of the cast…"

He drew the pause out for suspense.

"Yeah…?"

"Is Christopher Lee."

"HOLY SH—! What the… what… how did…"

"Tony? TONY!"

"Yes?"

"One condition: *do not* ask him about Star Wars."

"Would I?"

*　　　　　*　　　　　*

Our meeting place for Ghost Stories was Elton Hall, a spectacular gothic mansion dating back in parts to the 12th century. The immense building would be standing in for King's College, Cambridge, which was unavailable for filming due to being home to seven-hundred of the world's brightest (and richest) students.

"Wooooow..." was all Gill said, as our van curved through acres of immaculately-manicured gardens. The front of Elton Hall was a sea of pale stone, dominated by towers and crenelated battlements. You'd be forgiven for calling it a castle; only the number and huge size of its arched windows betrayed a more domestic nature.

"I can't believe you're going to be living in *that* for a whole week," Gill breathed.

"I don't think they'll let us stay overnight," I replied.

"Beg?" she suggested.

It's easy to find your way into a film set; just look for the vans, then follow the cables. I was escorted straight into the costume department, which had taken over a small dining room, and thoroughly measured to see if the details I'd given Robert Smith were true or not. They were – apart from a slight lie about my height, as I'm only six-foot in heels – but it didn't matter anyway, as period costumes never fit. The wardrobe lady had chosen a tweed suit for me, too small across the shoulders and too baggy at the waist, my body not being quite as old-fashioned as the melon on top of it. A scholarly robe went over the top of that, complete with matching black mortarboard hat. But I wouldn't be wearing the hat inside, which was where most of the filming would take place, so the make-up lady went to town on my hair, slicking so much oil on it I could see rainbows in the mirror, before giving me a severe centre parting. The props lady then placed a pair of delicate brass spectacles on the end of my nose, warned me not to damage them as they were over a hundred years old, and pronounced me finished.

To them, I appeared the very image of a Cambridge student at the turn of the century. Whereas I thought I looked like a paedophile.

Hopefully the viewing public would have a more favourable opinion.

Gill was waiting for me in the car park, and didn't recognise me when I came up to the van in costume.

"My God!" she said, after I tapped on the window. "Tony! Shit, I locked the doors when I saw you coming this way. I thought you were gonna ask me if I'd found Jesus!"

"Well, this is what I'll be wearing when I go out to the nation. At least no-one will recognise me on the street. Well, unless this comes back into fashion."

"That was *never* in fashion," Gill observed. "You look like Jack the Ripper in his school uniform. Hang on – I've got to get a photo of this!" She dug around in the back and produced the precious Polaroid camera. "Mum's always going on about you being so handsome... let's see her explain *this!*"

With that done, Gill set off on her first solo long-distance drive – two hundred miles across the country to Somerset, where she'd be spending the week helping Mum and Dad unpack.

I wandered back inside, and met my co-stars as they came out of make-up; Ed, a short, witty Londoner who made a living doing voice-over work; Mathew, tall, dark and handsome, whose hair had also suffered the oil-slick treatment; and Peter, with a fantastic collar-length blonde perm-job that landed him halfway between scholar and pirate.

Together we ascended a twisting wooden staircase, winding our way up one of the towers towards the library. Starting early tomorrow morning, almost the entire week would be spent in this room, and we'd been invited to take a look...

And meet a legend.

The library was a treasure. A massive room by any other standards, somehow the thousands of books lining every inch of the walls made the space feel closed-in and cosy. Ornate bookcases soared three metres up to the edge of the vaulted ceiling, their span broken only by tall bay windows on one side, and an enormous marble fireplace on the other. Above the mantelpiece hung a mirror the size of a double bed, reflecting the clutter of camera gear opposite. An awkward jumble of uncomfortable-looking antique furniture filled the space in between; mismatched wooden chairs and spindly-legged tables festooned with ornaments and candelabra.

And amidst all this ephemera from bygone ages, looking perfectly at home in a wing-backed armchair, sat the man himself; Sir Christopher Lee.

Not that he was a 'sir' at that point, but let's not hold that against him.

His silver-white goatee emphasised the leanness of his face; his dark eyes tracked us as we entered, not unfriendly, but intense.

I couldn't help but notice; his costume fitted him perfectly.

"You all know why we're here?" he asked, as we found places to perch around him.

We nodded, but I sensed Mr Lee was going to tell us anyway.

He didn't disappoint.

"M.R. James was the *provost,* the Dean, if you will, of King's College, at Cambridge, and then later, at Eton. I met him once; I'd like to say I knew him well, but I was only thirteen at the time, when he presided over my application interview. He was a medieval scholar primarily, but he had a secret fascination with the macabre. This year marks seventy-five years since publication of his last volume of ghost stories, so we will be re-enacting a tradition of his. Every winter he would write another one of his ghost stories. Then, on Christmas Eve, he would invite a small, hand-picked group of his favourite students up to his study. They were under orders to come promptly, and to come in secret. When they arrived, he poured them all a glass of sherry, and read to them his latest story. It was considered a great honour, to be one of Mr James's favourites. I must admit, I had my own designs to be amongst them; but he died, shortly after I met him, in 1936."

Mr Lee's tale was spellbinding. His delivery steeped even this simple anecdote in significance; the timbre of his voice was rich and deep. Each word came out as though it had been examined, polished and rolled off along its perfect trajectory. His manner, formal at first, softened with the telling, so that we leaned in close like co-conspirators. At seventy-eight years old, there wasn't a touch of rambling old man about him. He was alert and upright, poised and watching. His presence roared like a fire, even in the silence between words.

He could have read the menu at McDonald's and made it sound like Shakespeare.

He was literally *awesome*.

We left the library and wandered outside just in time to watch a filthy, battered minibus chug up the driveway. It shuddered to a halt, belching smoke, and disgorged a shifty-looking bloke in a tracksuit.

"Eh up lads, 'ow's it goo-in?" he said, in a Scouse accent so thick I could barely understand him. "I'm Dave. Yoose must be the other actors, areet?"

And behind him, a pack of the scruffiest-looking young hoodlums imaginable burst forth from the minibus.

Apparently, the rest of the cast had arrived.

It turned out, the director wanted a few more bodies to flesh out the group. Although the vast majority of shots would feature Mr Lee and the four of us, the rest of the library would look too empty in wide shots. Hence, the addition of four extra extras... and all Hell followed with them.

To save money, the BBC had hired their 'actors' from an extras agency, and as for their extras... well. I never figured out exactly what Dave was meant to be. Had he set himself up as an agent? Was he a sub-contractor? However it happened, he'd been given the task of providing the rest of the background artists. To say he'd done a piss-poor job would be an understatement on a par with saying 'he was a *bit* of a dickhead'. Faced with a request for university-age students with a suitably serious demeanour, he seemed to have sat outside his local high-school and offered sweets to passing children. The rag-tag bunch he'd assembled had precisely zero acting experience between them; not one had ever been on a film set before, which was immediately obvious from their behaviour. They bickered and pushed each other, swore and shouted, and generally made themselves as loud and obnoxious a presence as possible. I guess that was hardly surprising, seeing as how they were all fifteen years old.

I saw the look of horror on the director's face when she saw them for the first time. It was mirrored by the make-up and costume ladies, both of whom realised it was their job to make these kids look like mature, well-educated students...

When in fact they were the scruffiest bunch of delinquent scouser scallies ever to be assembled for a BBC production.

Even the make-up department can't work miracles.

The young lads still looked like young lads, no matter how many layers of robes they were swaddled in, and no amount of hair grease could disguise their childish faces. One of them was granted the dubious honour of wearing the most ridiculous false moustache I'd ever seen; 'slug balancer', we called him, and tried to stay as far away from him as possible. It was a natural instinct, for those of us who'd been in this game for a while. He looked bloody ridiculous, and we knew instantly that any shots he featured in would be going straight onto the cutting room floor. Anyone standing too close to him risked being edited out of the show entirely.

The appearance of these idiots put a damper on everyone's spirits. But there was nothing to be done about it; tomorrow morning the show, as always, would go on. For now, it was time to head off to the bed-and-breakfast that had been booked for us. Christopher Lee exited the make-up room, and headed across the courtyard towards a waiting car. As the man known to the world as Dracula passed in front of us, Dave eyed him suspiciously. Then he turned to me, spat out a chunk of whatever he was chewing, and leaned so close I could feel his breath.

"Oo's that owd geezer?" he asked.

Things That Go Bump
In The Night

Filming on Ghost Stories for Christmas was scheduled to take seven days.

For the duration of the shoot, we were all booked into a family-run bed and breakfast not far from Elton Hall. It was a comfy, quiet place, the owners a retired couple who'd extended their house to take in guests. I liked it – especially the part where the BBC was paying for it – and I respected the curfew the owners placed on us. By 10pm, all four of us principals were back inside, reading quietly in the lounge before an early night. Filming was set to commence at seven the following morning, so it made sense to be rested and ready for action.

The Scousers were a different story. They showed up, pissed as farts, banging on the windows at 1am. Their commotion woke us all up, including the furious landlord, who had to get out of bed to let them in. We thought that was bad enough, but later discovered that it hadn't stopped there; instead of going to bed, Dave had let himself into the private part of the house to raid the old couples' DVD collection... and their liquor cabinet.

On set the next morning there was a series of tense meetings with the director, a slender Scottish lady called Eleanor. First Dave and his cohorts were taken into a closed room and yelled at. They were told that, having ruined the accommodation arrangement for all of us, they would be fending for themselves from now on. It was down to Dave to find a place for them to crash the following night, and how it was paid for would be their problem.

Our meeting was rather more cordial; she explained what she'd told the Scousers, and then what she'd managed to arrange for us. The owners of the B&B had been persuaded to let the four of us stay for one more night – after that, there was nothing else she could do. So we'd be moving into the *Holiday Inn*, where the crew were staying! It was a fantastic result. Not only were the dickheads getting their just desserts – something which rarely happens in real life – we were ending up with a substantial upgrade. Although we'd be sharing rooms, the hotel had several bars, restaurants, an impressive breakfast buffet and a swimming pool! Nice as the B&B had been, this would be paradise.

The rest of the morning was spent filming our entrance to the library. As the room was standing in for the Dean's private study in King's College, we were instructed to enter with a mixture of enthusiasm and respectful dignity – not the easiest of combinations to pull off, which could explain why, in the end, they chose to film this sequence from outside, through the thick glass of the bay windows.

The four of us led the way, climbing the creaky wooden staircase and sliding one at a time through a narrow medieval doorway. The room was ablaze with flickering candle-light. A fire crackled in the hearth, and a silver tray sat on the desk, with a delicate glass of sherry for each of us.

It wasn't sherry, of course. It was ginger beer, and it was flat, which solved the problem of me drinking it too quickly. Ugh!

Christopher Lee sat in the corner of the room, in the same armchair as before. He looked like he belonged there, fitting seamlessly into the picture. The camera would be focused on him most of the time, shooting diagonally across the room from the opposite corner. Director Eleanor carefully positioned the four of us around him, filling the space so that most shots would include at least one of us.

Ed was given a low chair facing Mr Lee; he was right on the edge of frame, meaning he could either lean forwards and be in shot, or lean backwards and not be. Needless to say, he soon developed a hunch.

Matthew took the seat to the left of Mr Lee, so although the side of his face was in shot almost constantly, he was rarely shown face-on.

And I was sent to perch by the fireplace, closest of all to the man himself – and staring straight down the barrel of the camera. I was guaranteed to be in almost every shot, and was sitting within arm's length of *Christopher frikkin' Lee* – so close that, on occasion, and quite by accident… our knees touched.

It was beautiful.

For the first ten minutes.

You see, most of the others had bagged some kind of padded armchair to sit on. The Scousers had even scored a huge leather sofa, though it was far enough back that they were comfortably out of sight ninety-nine percent of the time.

Whereas I'd wound up perched on a narrow wooden railing that ran around the fireplace.

Sitting sideways so I faced Mr Lee, I could only get one arse cheek onto the bar at once.

Neither of them were keen on the job.

Every time 'cut' was called, I surreptitiously slid from left to right or vice versa, feeling the blood flow back into whichever leg I'd been balanced on.

Pins and needles is a weird feeling to start with. But pins and needles in one buttock? I wanted nothing more than to leap up and dance around the room, shaking my arse to restore feeling and end the torment… but somehow I thought that might be frowned upon.

So I sat, and I endured, as take after take passed, and the day wore on. It wasn't made any easier by the roaring fire right behind me. This provided a large part of the atmosphere and the lighting, but also gave out a substantial amount of heat. I was wearing a long-sleeved shirt, tie, three-piece tweed suit, and long black robes over the top of it all.

Consequently, I was sweating like a sheep in a Welshman's back garden.

I didn't realise it right then, but the positions we were allocated would be where we stayed, ten hours per day, for the rest of the week.

But none of that mattered at all. The pain, the discomfort, I could handle.

Because Christopher Lee was incredible.

I'd say he was the greatest living actor, except he's dead.

Reading from a teleprompter is hard. Doing it in such a way that it's not obvious you're reading from a teleprompter is bloody hard. Most TV hosts never fully achieve it.

Mr Lee was reading simultaneously from four separate teleprompters, one positioned behind each of our heads. The same spiel was scrolling on each device, allowing him to shift between them as though moving his eye contact around our little group. But jumping from screen to screen like this, I figured we'd be stopping every few seconds for a missed line, or while he found his place again.

Not so.

Mr Lee could read uninterrupted for ten minutes at a time, switching seamlessly from one monitor to another and back again, all the while giving the impression that he was speaking directly to us. He was passionate and engaging; considered and emphatic. His rich voice rolled out, a boom and then a whisper, as he narrated his tale; honestly, I'd have forgotten we were making a TV show, if half my arse hadn't been stabbing me with agony, the other half numb, and both bits sitting in a puddle of sweat. But I made no complaint. Only the crew let Mr Lee down; he was frequently frustrated with them, as they failed to match their camera movement to his absolutely perfect delivery.

In between takes, he regaled us with stories of his life. Although the new Star Wars and Lord of the Rings movies were a closed book, Lee having signed iron-clad confidentiality agreements (and in any case being far too consummate a professional to have told us anything he shouldn't) – the rest of his life was, believe it or not, actually *more* interesting.

He began with tales of his acting career, how he'd started out doing extra work and been repeatedly knocked back for being too tall and odd-looking. After dozens of movies, he'd worked his way into more prominent parts, but could never secure the vaunted leading man roles on account of his height. Then he'd struck it lucky playing Frankenstein's Monster alongside Peter Cushing, and he found his home in Hammer Horror movies.

All fascinating stuff, and a beguiling tale for a group of wanabee actors.

But then, as the days progressed, and we made him chuckle with amusing anecdotes from our own lives, his tone became conspiratorial and he began to share with us more personal stories.

He told us of his military service during World War II. He was a member of the British SAS (Special Air Service) at its inception, and described his missions to us in lurid detail. For the most part, his unit was tasked with parachuting into German-held landing strips under cover of darkness – then finding and eliminating the guards, one by one, until the airfield was secure enough for Allied planes to land! As he told us this, he took an item from his pocket and turned it over and over in his fingertips. Then he held it out for us to inspect: it was a metal pin badge, the kind a soldier would wear on their beret. "I took it off an SS officer that I shot," he explained, casually, before disappearing the tiny badge once more. "I carry it always, to remind me."

He dug around in his pocket a second time, and came out with another badge. This one was round, sort of like a small commemorative coin. "Delta Force," he said, handing it to me. "We helped train their boys, when they were just getting started," he explained. "We went over there to teach them how to conduct clandestine operations – night fighting, silent shooting, parachute drops in the dark and such. When we left, they gave us all those. If I ever get stopped by the police in America, I can show that button and they'll let me go automatically, with no questions asked."

I examined the precious token, then passed it around the circle to my new friends. Not one of them said anything; it was like we were so far under his spell, so awed by the gravity of what he was telling us, that we didn't dare sully the moment with our own paltry voices.

And then, like the snapping of fingers, it was back to filming. Another take was in the offing, we all repositioned ourselves to match our poses at the start of the previous take, and Christopher Lee went straight back into character. I haven't worked with many top-flight actors, so my opinion on this is incredibly bias, but for me he will always remain the perfect example of an actor; tremendously skilled, hypnotising to watch, a perfectionist of the highest order, and a consummate professional.

"What you're doing is brilliant," Eleanor told me that evening, over dinner. "We're so grateful!"

I was a bit confused by this. I was fairly sure she wasn't referring to my acting talent.

"Not a problem!" I told her. "But, ah, what are we doing exactly?"

"Keeping him entertained! Mr Lee *loves* talking to you guys. I think he's quite taken with you. Whatever it is, it's keeping the pressure off us a bit. He's an amazing actor, but my God he can be difficult! As long as he's absorbed with telling you his stories, he's not micromanaging, telling us what to do, demanding that we move faster. That's the problem, working with a perfectionist: he's so good, we can't keep up with him! It drives him mad. So, thank-you so much for, um, occupying him. Please keep it up!"

*   *   *

The Scousers showed up late the next morning, eventually arriving in a pair of taxis. Another meeting ensued, Dave was fired immediately, and his young protégés were sent home at the end of the day. They made it into the final cut on a handful of occasions – just enough to remind the viewer that the room contained more than five people, but not so much they'd start to wonder what the hell was on that bloke's upper lip, and who had accidentally let the children in.

I'll admit that I didn't like those guys, but I did feel a bit sorry for them. I'd spent the breaks trying to cheer them up, and as they grudgingly parted with snippets of information, I gradually built up a picture of what had happened.

Dave had found them a place to stay – a hovel by anyone's standards, but worse because he was making them pay for it. Having ditched them there, miles from anywhere, he had then taken the minibus and buggered off for reasons unknown. Somewhat predictably, his plan had been to get blind drunk, and this he had accomplished. Unfortunately, he'd then tried to drive home, and had crashed the minibus into one or more cars en route. Being hammered – and a dickhead – he'd resolved this situation in a spectacularly inefficient way.

I mean, there's an obvious solution to this problem, right?

Or there would have been, had the minibus been insured.

And had Dave been in his right mind.

Sadly, neither of those things were true.

So Dave had done something that, to his addled brain, must have appeared completely logical.

He'd driven the minibus into a field behind their accommodation, and torched it.

I know, right? *Who does that?*

Forget being fired – I had a feeling he'd be imprison by the end of the week.

And that was probably for the best.

All Good Things

I never got to say goodbye to Christopher Lee.

After a week of working with him, we were given a day off; I jumped on the train to my parent's new house in Somerset, and spent a night regaling them with ludicrous tales of my week.

We all arrived back at Elton Hall for the final day of filming, to find that Mr Lee had completed his part, and was already winging his way back to New Zealand to do pick-up shots for *The Lord of the Rings*.

I think we were all gutted; secretly, every one of us had hoped we'd get a final moment with the great man, a firm handshake perhaps, and an opportunity for him to impart some final wisdom. Or, you know, an opportunity for him to give me his phone number and tell me to call him if I needed help with my acting…

Instead, we spent a whole day filming our 'reaction shots' – where they moved the camera to where Mr Lee had been sitting, and took footage of us all frowning, nodding, smiling and trying to look scared. We each had a turn doing close-ups; with the camera at point-blank range, I spent a good half-hour staring, grimacing, sipping from my sherry glass and stoking the fire. It's a testament to the sheer quality of my acting talent, that from over thirty minutes of continuous footage, they managed to find approximately three seconds of useable material.

That night we filmed exterior shots for a title sequence, featuring us making our way through the grounds of the college towards MR James' study. Dashing around outside in the dark was good fun, but it eventually got old. Knowing this was their last chance, the film crew made doubly and triply sure to cover all angles, shooting and re-shooting the same sequences over and over again. It took until five am, before Eleanor was satisfied. Even then, I think she only stopped because the camera crew were getting hypothermia. It was the middle of November, after all; 5am is definitely not the most pleasant time to be standing around outside for long periods. There wasn't much ceremony to mark the end of the project; no glorious wrap party, just a frozen hug from Eleanor, a vague promise to the other guys to keep in touch (it goes without saying that this never happened) – and the first train home, which left at 6am. I arrived knackered, collapsed into bed, and slept for twelve hours straight.

The end of filming also meant a return to the Lynx job, which to be honest, I was ready to be over, too. I'd drawn heavily on my store of shaving jokes to keep Mr Lee chuckling, and hearing myself tell them, I could hardly believe it was me. That life had seemed so far away during filming, a shadow me from the past. In one short week I'd gotten quite used to being on set, to taking direction, talking in industry jargon and hanging around with the crew. I'd even been meeting Eleanor in the hotel pool before work each morning; purely plutonic, but we'd enjoyed a companionable few laps before getting ready for the day's schedule.

It had been... there's a word for it, that I can't quite grasp. Oh, that's right – it had been *fun*.

For a little while, I'd had a taste of what it was like to be a real actor. Now I wanted that more than ever.

But instead I was heading to the Super-Sava store in Gateshead to prance around in my knickers again.

There's something incredibly demoralising about going from the heady heights of intimate conversation with a megastar, to standing around in your underpants in the fresh produce aisle of Sainsbury's whilst some frumpy, fifty-something housewife tells you to be ashamed of yourself.

Gill, bless her, was getting over it, too.

She'd taken to driving around in circles while I did my shows, because as soon as she turned the van off, ice began to form inside it. We'd been sent up north once again, to a land where lesser vehicles required digging out of snowdrifts every morning. Luckily, we spent the whole last week in Newcastle, so we got to stay in one hotel, rather than traipsing off to a new one every night. Driving to work one morning, a speeding car had cut across in front of us on a roundabout, missing us by millimetres and forcing Gill to do an emergency stop in heavy traffic. We both shit ourselves; a split-second difference would have seen the driver plough directly into Gill's door. We reckoned the only thing that saved us was the missing bumper – those extra few inches had been the difference between life, and whatever came after being in the centre of a ten-car pile up.

When it came time to make the long trip back to London, to return the van to ID, Gill and I agreed that the time was right. We'd had a blast on the road together, shared many jokes, a few accidents, and had somehow managed to avoid having a single argument. It was a landmark victory for us, having fought like cat and dog for most of our childhood; Gill promised that, were I ever to need a roadie again, she'd be there. And I told her that if I was ever asked to strip off and start shaving in the middle of a supermarket again, she'd be the first to know.

There was a tearful moment when Gill surrendered the keys, then we sat with the other Lynx guys in the pub, waiting for our train back to Somerset. We all commiserated each other on the end of the job, and traded complaints about how few of ID's glorious promises had come to fruition. I'd never seen any of the billboards Sarah had promised, though I hadn't been in London; one of the other lads reckoned he'd seen one, but he couldn't remember where. The magazine and TV interviews never materialized, though with hindsight that was obviously just a subtle ploy to keep us keen. On the subject of dedication, though, I had a bit of a revelation. Sarah had told me that my feedback had consistently been the best by miles. My stupid requests had kept them entertained in the office, and they'd been hearing about my antics in phone call after phone call from the stores I'd visited.

Whereas the other four had hardly generated a whisper.

"So, what did you get up to?" I asked the guys, as we nursed our well-earned beers. "You guys pull any crazy stunts, or what?"

The lads exchanged disinterested looks, and shrugged at me. "Nah, not really. Just sort of stood there, pretending to shave."

"Boring as bat-shit, it was," added another.

"But… did you… *engage* with the customers at all?" I asked, struggling to keep the horror from my voice.

"Nah. If someone came up and asked something, yeah, maybe have a chat for a few minutes. Tell 'em a bit about the razors."

"So you didn't… dance around? Sing into a can of shaving foam, all that stuff?"

"Ha! In the audition, maybe! You think I'm doin' that shit in the middle of Tesco's? Get knotted!"

"So you just hung around your sets? For *three months?*"

There was a round of nodding.

"Yeah," the first guy spoke up again, "It was a pretty crap job, really. Tell you the truth, I couldn't be bothered."

He must have seen the shock and betrayal in my eyes. "Don't get me wrong though, it was good money," he added. "So, what did you get up to?"

*　　　　　*　　　　　*

So, what next?

It was a question I was having to ask myself more and more often these days. It was becoming clear to me that the life of an actor provided very little consistency or stability. Not that I was in need of such things; I loved the weirdness and unpredictability of my life. But it did highlight the primary vulnerability of a person in my position; no matter how much fun I may be having, I still had to eat. My parents would never let me starve, but my pride was inextricably bound up in this great endeavour; it would be a sorry day indeed that saw me crawling back home to beg for food.

(Although you could probably replace 'sorry day' with 'Thursday' in that sentence, and it would still be true.)

As ID had finally seen fit to pay me, I used the money from the Lynx campaign to pay off my credit cards. And then, to be honest, I went a bit crazy. I outfitted my room in Richmond Road with all new pine furniture; I bought a matching pair of mountain bikes for Dad and me, neither of whom has ever had, nor ever will have, any intention of biking up or down a mountain. I replaced my gigantic TV with one the same size, but marginally less shit, and added a state-of-the-art VCR (Hey! Don't laugh! There was such a thing, once upon a time.) And then I bought books. Ahhh! Books... I bought and filled three bookcases, which I arranged as a kind of screen between my bed and the door. And then I looked upon the breadth of my domain and wept, for there were no more purchases to conquer.

Which was probably for the best, as after paying Gill the last of her wages, I was back to being broke.

There was a certain inevitability about this cycle, I was starting to sense. Something about me making large piles of cash, and then spending it needlessly... I couldn't quite put my finger on what was wrong, but there was definitely a problem there.

For now though, my lack of funds meant I was back on the market. I'd bought a computer from my Uncle Gerard, complete with one of those dial-up modems that made sounds like someone was shoving a red-hot sparkplug up its Ethernet port. With access to the World Wide Web I began to cast my net a little further, listing my profile and photo on a number of casting sites that had sprung up. Few, if any were legitimate, but I figured if I threw enough resumes against the wall, eventually one would stick. Or else I'd get a nasty paper-cut.

My first success came in the form of an email from a man named David Yates, who informed me that he was recruiting people for a Yorkshire TV production of *Mutiny on the Bounty*.

He responded to my profile, told me he thought I had a good shot at a part, and then asked me to supply the following: a copy of my current CV, the ubiquitous headshot... and several pictures of my torso without a shirt on. This was because the casting directors were specifically looking for actors who could portray the emaciated, half-starved crew of the *Bounty* after a long and harrowing sea voyage. It was an unusual request, but certainly nothing to be concerned about. I'd got quite skinny during the Lynx job, and – this may come as a shock to you – I was a bit less self-conscious, too. I managed to convince one of my new housemates to take a series of photos of me in the back garden, stripped to the waist, posed (as requested) as though I was hauling on ropes.

I'm not sure if this contributed to my burgeoning mystique or not; the only thing he said about it afterwards was, "I feel a bit dirty, like."

I developed the pics, sent them off to the address provided, and waited with baited breath, for two long weeks. I'd just about given up hope of hearing anything, when I got an email back from David.

So fantastic was this message that I printed it out, and to this day I've kept it in a folder of memorabilia. When it came time to write this book, I dug the paper out, and I have copied it here faithfully:

'Hi Tony,

Sorry I have not been in touch for a while. I have some bad news and some good news. First, the bad news, I was unable to get you an audition with Yorkshire TV for a part in Mutiny on the Bounty, sorry about this, but they had already filled the parts. But on a brighter note, I may have got you an audition with Liquid Excitement productions, they are a small production company based in York. They are currently auditioning for a film called Euro

Boys 6, I don't have all the details to hand at the moment, but it looks like an excellent opportunity.

Could you get back to me ASAP if you are interested in the roll?

Many Thanks
David Yates'

The best part? I only just noticed this now, whilst transcribing the email. He even misspelled 'role' at the end there. Or did he…?

I don't know what it was, but something about this offer seemed, well, not quite right.

So I decided to pass on that roll.

Just in case.

Hospital Blues

It wasn't long before Robert Smith did me another solid.

He called up to talk about *Casualty,* and for a minute I thought he'd got his wires crossed. I was in the rare position of being represented by both of the casting agencies that sourced people for Casualty. This was a direct violation of both agency's rules, but I'd managed to iron out a deal over the years. TV shows are super-careful about over-using the same people in background scenes, lest they become too noticeable. It's the Star Trek red-jersey effect; "Hey, isn't that the same guy that got munched on by the space slug in last week's episode?"

To avoid this embarrassing faux pas, agencies were under strict instructions to rotate the people they supplied – the more prominently you were featured, the longer it would be before they would use you again. Working with two opposing agencies gave rise to the possibility of doubling up, which if noticed would reflect very badly on the agency that supplied you (as well as getting you fired).

But Southwest Casting had grudgingly allowed me to sign on with Robert Smith, on the condition that I did Casualty only through them. Because both parties trusted my professionalism, it had never been a problem. Southwest provided most of my extra work, and Robert Smith sought more substantial acting roles.

And that is what he was offering.

An audition, which could lead to a bit part in the show – with dialogue and everything!

"I've cleared it with the producers," he explained, "if you get it, you won't be able to do any more extra work with them for at least six months."

It was a sacrifice I was more than willing to make.

Because if this audition led to my first real speaking part...

It didn't.

Sadly.

I went through all the motions, showed up with a bunch of other hopefuls, strode confidently into the studio... and that's when it all turned to shit. Words clammed up in my mouth, my face turned to wood, and I gave them the same ham-and-cheese combo I'd eaten for lunch.

Argh!

I had to wonder – was I ever going to get any better at this?

Because aside from the near-impossibility of discovery, there seemed to be two major stumbling blocks on my path to become a world-famous actor;

1) I was crap at auditioning, and

2) I was crap at acting.

All things considered, it was a bit of a problem.

However.

Following the audition, I was over the moon to find I'd been offered a bit-part. Whilst I obviously hadn't done well enough to be rewarded with a speaking role, I was asked to do something that would require 'individual direction'. It was only a fraction of a step up from the usual extra work, and it came with a downside; even being featured this minutely in a single episode meant they wouldn't take me back as an extra for several months.

But it was worth it. I was determined to make the almost unheard of leap from supporting artist to main cast, and the only way that could ever happen was through taking whatever baby steps were offered. Even if they were – as this turned out to be – miniscule.

What they wanted me to do required no speaking. I was to play the unnamed boyfriend of a patient who was actually *in* the episode. Her storyline was that she'd stormed out after an argument with me, and had been in a car crash straight afterwards. What happened during her time in Holby General (the fictional hospital Casualty is set in), I never found out. But my scene came towards the end of the episode, when I walked towards her down the corridor, feeling guilty, armed with a bouquet of flowers.

"You're not happy to see him," the director explained to my co-star. "So we'll shoot a bit of you miming an argument, and then he'll offer you the flowers."

"Yep, that's fine," she said.

"And then I want you to slap him."

She looked at me, slightly taken aback.

"Okay by me," I said.

"Great!" The director span back to the crew, calling out a string of commands. Being part of the cast was quite surreal. The set was like a hurricane, with us in its eye; we hardly moved between takes, as total chaos ensued in every direction. Runners were running, Dolly Grips were gripping their dollies and Gaffers were doing… well, whatever the hell Gaffers do. Buggered if I knew. But on Casualty they were always festooned with rolls of brightly-coloured tape.

(For anyone who is wondering, a 'dolly' is a wheeled platform for the camera, sometimes running on rails, that allows it to be moved smoothly whilst filming. Oh, and FYI, extras get a severe bollocking if they try to ride on one when they think no-one is looking.)

Then, almost magically, with only seconds to go until the camera starts rolling, everyone shuts up at exactly the same time. Instant silence prevails; it doesn't matter if a member of the crew is hanging upside down by his testicles from a scaffolding pole, he'll quit whinging and hold his breath until the take is done.

Then, within a second of 'Cut!' being called, the set erupts into madness once more. Hammering starts up behind you, at least three people dash in with make-up cases and trip over cables being mysteriously unrolled by a chain-smoking sparkie with a back like a question mark. Lights flare, and others go out; smoke appears from somewhere and everyone ignores it. Is it part of the effects? Or is there a generator on fire? You wouldn't know, because people are trying to shout over the noise of the hammering, pressing their headsets into their ears so hard they'll need a screwdriver to prise them out again. Suddenly, off to the left, you hear a horse whinny. Is that... is that real? And someone's wafting the smoke away with a broken board covered in tinfoil, but his flapping disturbs the hair on one of the principal actors, and the bevvy of make-up artists make another cursing sortie. That's usually when you realise you're busting for the toilet, due to spending all morning sitting next to a table with the coffee urn on it. And you start to wonder if there's time to slip away, because from this angle it looks as though it'll be hours before anyone is ready for another take. Yet as soon as you have that thought, you hear someone counting down from five – and two seconds later, instant silence. Like a master switch was flipped, freezing time itself for everyone outside the camera's immediate field of view.

And then you remember you're meant to be arguing.

The first time we tried it, I felt we nailed it – right up until the slap. She swung at me so gently it was closer to a caress, barely making contact with her fingertips on my chin.

"Cut!"

CHAOS. EXPLOSIONS. MORE MAKE-UP.

"That's great," the director said, his tone implying something else entirely. "We need it to look more real, though. You guys are right in the centre of shot – we're going to cut back and forth between your fight and these guys." he waved a hand at the two principle cast members between us and the camera. They were having a reconciliation of some kind; I think the juxtaposition of our disagreement with their tender moment is what he was after.

"You can hit me," I told my co-star.

"Are you sure?" She didn't sound sure at all.

"It's fine, honestly."

So the director retreated to his monitor, the hush descended once more, and we repeated our performance. This time I was on the receiving end of a marginally less-feeble slap; the kind of lacklustre swipe you might make on a lazy summer afternoon when a fly swoops a bit too close.

"CUT!"

As the set sprang back into life around us, he made his way back over.

"*Like* that," he suggested, "but a bit sharper. Quicker. Like you *mean* it."

I braced myself for another round, and for the very real possibility that we'd be here for a long time. *Why the hell did I drink so much coffee?* I berated myself.

The girl shot me an apologetic smile. "Sorry," she said. "I'm just... I'm so worried that I'll hurt you."

I gave a little laugh. "Ha! Honestly, really, I *promise* you – you won't hurt me. Just go for it, I don't mind. He's not going to stop until we get one he likes. Give it some welly!"

"Okay," she sighed. "I'll try."

Hush descended. Cameras rolled. I flapped my hands, mouthing silent apologies for a minute, as my co-star glared back at me with venom. It was going great. The end of the scene approached, and I raised the flowers awkwardly between us.

She glanced down at them, miming something truly foul – and that was when I saw her arm go back. She wound up like she was about to pitch a baseball... then launched. She connected with the force of a sledge hammer, rocking my head back on my neck. Stars exploded in my vision and I reeled backwards, only just managing to stay on my feet.

"CUT!" the director bellowed.

"Oh my God, I'm so sorry!" the girl said, her hand going up to my face again. I flinched away from it before I could stop myself. "Sorry!" she repeated. "Are you okay?"

"I'm fine!" I said. "That was a good one!" One of the make-up guys was in front of me, head tilted as he studied my cheek. "Tsk. We'll get some ice for that," he said, then turned, snapping his fingers.

The director strode up to us, the crowd parting around him like the Red Sea around Moses. It was my turn to eat humble pie. "I'm sorry," I told him, "I didn't mean to overreact. I just… I wasn't quite ready for it."

"No," he boomed, a big grin on his face, "that was perfect! You really sold it. We messed it up at our end I'm afraid, a tech glitch, so we'll have to go again."

"Oh! Yeah, no problems," I said.

"Great though, just like that," he confirmed.

And so that's what we did.

Six more takes in fact, before all the elements came together perfectly.

In between each take, one of the junior make-up team scurried in with a cold wet flannel to press against my cheek, which was getting redder by the second.

The seventh time, half afraid she'd keep us here all week, my co-star made another heroic attempt to decapitate me bare-handed. It rocked me back on my heels, and I staggered, damn near ending up on my arse in the corridor.

"CUT!" the director bellowed. "Great! We'll keep that one. Now let's set up on camera two for the reverse, shooting towards the main doors."

And nice bloke that he was, he came over to thank us for our performance.

"That was a *really* good one," he said, "I could practically *feel* it."

"Really?" I asked, blinking away tears. "I didn't feel anything…"

"Ha!" the director roared, and clapped me on the shoulder. "Yes, I liked that one *a lot.*"

In fact, he liked it so much he spent the next hour shooting it again, in close-up.

Resignations

The main problem with doing extra work for a living is how
sporadic it is. Although the daily pay rate was good, the
limitations on how often I could appear on any given show,
coupled with the scarcity of significant TV and film
production outside of London, made it tough to earn even a
minimum wage.

But the Lynx job had opened my eyes to the world of
promotions. Companies like ID supplied 'brand
ambassadors' for product launches, sampling and special
events all over the country, and the main qualification was an
overabundance of enthusiasm. I found an agency in Cardiff
that recruited promotional staff, called *Fusion*, and signed up
with them.

Fusion's owner, a young bloke called Charles, had been
faced with same dilemma as me; no decent acting agents
outside London, and no desire to join the migration of
desperate wannabes flocking there. So he'd set up his own
agency – an idea which had occurred to me a few times. But
Charles had done it properly, building up a business that
now had big-name corporate clients and hundreds of
hopefuls on its books.

"I'd like to get more acting work for everyone," he
explained, "but there's so little of it around here. The

promotions jobs help pay the bills, and fill the gaps between auditions."

Charles booked me into a promotion for *Grand Marnier,* an orange-flavoured cognac that was undergoing a re-brand. The drink's image was old-fashioned and stuffy, and the company wanted to connect with a younger demographic – because in the UK, that's who does most of the drinking.

"Call me Charlie," he said, when he came to pick me up. Charlie was tall, dark and handsome, with an easy smile and prefect white teeth. He did modelling, as well as acting, singing… and some other stuff, which I'll tell you about later.

"Drinks promos are great," he promised, "you'll have a blast."

And we did. The premise was simple; we donned tight black t-shirts with the Grand Marnier logo on, set up a portable drink dispenser in the corner of a bar, and spent the entire night handing out free shots.

Who doesn't like free shots?

I did.

I drank dozens of them.

But that was all part of the job – get buzzed, have a great time, and encourage everyone in the place to do the same. If you want to become the instant best friend of every single person in a bar, all you have to do is give out unlimited free drinks. I haven't been kissed, groped and spanked so much in one night since I was a choir boy.

"Not a bad gig, eh?" said Charlie, as we hauled our empty dispenser back to his car.

"And we get paid for that?"

"Sure do!" he grinned. "Same time next week, then?"

Alas, man cannot live by booze alone.

I know, because I've tried it.

Promotions, like extra work, are sporadic and unpredictable. With Christmas fast approaching, there was a 'Staff Wanted' sign in every shop window, and I reluctantly resigned myself to doing something I'd sworn never to do again.

I was going to get a real job.

I went for an interview at *The Entertainer,* a toy shop in Cardiff. I figured if I was going to re-join the workforce, at least a toy shop would be a fun place to do it.

And it probably would have been, if that's where I was working.

But the boss, an overbearing, self-important arsehole, had neglected to mention that what they were hiring was a stock-room monkey. In the sunless, frigid catacombs beneath the store was an acre of shelving crammed with boxes of products, and my job was to live down there, hauling it back and forth to the freight elevator as the boss demanded.

It was freezing cold, knackering, painful and lonely. The one other bloke down there hated it too, hated the boss's constant criticism, and told me every day he was going to walk out. I asked him why he hadn't quit already, and he couldn't come up with an answer. So later that day, he did – leaving me alone in that miserable concrete basement, heaving crates around for ten hours per day.

I worked for nine days straight, and didn't see the sun once.

And not just because I was living in Wales.

On my tenth day, late for work, I was sprinting through the pre-dawn gloom when I got hit by a car. It only clipped me, just enough to spin me around and scare the shit out of me, and the driver drove off again after getting out and swearing at me. Neither of us had been looking, and we'd both been going too fast, but since I'd been on a zebra crossing when he hit me, I was pretty sure it was his fault.

When I got to work, the boss bawled at me for being late. Upon hearing I'd just been bounced off a car, he generously offered to let me sit down for ten minutes to recover.

Then he sent me back to hauling boxes for the next ten hours, with just one slight difference; on account of the nice little rest he'd given me, he docked ten minutes off my lunch break.

That night, I got drunk. Sally and Katie came round and helped me.

I was still drunk the next morning – hadn't even been to bed, in fact – and I waited until it was fully light, before sauntering into work.

The boss went a dangerous shade of red when he saw me, but before he could explode, I held a piece of paper out to him. "I just came to give you this," I said.

He took it, confused, and opened it to see 'I QUIT!!!' written in huge letters.

"What the fuck am I meant to do with this?" he demanded.

"Well, I've got one suggestion," I told him.

Later that morning, strolling around Cardiff city centre in the daylight, I felt fantastic. And naughty, like a rebel; liberated, vindicated, and deliciously, blessedly, *free.*

Damn, I thought, *this is fun! I should quit more jobs.*

And then, wandering randomly through a shopping centre, I spotted another 'Staff Wanted' sign, this time in *JJB Sports.*

I'd sobered up a bit by then, and it had occurred to me that, blissful as unemployment was, it wasn't really a sustainable long-term strategy.

And I'd had a few hours to enjoy it.

So I popped a Tic-tac into my mouth, nipped into JJB, and walked out half an hour later with a job in their footwear department. Fortune favours the brave... as well as the mildly inebriated.

I wish I could say that selling gym shoes fulfilled all my dreams. Maybe I'm just not cut out for real work? Long hours of boredom and a thorough snubbing from the male staff clique, all of whom were football-mad athletic-types, made for an uninspiring first week. Predictably, the manager was petty and belligerent, the undisputed big fish in his miniscule pond, and keen to make sure everyone knew it. The other lads took absolutely no notice of him, and spent most of their working day throwing tennis balls at each other in the stock room – so he took out his frustrations on me. As the newest member of staff, I was given all the shifts everyone else had refused to work: Christmas Eve and Boxing Day, New Year's

Eve and New Year's Day, and pretty much every day in between.

That was to be expected, really, but it was a bit demoralising.

It meant that, for the first time in my life, I wouldn't be able to spend Christmas with my family. Sally, Katie and Chris would be going home to visit their folks; the big house on Richmond Road would be empty. And I'd be spending the entire festive season on my own.

Well, when I wasn't selling shoes.

On December 23rd, I ducked out on my lunch-break to buy a sandwich.

By pure chance I bumped into Charles, of Fusion, who was in town doing a bit of last-minute Christmas shopping.

"You alright, matey?" he asked.

"Yeah... not too bad."

"Really?" Charlie was a clever bloke, shrewd and intuitive. He knew straight away that something was wrong. And, as I was to discover, he was a supremely decent fellow, and a man of immediate action.

"You're not happy, are you?" he said.

"Meh. Well, no, not really."

"Right, come on – I'll buy you a pint, and you can tell me all about it."

I brightened at the offer. The manager at JJB would kick my ass for sure... but he'd find a reason to kick my ass at some point today, no matter what happened. He had done every other day. I might as well get some benefit from the inevitable bollocking.

"Yeah! Why not!"

In the pub, I shamelessly unloaded my frustrations. Charlie was a good listener, and asked pointed questions that cut through the turmoil in my mind to find the source of my unhappiness. It was more than just the crappy job; more than missing my parents, and Gill, missing my friends, and feeling alone and left out. It was the sudden stagnation of my acting career that had given rise to this bleakness of spirit. Accepting the shop jobs had been like admitting that I'd failed; no matter how temporary I told myself the situation was, I was deeply afraid that it wasn't. That all the promise and potential I'd seen in my future had leaked away, and would be reduced to an agonizing succession of minimum-wage jobs, until one day I looked back and laughed bitterly at the ridiculousness of the dreams I'd abandoned.

Fortunately, Charlie had a solution.

"Why don't you come and work for me?"

He explained that he was in need of some help in the office. It would be primarily an admin job, and only part-time, "But you're welcome to steal any extra work or promotions that come in. And of course, you'd have your pick of any auditions we find out about…"

It was the answer to all my prayers.

Well, most of them.

"Awesome! When do I start?"

"Let's kick it off in the new year, shall we. How about January the second?"

We celebrated the deal with another pint, before Charlie had to leave to get his shopping done. I stayed for one more drink, marvelling at how suddenly my fortunes had flipped. Was this Fate, taking a hand in my life once more, I asked myself?

I left the pub and went straight home. I packed a bag, jumped on the train to Somerset, and three hours later knocked on my parent's front door. I was just in time for dinner.

Christmas and New Year passed in a happy blur of too much food, too much TV, and too many stupid jokes. Family time, for me, has always been the best time.

On January 2nd, I found my way to Charlie's house in an outlying suburb of Cardiff, and commenced my employment.

I'd been working there a week – and thoroughly enjoying it – when it occurred to me that I should probably tell JJB Sports I'd quit.

After all, I'd left for a lunch break and never come back. My jacket was still in their staff room.

I wandered in the next morning, and immediately found myself face to face with the manager.

"YOU!" he roared, stabbing me with a finger.

"Oh! Yes," I admitted, backing away. "Sorry, I've just come to get my jacket."

"YOU LITTLE BASTARD!"

My instinct was to cringe, but then I realised that now, I didn't need to.

"Don't worry," I told him, "I don't work here anymore."

His whole body trembled with rage, as he took a deep breath and bellowed, "You're damn fucking right you don't!"

The Office

Fusion Acting and Modelling Agency was run from Charlie's home, a very nice three-bedroom detached house in a quiet suburb of Cardiff. The kind of wholesome neighbourhood where kids walked to school, past white picket fences and proud homeowners mowing their front gardens.

I bet not one of them suspected what was going on inside no.37.

In fairness, even I didn't have much of an inkling.

Not in the beginning, at least.

Charlie's partner in crime was also his partner in life, and in business – his wife, Eleanor. The pair were high school sweethearts; her a tiny dark-haired temptress, him a tall, muscular stud. And to be honest, they hadn't changed much. They were both exceptionally attractive, confident and outgoing individuals.

Which could explain why they'd both decided to become strippers.

Charlie booked himself out doing kissograms and stripagrams, through a sub-section of the agency, whilst Eleanor worked nights in *The Fantasy Lounge* in Cardiff. I guess that's one way to deal with any insecurities that could arise from being married to a stripper – if you can't beat 'em, join 'em!

But Charlie and Eleanor had many more strings to their bows. As well as running the agency, both worked professionally as actors and models, and neither were too proud to take on extra work and promotions. But by far their most lucrative income stream was glamour photography – of the kind that would have graced Page Three of certain newspapers in the UK, or the classier of the top-shelf men's magazines. Using the superbly appointed rooms of their house as a studio, Charlie was the man behind the camera, and Eleanor was his Top Model.

And she was famous.

Her cheeky, girl-next-door innocence was part of her appeal; the rest came from her absolutely enormous, yet completely natural boobs – from memory, I seem to recall her being a 32-double-G. It made her somewhat top-heavy, being as she was otherwise slender, and a pocket-sized 5' 3" (160cm) tall.

It wasn't a bad job, all things considered. She got to work from home most of the time, but regularly jetted off to photo shoots all over the world. She spent time in exotic locations, was incredibly well paid, and had her own international fan club. It was still early days for the internet in many regards (this was three years before MySpace debuted; Google was being run out of a garage) – but Eleanor's email newsletter already went out to over 30,000 subscribers. Aside from Christopher Lee, she was probably the most famous person I'd ever met.

As befitted her superstar status, Eleanor's office was in the big bedroom upstairs. Charlie's was in the box-room next-door, and he cheerfully squeezed in an extra desk and chair for me.

At first, I manned the phones. Charlie had installed a nifty intercom system, so we could call each other from one office to the other – much easier than crossing the nine feet of carpet and two internal doors that separated us! I made the tea and coffee, opened and sorted the post, dealt with email requests and sent out application forms.

As my experience and understanding of the operation grew, I began booking staff for promo jobs, dealing with new applications, and uploading their photos to our fledgling website.

Genuine modelling jobs were as scarce as genuine acting jobs. What we really needed was more promotions staff, and the vast majority of companies requested girls – the more attractive, the better. There's nothing dodgy about it; that's just the way the world works. People are more inclined to pay attention to, or take a product sample from, an incredibly hot girl in a tight t-shirt than they are, say, a beardy old fat bloke wearing a trench-coat.

So from time to time, we charged up battery packs and took Charlie's new-fangled digital cameras on a night out, hoping to find recruits for upcoming campaigns.

We took it very seriously.

We couldn't risk appearing unprofessional, or we'd soon find ourselves unwelcome. And few things react more poorly with expensive camera gear than being thrown out of a nightclub. But it was hard not to get caught up in the current of excitement. Everyone we met was out to have a good time, to dance and drink and forget their troubles. With no stuffy company policies weighing us down we were free to indulge in the odd drink ourselves, and as the evening wore on and the crowds became merrier, we took our cameras onto the dance floor.

No two ways about it, this was fun. As jobs go, it was about as sweet as I could imagine.

Not that I was actually getting *paid* for this part of it, but who cares?

Towards the end of our first such adventure, we stepped outside for a breather, the camera straps starting to chafe our sweaty necks. The night air was cool, the sudden absence of noise left our ears ringing.

Charlie took his camera off and checked the battery level.

"We'd better pop in and see Eleanor at work," he said. "She'll be pissed off if she finds out we were in town and we didn't go and say hi."

This sounded perfectly reasonable, so I trailed alongside Charlie as he led the way through Cardiff's busy streets. At this time on a Saturday night the pavements were crawling with revellers, spilling into and out of the numerous pubs, bars and restaurants that dominated the city centre. I loved the hustle and bustle, the atmosphere of expectation and merriment. For the good citizens of Cardiff, the working week was over at last. Now it was time to party.

It wasn't until we turned onto the main drag, strolled a few blocks further down and stopped, that I realised we were standing outside the entrance to *The Fantasy Lounge* – Cardiff's premier lap-dancing venue.

Ohhh… I thought, as it dawned on me, *of course! Eleanor's work…*

This could be awkward.

As a young, red-blooded male, I hadn't been able to foresee many downsides in working for a stripper. But now it suddenly occurred to me that somewhere in the underground club below me was my boss – and that quite possibly she was naked. Or writhing seductively on a stage. Or both. And I was going to have to walk in here, into this den of sin and iniquity… and be professional. No matter what sordid sights my eyes beheld in this place, I would have to conduct myself with respect and maturity. More to the point, I would have to make Eleanor's coffee every morning for the rest of the week, and I could do without seeing her pole dancing in my mind's eye every time I did it.

Right, I told myself, *you can do this! Eyes straight ahead. Look but don't touch… NO! Don't look. That's much safer. Look at the floor. Look at the walls. Don't look at that naked chick grinding against the old bloke on the sofa. Holy crap! No wonder he's breathing heavily. I think he's about to have a heart attack…*

We made it inside, down a sumptuously carpeted staircase and into a spacious basement lounge. Everything was red, from the upholstery to the drapery to the outfits. Not that there was much *to* the outfits…

A handful of particularly attractive girls were strolling around in red lingerie, shooting suggestive glances at me. This was more than I could handle. I was poised for flight, when one of the girls gave a little squeal of joy, ran up and threw herself onto Charles.

"Hey Charlie!" she said, wrapping him in a hug. I was a little unsure of strip-club etiquette, never having been to one, so I resisted the urge to join in.

"Is she here?" Charlie asked the girl.

"Yeah," she replied, "she's in the back. I can get her for you?"

"No, it's okay. We can wait. We only nipped in to say hi."

"Okay! Hi!" She giggled.

Then Charlie steered the girl towards me. "Amanda, this is Tony," he said, with a vaguely sarcastic flourish. "Tony... this is Amanda."

Amanda.

She was, in a word, exquisite.

Tiny, elfin even, perfectly formed, with smooth, flawless skin and long blonde hair trailing down to her...

NO! Don't look at them!

"Hi... Amanda? I'm Tony."

I offered her my hand, and she shook it. It seemed oddly formal, being as how she was wearing less than I do to sleep in.

"Hi," she said. But nothing else. No squeak of delight for me. She gave me a slight smile, and just stared at me, as though waiting for me to speak.

Words can't express how awkward I felt, standing there with her in her lacy bra and microscopic panties. It's just not natural to meet people that way.

"Sorry," I said, "I'm a bit, ah, nervous, you know, coming in here. I mean, I've been past it loads of times. I always wondered what it was like inside." I glanced around. "It's nice. Very... very red. I like the curtains."

Now Charlie was staring at me, too. "Whaddaya mean, you've never been in here? Seriously?" He looked shocked.

"Well, yeah. I don't know, I've just... I've never really had the chance."

"But you're okay?"

"Yeah, fine, fine, you know..."

"Oh no," Charlie shook his head in fake exasperation. "We can't have you being like this! We have to come in here a lot, you know."

He dug out his wallet and pulled a sheaf of notes from it. "Here, have a dance on me!" He held the cash out to Amanda. "Whaddaya think?" he asked her. "Can you help him loosen up a bit?"

All the blood drained from my face. I mean, I could actually feel it happening.

"Oh, ah, no, that's okay, Charlie, I don't really need…"

"Don't be crazy! It's my treat. Amanda's the best!"

Amanda, however, didn't seem to think so. "I'll just go and find one of the girls," she said, backing away apologetically. "I think Gemma's about to start her shift…"

And she was gone.

Charlie quirked an eyebrow. Confused, or amused? I used the breathing space to thank him for his kind offer, and was trying to politely decline when Eleanor dashed up and wrapped him in a gleeful hug. "Yay! I'm gonna finish early, so I can get a lift home with you guys!"

"Great!" Charlie said. "Go grab your things. Tony's never been inside a Gentleman's Club before, so I'm treating him to a dance."

"Oh-oh!" Her eyes went wide. "Ohhhh, you're a virgin, are you?"

"NO! No, I'm not a… I mean, I'm not, like…"

"*Relax!* I meant you've never had a dance before. And boy is it obvious! You're wound up tighter than a drum. There's nothing to worry about. It's harmless fun! No touching, nothing dodgy. Nothing to get worked up about."

"Oh. Ah… okay then? I guess…"

Eleanor suddenly chuckled to herself. "Ha! I was going to ask you to shag Lauren. She's the head dancer here, and she *badly* needs to get laid. She's got a stick up her arse."

I gave Eleanor a questioning look.

"No, not literally!"

"Oh! Okay. Sorry, it's just…" I spread my hands to indicate the room around me. "I'm sort of… new to all this."

"And that's why Gemma is here, to sort you out," Eleanor explained.

And Gemma, the slender redhead Eleanor indicated, took me by the hand, led me over to a booth along the back wall, and spent the next ten minutes gyrating so close to my face I could feel her body-heat on my forehead.

It was certainly educational. At least from an anatomical standpoint.

"You more relaxed now?" Eleanor asked me, as we headed up the stairs back to street level.

"Uh, yeah…" I said. It was a lie; my heart was racing, my limbs were trembling… I was on the verge of cardiac arrest. God knows how anyone could ever find a lap-dance 'relaxing'.

"Good!" Eleanor replied. "By the way, what did you say to Amanda? She went all weird when she came in to get me."

"Really? Nothing, honest! I only introduced myself."

"Interesting…" Eleanor and Charlie exchanged sidelong glances. "I haven't seen her flustered like that in a long time. And Amanda's never turned down a dance before… even when this cheap bastard's paying!" She gave Charlie a playful elbow in the ribs.

Shame burned my cheeks at the realisation that such a beautiful, delicate girl could be so disgusted by me, she'd actually run away.

"Oh dear," Charlie said, clapping an arm across my shoulders.

"Yep, you're in trouble, Tony…" Eleanor continued. "I think she likes you."

Job Satisfaction

I loved working at Fusion.

Eleanor and Charlie were great as bosses, and became great friends as well. For the first time in weeks, I didn't wake up dreading the day. The wages barely covered my rent, and the commute to and fro – a half-hour walk followed by a half-hour bus followed by another twenty-minute walk – was a bit excessive, but I didn't mind any of that. It felt great to be a part of something; I had a real sense that Fusion was on its way up, that it would become something to be proud of, as well as being a stepping stone to bigger and better things.

I loved sharing an office with Charlie. He treated me like an equal, and was genuinely interested in my thoughts and opinions. We spent many an hour in philosophical debates that bore only the most tenuous connection to work. Sometimes I used to think that he was lonely, sitting alone in his office all day, with one wall, two doors and an intercom system between him and his wife. I often wondered if the business really *needed* me, or if Charlie just wanted someone to talk to.

My bosses spent a large part of the day on the phone to each other. It was an arrangement that worked well; whilst they needed constant collaboration over many aspects of their jobs, they still preferred to have their own space.

When we needed to discuss something with Eleanor in person, Charlie could either phone and ask her to come over, or just yell for her through the partition wall.

Of course, there was a third option. While we were overhauling the office systems, Charlie discovered a nifty trick. Because his PC was the dominant one on their tiny network, and he had all the administrator privileges, with a few clicks he could completely take over her computer. Inevitably we'd hear Eleanor start to curse in frustration, as her mouse pointer no longer obeyed her commands. The swearing would rise in frequency, volume and vehemence, whilst we sat there giggling like schoolboys, waiting for the inevitable scream of, "CHAAAARLIIIEEE!"

"What's wrong, my love?" he'd shout back through the wall, all innocent whilst I chuckled away next to him.

"My computer's doing that weird thing again! Can you fix it?"

"Sorry, what's that?"

At which point we'd hear a frustrated sigh, followed by the creaking of her chair as she got up and made her way across the hall to our office. She open the door and poke her head in, greeting us with, "That bloody computer!"

"Oh, doing that thing again, is it?" Charlie would ask, barely repressing a smirk.

"Yeah! I don't know what the hell's up with it."

"Okay," he'd relent, "I'll take a look. Don't suppose could you make us a coffee while I fix it?"

As she stomped off downstairs to the kitchen, he'd relinquish control of her computer without leaving his desk, and we'd congratulate each other on having our own unique coffee delivery service.

Poor girl, she never figured it out.

Most of all though, I loved how *weird* it was to work there.

I'd be sitting at the desk I shared with Charlie, quietly working my way through a string of emails, when he'd break the silence by asking, "Whaddaya think of these?"

And I'd glance up as he swivelled his monitor around for me to look at.

Invariably, it would be covered in close-up photographs of female genitalia.

"Ah… they're… very nice?" I'd hazard.

"Yeah…" from his pensive tone, I could tell he was after more than general compliments.

"Well, they're very bright," I'd say, squinting across at his screen.

"That's what I thought! I'm trying to remove the shadows, because I didn't use enough light when I took these. But I think I'm losing definition as I brighten them. Can you tell?"

"Um… not really. Not at this scale, anyway."

"Hmm…" He'd zoom in, presenting crotch number three in full 22-inch widescreen glory. "It's the edges, see? Are they slightly blurry?"

"I dunno, man. I don't think so."

At this point he'd sink back in his chair and rub his eyes. "Maybe I've been staring at vaginas for too long."

I was hard-pushed to think of an answer for that.

Charlie was a great thinker. He never parroted answers he'd heard, or made rash statements about things he didn't understand. If something confused him, he'd devote the next half-hour to reading about it, until he understood it well enough to explain it himself. And without consciously trying to, he encouraged those habits in me. It was an education of sorts; I didn't know many intellectuals, and the chance to discuss something other than the evening's drinking plans was quite welcome. And because Charlie always considered his point of view, and crafted it based on evidence and experience, he gave the best advice.

One afternoon I was feeling pretty low. I'd taken the previous day off to do extra work on Coronation Street, and it had been a demoralising experience. It was a gruelling and expensive trip, from Cardiff to Manchester on the train followed by a bus to my Uncle Paul's house, and minimal sleep before a crack-of-dawn bus back into town and a substantial walk through central Manchester to reach the studios. The usual ten-hour filming day went smoothly, but the four-hour trip back to Cardiff had been made under a cloud. Instead of chatting away to random strangers on the train or relaxing with a good book, I'd spent those hours brooding on my future – or more specifically, the lack thereof.

You see, Coronation Street had a brand new cast member. A young lad, the same age as me, slim and not bad looking, but nothing special; I'd chatted to him briefly, determining that whilst friendly, he wasn't the brightest crayon in the box.

I couldn't help but draw parallels; this lad had no formal training, and no real experience. To all intents and purposes, he was me. Only less qualified, less intelligent, less experienced, not as attractive, and he hadn't spent the last four years travelling for four hours in each direction just to work a single day on the damn show. What he did have was an uncle on the production team – and that was why, when the writers decided they were in need of a fresh young face, they'd looked no further.

It was more than a little galling.

I'd never let myself hope I'd be plucked from obscurity as a supporting artist and catapulted to instant stardom, but it still felt like a slap in the face that I hadn't even been considered. Not that I wanted to spend the rest of my life in the most boring show on the planet; rather, it was a wake-up call. A reminder that no matter how many shows I worked on, I was still the lowest of the low in this industry – far beneath the notice of people like casting directors, or anyone with the power to kick-start my career.

It illustrated a harsh truth, one I'd been trying to ignore for the last few years.

At current speeds, I was getting precisely no closer to my dreams.

If I kept doing what I'd been doing, I would keep getting what I had got.

Which was nothing.

I was wasting my life.

"I should apply for a post-graduate course in one of the proper acting schools," I said to Charlie, as I leafed through a pile of application forms. Fusion was a fairly small-scale operation, but we still received a ton of applications from wannabe actors and models. Sometimes I felt like everyone in the world was trying to get into this industry. It didn't make me feel any better about my chances.

"You want to go back to school?" Charlie asked.

"Yeah, well… my degree was pretty useless. The acting classes were crap, and they didn't even invite any agents to our final performance. I can't think of a single advantage it's given me, in terms of creating an acting career."

"And so you want to do more of it?"

"Ha! Not really. I just think, if I'm to have any chance at all, I need to attend a *real* acting school. One of the prestigious ones. In London."

"Hm. Those places aren't cheap. Neither is living in London for a year. Do you know how much a postgrad would cost you?"

"Nah, not exactly. But I reckon about ten grand."

"Is what they'll teach you in that year worth ten grand?"

"Probably not. I mean, my acting would have to be pretty good just to get in. I'd have to audition – crazy, really. They only take people who can act already."

"So, could you buy yourself private acting lessons for a year instead? That wouldn't cost you ten grand."

"Yeah… but that wouldn't help me get an agent. That's the real stumbling block, the Catch 22 of it all."

"And the postgrad course would get you an agent?"

"Well, they do a showcase at the end of the year. They invite a whole bunch of agents, and after the show quite a lot of the students get signed up."

"And what if you don't get picked up afterwards?"

"Well, then you're screwed."

"It's a lot of money to gamble on such a dicey outcome. If you're given a crummy role in the showcase, or you're having an off day, you end up ten grand in debt for a single line on your CV."

"Yup. It's a bit of a shitter." I stared glumly at the paperwork spread out on the desk. Two dozen more hopefuls grinned up at me from their mug shots.

Jonathan sat quiet for a minute, mulling things over. Then a conspiratorial smile stole across his features. "Here's what I'd do," he said. "Take that ten grand. Find out when the top acting schools, RADA, LAMBA, Central et cetera, do their showcase. Most likely they'll all be within a week or two of each other. Just before they start, go to London, and spend half the money on renting the snazziest apartment you can find for a month. Spend the rest of the money on booze. Throw a party every night. Go to all the showcases, sit in the audience, and dress like a businessman. In the bar afterwards, talk to the agents – about anything *other than* acting. Agents are all alcoholic; it goes with the job. Tell them there's free booze at your party, and they'll all come. Tell a few students that all the agents are coming – that will guarantee a full house. Then, be the life and soul of the party, and make sure everyone has a great time. Repeat the process every night there's a showcase. By the end of the month, you'll be on first-name terms with every agent in London. Better still, they'll *like* you. If that doesn't open more doors than a year of pointless lessons and ten minutes in a showcase, nothing will! And instead of wasting a year, you'll have the best month of your life. You'll end up with a book full of phone numbers and a head full of good memories. Now *that* might just be worth ten grand…"

I sat in silence, letting my mouth hang open a little, while the concept played over me. It certainly was a bold plan.

And far more tempting than sending out applications of my own.

It was audacious. *Brilliant*, even.

It was pure Jonathan.

Somehow though, I couldn't see the bank agreeing to lend me ten grand for a gigantic piss up. And my poor parents, bless their hearts, had already funded me through one degree course.

I could just imagine the phone call. "Hey Dad, I was thinking of going back to university, but then I had this great idea instead…"

Awkward Situations

A few blissful months passed in Charlie's employ.

My routines were well established. I skipped on the way to work. I had a key to the house, so no-one had to come downstairs to let me in. And I looked forward to my latest project; compiling an elegant brochure, featuring photos of the best artists on our books. I'd taught myself several computer packages to design the thing, and Charlie had invested over a thousand pounds in a state of the art printer to produce it.

Ironically, it was the first work I ever self-published.

But nothing was printing today.

All was quiet inside the house.

Normally, within a few seconds of entering, I'd hear the sounds of busy-work emanating from the offices above. But not this time; silence greeted me as I poked my head into the empty, spotless lounge.

I had that horrible thought: *Is this the right day? Did I get something wrong?*

I checked my watch. I was where I should be – and *when* I should be. Just, no-one else seemed to be…

Ah well. Maybe they'd nipped out for a walk.

At any rate, I was well-versed in my first duty of the day. Like any good Englishman – especially one employed by foreigners in a foreign country – I began by making tea. I flicked on the kettle, readied the various milks, sugars and sweeteners, and brewed a fresh pot.

Transferring the tea to a pair of mugs, I made my way cautiously along the hall. Still no sound betrayed any presence above me; it was getting quite eerie. I all but tip-toed up the stairs, so strong was the urge not to disturb the stillness.

Daylight spilled through the gap under both bedroom doors. I paused between the two, deciding which to try first, when I heard a sharp *click!* from Eleanor's room. Aha! So someone was in there! I grinned. Without really intending it, I'd hardly made a sound on my approach, the lush carpet absorbing my shoeless footsteps. There was a pretty good chance that whoever was in there was still unaware of my presence. Which meant they were going to shit themselves when I walked straight in.

True, it was a bit of a childish trick, but if you know anything about me by now, it must be that my sense of humour stopped developing at about eight years old.

Juggling the full mugs into one hand, I knocked to announce my presence and opened the door in the same motion.

And froze.

There were three people in the room, and they all froze too.

Eleanor was facing me, reclining in her leather-backed swivel chair. Both legs were in the air, her feet above her head; she was holding them there by gripping her own ankles.

And she was naked.

Kneeling between her knees was a man I didn't recognise; a photographer, judging from the size of his lens. The instrument in question was poised less than six inches from Eleanor's crotch – he couldn't have gotten it any closer without applying lubricant.

Charlie was stood in the far corner, fiddling with a light umbrella.

By mutual agreement we shared a few seconds of stunned silence.

Then Charlie spoke up. "Oh, sorry Tony! Didn't we tell you there was a shoot going on today?"

"Ah…" I finally managed to drag my eyes away from the scene in the centre of the room, and looked at him. "No. No, you didn't."

"Oh! Right. We've, um, got a shoot going on today."

"I… I see."

"So if you like, you can get started in the other room?"

"Yes! Yes, of course." I glanced down at the mugs in my hand, amazed to find I hadn't spilled either of them. To say I felt ridiculous, standing there in the doorway with one hand on the door handle and the other laden with hot beverages, is an understatement on a par with saying, "this was unexpected."

I was still a little wary of making eye contact with Eleanor, what with the camera lens practically embedded in her groin. Not to mention her groin itself, which seemed to exert a powerful magnetic influence over eyes; best to be avoided, less it pull me in and drown me.

Instead, I trained my gaze safely on Charlie.

"Erm… would either of you like a cup of tea?"

"Oh! Yes please, matey," he said, and reached out to take his brew.

"I wouldn't mind one," Eleanor added.

"Okay…" My eyes strayed back to the scene below me. There wasn't an obvious place to put a cup of tea. Not without the risk of third degree burns, anyway. "Ah, okay Eleanor… where do you want it?"

A short while later I sat alone in Charlie's office, musing on the weirdness of a life that had just seen me carefully pass two hot cups of tea, one at a time, over the body of a naked woman.

It was very nearly the strangest thing I'd done all week.

*   *   *

My reputation amongst my housemates had gone from impressive to stellar, when I grudgingly admitted that, yes, I was working for a lap-dancer; yes, I did get paid, at least in part, to look at pictures of naked women; and that whilst I wasn't quite dating a lap-dancer yet, things certainly seemed to be heading in that direction.

A night out with Charlie and Eleanor had ended with Amanda and I kissing passionately for so long that the others got bored and went home.

"Did you tell him what she said afterwards?" Charlie asked, with a grin.

"No," Eleanor replied.

"That Tony's *so dreamy* that she forgets how to speak whenever he's around?"

"Don't tell him that!" Eleanor scolded, "It'll go straight to his head!"

And it would have done, too, had it not been for the crippling nerves I felt in her presence. She was so far out of my league, I went like a rabbit in the headlights whenever we met; I was every bit as tongue-tied as she was.

Which was making it spectacularly difficult to start a relationship.

My best chance to turn this around came on Amanda's twenty-first birthday.

Not that I realised it at the time.

Bless them; Charlie and Eleanor were working so hard behind the scenes, trying to set us up – only, I was too damn stupid to realise it.

And far, far too gentlemanly to take advantage of it.

My bosses organised Amanda's birthday party, and made sure I was coming. They were having it at their house, a small gathering only, and I was invited to stay over.

Never one to turn down a party, I put my glad rags on and caught the bus there.

Amanda had already arrived, and was chatting to Eleanor on the couch. I took a chair opposite, beneath the front window, and hoped Charlie would get his ass there before I ran out of jokes.

"That might be him now," Eleanor said. "Check, will you Tony?"

I turned around and leant on the windowsill to look out. "Nope, nothing there," I reported, sitting down again.

"Oh. But that might be him, now! Did you hear that?"

"No..."

"Would you mind checking again?"

This went on every few minutes, and whenever my back was turned I could hear whispering and supressed giggles. I was starting to get a bit paranoid when Charlie finally showed up to rescue me.

He'd come bearing gifts (appropriately enough for a birthday party), and more booze, but he needn't have bothered; the liquor cabinet he showed me contained enough strong drink to stupefy a garrison.

I took the chance to describe the girls' odd behaviour, and it instantly generated a smirk. "Oh, Tony," he said, shaking his head at my ignorance. "You silly bugger! It's those tight jeans you're wearing. They were getting you to bend over so they could check out your arse."

There wasn't much I could say to that.

As the evening wore on, it became obvious that no-one else was coming. I'd half hoped the place would be awash with strippers by now, but realistically I wouldn't have dared talk to any of them. I'd have been hiding out in the kitchen, talking to Charlie... which is exactly where I was. For some reason I had a kind of mental block around Amanda. It's like some part of my brain had evaluated her hotness as so far out of my league that it just shut down in her presence. Knowing that she was a stripper, and thus even *more* unattainable to the average man, made it worse. Normally, when I'm nervous you can't shut me up. In fact you normally can't shut me up, period. But for some reason over which I had no control, being around Amanda rendered me completely speechless.

It was a situation I was determined to remedy with alcohol.

Particularly as Eleanor had explained the sleeping arrangements; they would be inflating a queen-sized airbed in the lounge for Amanda and I to share once the party was officially over.

Looking back, it's hard to believe just how naïve I was. Raised a good, honest, Catholic lad, I'd instantly determined that the gentlemanly thing to do was to make it clear that I wasn't about to push my luck. So we'd be sharing a bed – I didn't want that to make her feel *awkward*, did I? No, I would be a good boy – not the kind of lecherous desperado she had to deal with every night at work.

Sometimes I wish I could reach back in time and slap myself. How could I not have noticed the set-up? The private party... the convenient airbed... despite there being plenty of floor-space available, and sofas in both office bedrooms...

Eleanor had asked Amanda what she wanted for her birthday, and she had said she wanted me.

And as Amanda was her closest friend, Eleanor had decided to give me to her.

If only I'd known.

Safely ensconced in the kitchen, I convinced Charlie to broach the liquor cabinet. He pulled out a bottle of 'Aftershock' – a disgusting purple spirit that tasted like perfume – and we proceeded to drink the entire thing.

So much for Dutch courage!

Eleanor's description of that night pretty much summed it up. "All I could hear the entire night was Charlie throwing up in the en-suite, while you were throwing up in the bathroom downstairs. Synchronised vomiting! I hardly slept a wink."

I doubt Amanda did either, though at some point I must have passed out on the airbed next to her; stinking, sodden, and slightly incontinent.

I never saw her again.

I have since made an agreement with myself that the next time an astronomically attractive lap-dancer is so keen to sleep with me that she arranges a private party, gets her friends to help her seduce me, and even provides the bed – I will *not* drink myself insensible and collapse in a puddle of puke.

It hasn't happened yet, but I remain ever hopeful.

Strange Days

Life is divided into the opportunities you seize, and the ones you don't.

For most people, anyway.

For me, it's divided into the opportunities I seize, and the ones I spend the rest of my life kicking myself for not seizing. I'm a bit manic, it must be said; I think I was born with Fear Of Missing Out.

So when my long-time friend and kung fu mentor Mark Strange called me out of the blue, and asked me to help him make a movie, I seized so hard I nearly bit my tongue off.

The film had begun as the germ of an idea, back when I'd had nowhere to stay after my Thunder Wolf tour. I'd spent a few days up in Lancashire, training with Mark and sleeping in his gym. He'd been given a bunch of old army uniforms by one of his students, and was trying to figure out what to do with them.

Our first idea hadn't been the best.

We'd decided to go hiking, and camp out in the forest overnight. However, neither us, nor Mark's new friend Martin, who'd come with us, had ever done anything like this before. Our preparation had included extensive uniform selection, careful packing of all Mark's replica guns... and nothing else. I'm not sure what we thought would happen. In our minds, I think we saw ourselves living off the land, trapping animals and roasting them over a fire, and returning to civilization as hardened survivalists. What actually happened was Martin drove us to a local hillside called Rivington Pike, we blundered around in the dark for hours, got hopelessly lost in a small stand of trees, and 2am found us all back at Mark's gym, soaked to the skin and borderline hypothermic.

Note to self: if you're going to camp out in the north of England, in October, with no tent, no sleeping bag, no cooking gear and no clue – at least check the weather first.

But the experience – which we agreed never to mention again, to anyone, *ever* (sorry, Mark!) – had produced one notable idea. Stumbling around in the woods, our heads filled with invisible enemies crouching behind every tree, Martin had told us of his ambition to make an action movie. Martin made wedding videos for a living, but he was (understandably) rather bored of them. He was forty, single and still lived with his mum, so he'd been able to afford some really high-end camera gear. He also had, *err...* plenty of spare time in his social calendar, shall we say, to do a spot of amateur film-making.

It was a match made in heaven. Or more accurately, made whilst hopelessly lost in a pitch-black forest in the pissing it down rain – but that didn't mean it was a bad idea. Did it? Indie films got made all the time. How hard could it be? We had the army uniforms, we had a bunch of replica weapons... and we had each other.

More importantly, we had journeyed into the savage wilderness, and we had SURVIVED! We felt we could accomplish anything.

What really swung it was Mark's kung fu school. He had dozens of talented students, all of whom would be keen to get involved.

The word went out, and the planning phase got underway. At least, I assumed that's what had happened. Martin had offered to take creative control, while Mark concentrated on securing the rest of the cast, and a location to film in. As for me... well, I went back to Cardiff, and got offered a job dancing around in a towel.

And as it turned out, what Martin contributed during this time period was even less useful than what I did.

Mark, on the other hand, was a genius. His ability to smooth-talk people and recruit them to our cause was almost other-worldly. Perhaps because he'd spent most of his life doing something he loved, Mark had never become cynical. His honest enthusiasm and boundless self-belief was contagious, and drew people in wherever he went. In this way he was able to commandeer every replica firearm in a twenty-mile radius, a veritable fleet of posh black cars and minivans – even an off-duty police dog handler showed up to get involved. But by far his best score was our filming location: a gigantic abandoned rubber factory set on five acres of industrial wasteland. Mark had met with the owners and convinced them to let us use it – how, I'll never know. The place was a death-trap; condemned buildings, massive machinery, piles of rusty junk everywhere...

It was a hundred accidents waiting to happen all at once.

I imagine the conversation went like this:

"Please can we use your derelict factory to film our movie?"

"That depends. What do you want to do there, exactly?"

"I dunno, really. Just lots of fighting, maybe shoot at each other, try a bunch of stunts and blow shit up."

"Okay! That sounds fine. You kids be careful, now!"

For our first filming day, a handful of Mark's students showed up. Between us we possessed a platoon's worth of ex-army gear and a disturbing array of weaponry; it was like an amateur vigilante convention.

We began with no clear intention beyond making something that looked awesome – not even a rough idea of the plot. We all assumed that Martin, who was directing us and operating the camera, had at least a vague idea of the story he was making.

We were wrong.

In the beginning, it didn't matter much. We knew we wanted plenty of action, and it had already been decided that

Mark would star, ass-kicking his way through as many of his students as were game. The rubber works could have been purpose-built for our needs; the kind of venue that would cost millions to reproduce on some gigantic Hollywood back lot. We explored cavernous warehouses, overgrown alleyways, ruined workshops and a wing of offices that looked like a hurricane had blown through them. At every turn we, found stunts just begging to be filmed.

"Wow! Look at that mechanical thingumajig! Wouldn't it look cool if someone got their head smashed against it..."

"I found this great pile of rubble. We should do a scene where it all collapses on someone..."

"This window still has glass in it! Try to punch through it, and smack a guy on the other side..."

"We're two stories up... you can land okay from that height, right?"

Our movie started out as a short film, which we called 'Insidious', for no other reason than it sounded cool. We worked on it every weekend for months; I travelled up from Cardiff most Friday evenings, staying with Mark or sleeping in the gym. Our filming days followed a regular schedule: divvy up the costumes and weapons, rock up to the rubber works, and beat the shit out of each other for a couple of hours. As each fight was completed, those of us who'd been killed swapped bits of kit around to become new adversaries. A job lot of balaclavas Mark had bought from the Army Surplus Store made us suitably anonymous, and allowed ten guys to become an army. I had the dubious honour of being voted 'best at dying'. Reacting to blows, I threw myself around with reckless abandon. I knew that selling the shot was far more important than saving myself from injury. Cuts and bruises would heal, but the camera never lies; if it didn't feel real enough to hurt, the chances were good it wouldn't look real, either. Which basically meant you'd done it all for nothing.

There's one rule to remember when getting your ass kicked; *be floppy.*

Young children and drunks survive truly epic spills without injury, because they bounce; tensing up in anticipation of pain is something programmed into us on the path to adulthood. It's a huge mistake. Tense parts tear and snap and pop out, whereas floppy ones can absorb much more punishment without damage. And in this gig, punishment was the name of the game.

I believe I held the record at over twenty different deaths in one day.

By mid-morning we were all getting hungry, so we piled into the cars and headed to McDonald's for breakfast.

The staff fair shit themselves when we strolled in – a dozen guys in battered army gear, covered in fake blood, festooned with knives and handguns. Mark had to do some seriously fast talking to stop the manager calling the cops.

After that, we mostly used the drive-thru.

The rest of the day featured more of the same.

I was always absolutely knackered when I caught the last train back to Cardiff. One time, no-one talked to me for the entire three-and-a-half hour journey. No-one even sat next to me. It wasn't until I got home and looked in the mirror that I realised I'd forgotten to wash my face; it was caked in blood, dirt and camo make-up. No wonder I hadn't been a popular seat-mate – I looked like I'd just finished burying the body of the last person who sat next to me.

As time wore on, Martin decreed that Mark's character was really an alien. This allowed him to try some special effects, filming Mark in a mix of slow and fast motion to give him superhuman speed. When we came across a room full of filing cabinets, Martin decided to film scenes with Mark searching through them, and of a soldier stealing a file and hiding it in his backpack. He then revealed that Mark's alien had come to Earth to find this file – as though that had been his plan all along. Later still, playing around with costume combinations we hadn't used yet, Mark found that wearing goggles under a balaclava looked particularly bad-ass. Thus was born a new character: 'Radius' (again, because it sounded cool). Radius was originally a 'surgical soldier', but later became an alien bounty hunter in pursuit of Mark. By this point the project had morphed into a full-length feature film, and the name had been changed to 'Displaced' – if you can guess why, I'll give you a donut.

To say the storyline was confusing would imply that there *was* a storyline – but for the most part, I was content to show up and die authentically on cue.

In the wide world of acting, it seems I'd finally found something I was good at.

Strange Nights

We had one rule about Fight Club: tell everybody about Fight Club!

We needed as many bodies as possible to do the dying, as most people only filmed a couple of days before they got hurt, and suddenly started being unavailable on weekends.

We could have one balaclava-less scene each; once a person's face had been seen on camera, and they'd been brutally killed, they couldn't used again. I didn't mind the endless balaclava work, as this project was my baby almost as much as it was Mark's, but I'd been secretly hoping for my chance to shine.

And today was the day.

Extreme close-ups were filmed of me hiding behind a huge sliding door, my panicked eyes just visible through the thick lenses of a gas mask. Mark could be heard coming up a rickety stairwell beyond, and I readied my MP4 (that's a machine gun – I wasn't about to show him the Special Edition of Avatar on my iPod).

Then the door flew open, and Mark's hands shot through the opening, tearing off my gas mask.

I was free!

And we had a long, extensively choreographed fight sequence to capture.

The fight went on all day.

Which is impressive, as on film it only lasted around thirty seconds. And years later, when the final version was cut together, it was closer to three.

But in that dusty, atmospheric warehouse, it was impossible not to take advantage. Martin wanted shots from every angle, and both Mark and I were fighting fit and eager to make the most of it.

After launching a vicious series of kicks, Mark pursued me around a steel column. I blocked a dozen rapid punches and backed away from him, crouched and ready – but not for his next move. He leapt up and caught hold of a rusty chain hanging from the ceiling, swung forwards at top speed, and planted both feet on my chest. It was a powerful attack, only slightly cushioned by the bubble-wrap-filled ammo pouches on my jacket. I let the kick tumble me into a backwards roll, then regained my feet for another flurry of blows. We'd battled the whole length of the room when it ended; Mark stunned me with a kick to the face, slipped behind me, hauled me across his knee and broke my neck. My body fell slack to the floorboards, as dust motes danced in sunlight streaking through a broken window.

Beautiful.

"CUT! Again!"

Always again. I didn't mind, but I was getting tired. Bruised and cut from many encounters with the floor, the sweat and dirt and fake blood comingling with the real stuff, I was reaching my limit.

Around the thirtieth take, my blocks coming slightly slower than before, I didn't manage to retreat as far past the column as I had on previous attempts. I was too close; Mark's double-footed swing-kick caught me full in the chest, throwing me backwards so convincingly that I smacked my head on the floorboards and was knocked out.

I came around a minute later, to see anxious faces arranged above me.

"You alright, mate?" someone asked.

"Yeah, fine," I groaned.

"Shit, you had us worried there!"

I sat up, and felt myself for injuries. There were too many to list, but none of them seemed new. Which is to say, none of them seemed younger than five minutes or so. My head still rang, but my blurred vision was clearing.

Bloody good job the floor is wood up here, instead of concrete, I thought.

"Yeah, I think I'm okay."

"Phew!" This came from Martin, who was resting his camera on the floor. "You're sure?" he asked.

"Yeah. Sure."

"Great! Let's go again."

The next take was a carbon-copy. Still dazed, and moving too slowly to reach my mark, I took the full impact of the swinging kick and flew through the air, landing in a heap.

This time, when I woke up, they'd decided to move on.

"We'll just film your death," Martin explained, for which I was extremely grateful; dying was by far the easiest part.

That night, for a bit of a change, we decided to head slightly further afield, to a town called Blackburn. About ten of us went, all dressed in our glad rags, all pumped from the successful day of filming.

But we seemed to have picked the wrong pub; within minutes of sitting down, I could feel eyes on me. Hostile stares were coming our way; it was soon quite obvious that we'd wandered into someone else's territory. I've no idea how many blokes in that bar were sizing us up, but the aggression in the air was a palpable thing. There was going to be a fight, and soon. We'd been marked as intruders, and any opportunity would be taken to make an example of us.

I knew Mark could tell. Patrice, a skinny French guy with muscles like steel cables, was glancing around warily. A trio of Mark's private students, black-belts all, had gone strangely quiet. It's funny; around that table were people with more than a decade of kung fu experience. Masters of swords and knives, of steel whips and the Chinese long staff. People whose knowledge and skill vastly exceeded my own, and at that point I could have bitch-slapped Chuck Norris and walked away from it. And there was Mark himself of course, crowned the Euro-British full-contact champion just one year previously, and the fastest kicker I'd ever laid eyes on.

Between us, we could have taken that place *apart.*

I looked at Mark. "Let's go," he said. "Quick."

On the long, cold walk to the furthest-possible pub, we congratulated each other on a situation narrowly avoided. No-one wins in a real fight; one person gets badly hurt, and the other person gets to live with the knowledge that they've badly hurt someone. Violence is a lose-lose situation; the only way to genuinely win is not to fight at all. And in this instance, by fleeing with our tails between our legs, we'd saved a whole bunch of people from a lengthy hospital stay.

I considered that a victory.

Our next Displaced social was a more subdued affair.

Mark had been offered a pair of chemical warfare suits by the owner of Leyland's Army Surplus Store. They'd gone unsold, so Mark took them in exchange for a private kung fu lesson, and we decided to wear them to a fancy dress party. Each suit consisted of a heavy jacket and trousers, which protected us well from the cold night air as we walked to the pub. Inside was a different story, though; the heat was cranking, and I reluctantly stripped off my jacket.

Mark was staring at me. "Tony? Shit! Look at you!"

I did.

I'd gone black.

A dark liquid stained my t-shirt and my arms; it looked like I'd rubbed myself all over with shoe polish.

"What did you do?" Mark asked.

"Nothing!"

A quick trip to the bathroom revealed two things: the black would not come off, no matter how hard I scrubbed – and it was *everywhere.*

Sweat had mingled with some sort of powder in both jacket and trousers, to form a black goop that seeped through underpants with alarming efficiency.

And Mark was in the same boat.

In this way, we discovered why the outfits had been unsalable. Being designed to protect against chemical attack, they were thickly lined with inert charcoal. Apparently charcoal absorbs all sorts of nasty gasses; it also stains the wearer indelibly black from neck to ankles. I guess you wouldn't care about that so much, if you were being attacked with chemical weapons.

But it made for a bloody miserable night out.

Returning to Cardiff every Sunday evening covered in a fresh round of battle damage did wonders for my reputation in Richmond Road.

No matter what time I hauled my weary body through the door, except for a handful of ungodly hours between three-ish and seven in the morning, there was always at least one person awake in the lounge – generally drinking and/or getting stoned. Even between those hours there was quite often at least one person asleep in the lounge, as the place frequently became a doss-house for friends, relatives and the occasional stranger. I distinctly remember one bloke living on our sofa for about a week, before I thought to ask who he was and why he was there. I asked everyone, eventually – no-one knew! He'd simply shown up for the last party we'd had, and never left. Everyone assumed he was a friend of someone else, and it wasn't until I started asking questions that we figured out he knew none of us. There was a slightly awkward moment when he was asked to leave, but he'd been friendly enough and he left without argument. He even left a few beers in the fridge.

I bloody loved living in that place!

Every so often, as I bowed out of the never-ending house party for a trip to Manchester, I'd hear one of my housemates explaining me to a newcomer.

"Serious, now – on *telly*, he is."

"No way! Cora-NA-shun Street, is it? That's mad, like."

I had to grin. It was the truth, after all. Just because I knew it was about as exciting as being run over by a golf cart, it didn't stop them from being impressed. I was supplementing my Fusion wages with as much extra work as I could get my hands on, so several times a week I'd be leaving or getting home at odd hours, from shows like Casualty, Pobol-y-Cwm and East-Enders. When asked, I said little about any of it – mostly because there wasn't much to say. The jobs continued to follow the standard pattern; arrive early, sit around doing very little, eat breakfast, return to doing very little, then a flurry of activity – by which I mean, ten minutes standing in a corner of the film set doing very little – and then home. I couldn't really dish the dirt on the various actors and actresses, because my relentless professionalism kept me from peppering the cast with questions. And I rarely knew who was who on set anyway, as I hated most of the shows I worked on, and never bothered watching them.

My housemates, however, took my reticence for secrecy. As far as they were concerned, I'd seen things mere mortals were seldom allowed to glimpse, and was bound by confidentiality from spilling my forbidden knowledge.

Without even trying, I became known as The International Man of Mystery.

I have to admit, I revelled in it.

Many were the times I'd get back from some dismal day sitting on a bus in the middle of the North York Moors, or from ten hours spent pacing the rain-swept grounds of a stately home dressed as a butler. I'd ditch my bags and stride straight into the lounge, where inevitably a gathering of some sort was taking place.

"TONY!" someone would yell. "Where've you been, mate?"

"Ah, you know, just work," I'd say.

Anyone who didn't know me would turn back to their conversations, until someone else yelled, "TONY! Tell us what you did at work today!"

To which I'd reply, "Ah, you know. Same old shit."

"But what? LISTEN guys! Tony's gonna tell us what he's been doing at work."

By this point everyone else would have given up trying to ignore the situation, and would be shooting me confused glances.

"Come on, mate! Spill the beans. Were you doing that porn job today?"

"No," I sighed, "it's a *glamour modelling* agency, and that was yesterday."

"So what about today?"

"Today I was up in Lancashire, filming this kung fu movie called *Displaced*…"

"SOMEONE GET TONY A BEER!"

Blood, Sweat And Tears

Mark's number one pupil, Steve had been with us on Displaced since the beginning. Short, bald and muscular, he was undoubtedly the toughest amongst us. His job as a doorman at a rough nightclub in town meant he had more real-world brawling experience than the rest of us put together. He always came to shoots in his flame-red convertible sports car, a top of the line Mazda Roadster.

"Can I drive it?" I asked him once.

"Can you drive?"

"Um… no. Not really."

"Then no."

There wasn't room for me in anyone's car that day, so I piled into the back of a white van driven by one of Mark's students. We planned on using it as a coroner's vehicle, to collect bodies in bags, but I had a better use for it. We weren't driving far, as Mark's gym was in the same industrial estate that bordered the rubber works, so I thought I'd have some fun. I opened the sliding door, pulled myself up onto the roof, stood up, and surfed the van the whole way there.

Even Steve was impressed.

"I'm doing that on the way back," he said.

"But Steve, how are you gonna get your car back?"

He glared at me. Then threw me the keys. "Be careful."

"Don't worry, I'll drive slow."

He shook his head at me. "That car doesn't go slow."

He was right, too. It was fast as hell, that thing; not a bad choice for the first car I ever drove on my own.

When the day came for Steve's balaclava-less fight, we knew it would be epic.

We set aside a full afternoon to film it, and scouted a new location; a disintegrating warehouse big enough to park a jumbo jet in.

It was perfect for a shoot. Long disused, it had piles of dungeon-worthy chains in odd corners, ominous crates and barrels stacked here and there, and a pervasive, horror-movie ambiance.

The rusted steel roof was a good ten metres above us as we explored the ground floor. Towards the back of the warehouse was a mezzanine level about the size of a tennis court, accessed by a scaffolding staircase. Along one wall I discovered hundreds of bales of glass-wool insulation, still shrink wrapped in plastic. They could have been worth a fortune, for all I knew; then again, judging by the age of the place, they could have been 100% asbestos. What I did know is that they would be perfect for the stunt Mark and Steve were planning.

Up on the mezzanine, they were blocking out a fight sequence. Martin was testing camera angles from above and below. It was time to add a third dimension to our otherwise claustrophobic movie.

We had our million-dollar film set. We had the kind of martial arts talent that would have cost a fortune in Hollywood (unless they hired us; every one of us would beat each other bloody for two pints of beer and a screen credit). The only thing we didn't have access to was special effects. Anything we wanted to accomplish had to be done for real, and we were always looking for ways to push the envelope.

And now we had found one.

As Mark and Steve worked on their choreography, I directed the handful of people who'd showed up to take part. Together, we moved the entire stock of insulation bales, stacking them together beneath the edge of the mezzanine. It took an hour, but I was well pleased with our efforts. We'd created a giant crash mat, five metres square and three bales deep; the top edge came up to my shoulder. I'd made sure the bales were stacked in a kind of running bond, like bricks, so there were no weak spots where a person could easily fall through. I climbed up the stairs to the mezzanine trembling with excitement. And, it must be said, with a modicum of trepidation – as the creator of the huge landing pad, it was my responsibility to test it.

The safety rail along the edge of the balcony had been removed in the middle, and I stood there for a moment, looking down on my creation. Four metres below me, the shiny black plastic reflected daylight from the distant roller door. Then I jumped into empty space, and whooped in delight as the insulation absorbed my impact. I scrambled out of the pile, replacing the bales I dislodged, and gather up the few that had rolled away.

And it was good.

So I gave Mark the thumbs-up.

Of all of us, Steve was by far the most ambitious with his stunts. Whilst Mark and I had visions of becoming actors, Steve's dream job had always been stuntman. He was actively working towards it too, studying gymnastics, excelling in kung fu of course, and driving that Roadster like the FBI were chasing him.

Well, I assume that was part of his preparation for stunt work.

Steve usually played whichever balaclava-man met the most acrobatic end. So far he'd been run over, kicked into a log pile and thrown out of a second storey window.

But this was going to be the fight of his life.

The choreography the pair had worked out involved a short but brutal fight, finishing with Mark delivering a series of kicks to Steve's chest, driving him back towards the edge of the balcony. The final mighty kick would send Steve flying backwards to a gruesome death below. And it certainly would, if my jerry-rigged landing pad didn't work out.

Steve took a few practise jumps, proving his gymnastics lessons had furnished him with an impressive backflip. I'd only dared jump off forwards, but fear was never an option for Steve. He wasn't as hard as nails – he was so hard that nails shit themselves and crossed the road to avoid getting bent out of shape.

And so, filming commenced.

Somewhere between ten and twenty takes passed flawlessly, with Mark and Steve demonstrating just how perfect their timing was. Martin filmed them from every close-up angle possible, pulled back for wide shots, and then came downstairs to capture the whole fight from a distance.

Then he decided to try sitting on the leading edge of the stacked insulation, filming upwards as Steve tumbled through the air above him. This was classic action movie stuff, and would look great in the final edit. Batteries were changed, the insulation bales re-stacked for the twenty-oddth time, and the cast resumed their positions.

Action was called (by Martin), and the fight scene began again in earnest. Steve parried the same flurry of blows, then took his first kick to the chest. He bounded back, took another, and ended up perched precariously on the edge of the balcony. Then Mark leapt in with his devastating side-kick, connecting only lightly with the padding inside Steve's costume.

And Steve, launching his photogenic backflip, yet mindful of the cameraman now sat beneath him, pushed off just a little bit harder.

Almost twenty years later, I can still see it if I close my eyes. I swear it happened in slow motion. Steve flipped gracefully through the air, missing Martin by a mile, and arced towards me. The extra power he'd put in made him travel a good deal further than on previous takes, and instead of landing in the middle of the insulation pad, he overshot it.

The middle of his back hit the edge of the mat, and a split-second later the back of his skull hit the concrete floor.

It exploded like a dropped egg, with a mushy pop that I'll never forget.

I was less than three feet away; the splatter of blood and what looked like brain matter lightly speckled my shoes.

CHRIST! I thought. *He's dead!*

I ran to where Steve was sprawled, his legs splayed awkwardly up the stack of bales. I was the first to reach him.

His eyes were open, but rolled back in his head. Mucus was coming out of his mouth, and the insides of his head were slowly forming a puddle underneath it.

I didn't know what to do. There was nothing I could do! Someone who had a mobile phone on them must have called for the ambulance, and it was there in minutes. By this time Mark and Martin were there with me, with the rest of the group forming a ring around Steve's body. He hadn't moved.

Mark accompanied Steve in the ambulance, and Martin flung his camera gear in his car and followed them. I stayed behind to organise the clean-up, and I must have been in shock, as all I remember is collecting fragments of Steve's skull, and scrubbing at the small pool of blood and blubbery stuff that I could only assume was his brain. I used a handful of glass-wool from a torn insulation bale for this, and my bottle of drinking water. I don't even know why I did it – it's not like anyone was going to use that warehouse in the near future.

We finished putting the venue back to rights, and the rest of the cast dispersed. One of the lads gave me a lift to the hospital, and I walked into the Accident and Emergency Department past a pair of idling police cars.

Indie A&E, the bright lights and the calm, efficient atmosphere were as much of a shock as the accident itself. I half expected screams of pain, sobbing relatives, running and panic and terror – possibly because that's what was going on inside my head.

Instead, I found Mark and Martin sitting next to each other on plastic chairs, staring into space, saying nothing.

"How is he?" I asked.

"Dunno," said Mark. "Alive, maybe. They've taken him straight into surgery."

"Is he… is he gonna…?"

Mark just shrugged.

I collapsed wearily into the seat beside him. The adrenaline was leaving my system, and suddenly I understood Mark's zombification. It had been a full-on filming day even before we'd reached the warehouse. We'd been fighting and running and fighting again for nearly eight hours straight. I was covered in cuts and bruises, blood from more than a few incidental injuries mingling on my hands with Steve's. All of us were exhausted, and deep in shock. Steve's head hitting the floor replayed every time I closed my eyes. I'd cried while cleaning the floor, and I did so again now, trying and failing to control the sobs. I could see that both Mark and Martin had been doing the same.

And then we sat there, three lost souls, heads in our hands, contemplating mortality.

We stank, I suddenly realised. Sweat coated me and chilled me; the honest kind, from the exertion of fighting all day, and the sour-edged sweat of stress and fear. Dust was bound up in it, turning to mud on my hands and face, where it blended with fresh tears and day-old make-up. Blood too, real and fake, was very much in evidence.

And both Mark and I were still wearing our costumes.

This wasn't much of an issue for Mark, as his outfit consisted of baggy trousers and a jacket, but I was in full-on camouflage fatigues.

I cast a glance at the pair of policemen seated opposite. Between them, a filthy-looking bloke was hunched over his handcuffs.

"I hope they don't come over and question us," I said, nodding towards the coppers.

"Yeah," Mark agreed. "I want to take my gun holster off, it's really digging in, but I'm a bit worried about them seeing it."

"What?" I hissed. "You're still wearing it?"

Mark flapped his jacket open slightly, giving me a glimpse of the shoulder-holster strapped around him. Thankfully, his movie-quality replica Beretta wasn't in it.

"Holy shit! Yeah, that could be real awkward…"

And then I looked down at myself.

Specifically at my right leg, which had a two-foot-long machete strapped to it.

There was nothing replica about the razor-sharp blade; it was from my own personal collection, donated to Mark's stash for the duration of the movie.

Mark was also looking at the weapon. "You might want to think about taking that off…" he said.

SHIT!

The last thing I needed now was to be arrested. Knives of all sorts had recently been made illegal in Britain; you now had to be over 18 just to buy cutlery. Anything bigger than a folding pen-knife was liable to get you in big trouble if it was found on your person – and by 'big trouble', I mean an unlimited fine, and up to four years in prison.

"I'll just nip to the bathroom," I said, sliding out of my seat. I turned away from the seated policemen, the machete now riding my opposite thigh, and I strolled out of the waiting room as casually as I could manage.

In the bathroom, I wrapped the sheathed blade in my camo jacket and tried to scrub the mud, blood and make-up off my face.

It's quite disturbing how often in my career I've had to do that.

Unfortunately, I also took off the gorgeous Celtic gold ring my parents had bought me for my 18th birthday, and placed it on the side of the sink while I cleaned myself.

And what with my mind being rather occupied with the events of the day, I completely forgot to put it back on. By the time I realised my mistake, the ring was long gone, and presumably ended up in Cash Converters.

I was pretty cut up about that.

Aftermath

I never saw Steve again.

He survived the accident, after being in a coma for three days, and spent months in hospital.

People who knew him later said that when he came out he was crazier than ever – which, for Steve, is really saying something. As though cheating death had made him immortal, he threw himself into ever more dangerous situations, but it seemed to work out for him; as far as I can tell, he is now a perfectly respectable husband and father. And still a stuntman, of course! I can't imagine him as anything else.

Filming on Displaced went on, after a short break, but I was finding it harder to stay involved. Travelling to and fro was costing me a fortune, and there was a growing twinge of doubt in me that this zero-budget action flick would constitute my big break. Despite months of filming and countless minor injuries, I was effectively invisible in the movie. Some of the less confident fighters had been given an odd line to say, and as the need for a storyline grew, Martin had built on these rare snippets of dialogue to create characters. Hence, we were increasingly featuring a few of the guys, none of whom had any aspirations towards acting. I had a horrible feeling that the hundreds of pounds I'd spent riding the train back and forth to Lancashire, and the nights spent on various cast member's floors, would eventually come to nothing. I mean, no film made without a plot is going to end well, is it?

But Displaced had Mark.

His audacity knew no bounds. In a move I would have considered ludicrous, had I known about it at the time, he took a trailer Martin had edited to the Cannes Film Festival in France.

Like any action movie trailer it comprised random, unconnected fight sequences scenes – but it looked superb.

In truth, all we had were random, unconnected fight sequences. But no-one else knew that. The trailer looked slick, the stunts impressive, the ass-kickings amazingly realistic. It was almost as though hundreds of people had really had their asses kicked…

Or a handful of people had their asses kicked a whole bunch of times.

Whatever the case, the trailer drew interest from several big names in the world of film production.

It didn't open any doors for me, but it certainly did for Mark.

Meanwhile, I had something else to think about.

James, my hairy friend from uni (he's gonna *hate* me for saying that) had got himself involved with one of Cardiff's best amateur theatre companies, and he invited me to join in.

Technically, *Orbit Theatre Company* was semi-professional; that means the director gets paid, and a few other people, but the cast are still doing it for free. Generally though, these outfits take themselves a tad more seriously than the purely amateur bunch, and Orbit was no exception. The show they were currently rehearsing, a musical about the Deep South of the US, called *Showboat,* would be playing in the New Theatre – one of Cardiff's most prestigious venues.

It's a tough gig, being in a musical when you can't sing to save your life.

And, you know, when you hate musicals.

But I *did* love performing, and hadn't done any for months. So I eagerly accepted the small role of an unnamed redneck, which gave me the chance to practice a ridiculously over the top southern drawl. I also got to fire a pistol into the air at one point, which meant I'd be using a blank-firing gun – something I'd had plenty of practice at.

Rehearsals for the show went well. Everything went well, in fact – right up until the first night. Then, after one performance, the young guy in the lead role gave in to his nerves and fled, never to return. In desperation, the director turned to his understudy, an older guy who was playing my cowboy partner. He stepped into the lead role, and did it brilliantly, and I had to figure out how to do both our parts by myself. We didn't have many lines though, so it wasn't too difficult.

Until, on the second night, James fell badly on stage, and broke his ribs.

Which meant I had to do his part as well.

The show was a triumph, and the director was so grateful for my help that he gave me a part in his next musical – *Jesus Christ Superstar.*

I couldn't decide if this was a good thing, or not.

Then I got a phone call from Mark Strange.

Something amazing had happened.

"I'm going to be in a film with Jackie Chan!" he told me. "They want me to fly to Hong Kong in a few weeks, and I need to be in the best shape of my life. Can you come and be my training partner?"

I dropped everything and caught the train to Leyland the next day.

For the next week I slept on a gym mat in Mark's tiny, two-room flat above an antique shop. It was bare floorboards and crumbling plaster, but he knew the owner and was paying heavily reduced rent in exchange for private kung fu lessons. Likewise, he'd negotiated with another student who worked as an Artexer. (Artex is that hard plaster stuff they apply in circular patterns to ceilings.) A few private lessons was enough to get Mark's ceiling done, and loving the speed it went up with, Mark offered the bloke a couple more lessons to get his walls done, too. Mark was also broke; he'd had to close the gym when the landlord doubled the rent for no reason, and he'd poured what little savings he had into Displaced. But kung fu was currency for Mark – there was always someone willing to exchange what he needed for an hour of expert tuition. It also helped that he was one of the nicest, most likeable blokes on the planet; people just *wanted* to help him out.

I spent the whole week with Mark, working out, sparring, jogging, and trying to teach him how to swim.

Then he got another unexpected phone call from Hong Kong – the filming dates had been brought forward, and he had to leave right away.

Three of us coppered up, managing to find a few hundred quid between us to keep him in food until he found his feet over there.

I remember thinking, as we put him on the train to the airport, *'There goes a star. He's on his way at last!'* It was a triumphant, yet wistful feeling. Mark was going to be the first of us to hit the big time, and I was absolutely thrilled for him. But it made my trip back to Cardiff, and my desk job at Fusion the following week, seem even further from my goals.

Mark ended up staying in Hong Kong for two months. He met Jackie Chan, and worked on two films with him; fan-favourite *The Medallion,* and *Twins Effect,* in which he played a vampire and scored a fight scene with the man himself.

But my favourite story of the trip was when, at a bar with several prominent directors and producers, he got chance to show off his legendary axe-kick. Familiar to fans of the Matrix, this is where the hero's leg swings straight up in front of them, going so high it lets them kick someone stood behind them.

It was Mark's signature move – but he'd reckoned without the bar's low roof. His leg went up, but never came down; he'd got his foot wedged in an air-conditioning vent, and had to be cut free.

Man, I wish I'd been there to see that!

As for Displaced, Mark's confidence and ability to charm the pants off anyone was running on steroids when he got back. Already featured in prominent martial arts magazines, he started giving talks at local events, set up countless fundraisers, and somehow arranged to film at Jodrell Bank, site of the third-largest steerable radio telescope in the world. Coups like this kept coming; the icing on the cake was when Sir Ian McKellen, fresh from playing Gandalf in Lord of the Rings, heard about the project and agreed to record a voice-over for the opening scene. Eventually, six long years after that ill-fated hiking trip, Displaced gained a theatrical release in the US.

Sadly, it was rubbish.

But whilst Mark was making a name for himself in Hong Kong, I was going through another rough phase in my life.

Inevitably, I was penniless. Despite all my efforts I was still single, and still pining pathetically over Sally – even though she'd made it clear that our relationship was firmly behind us.

The shock of Steve's accident continued to haunt me for months; every night I woke in a panic from the same vivid nightmare of his head exploding right in front of me. It bled over into my work; I was tired from lack of sleep, depressed that my career had stalled, and frustrated that I didn't know how to fix any of it.

Mostly, I was afraid of failure; that I had already failed, that I was continuing to fail; that I was, in fact, a failure.

Then a girl I knew came to visit me in Richmond Road, and slit her wrists in my bathroom. She survived, but it gave me quite a turn. A few days later I broke down at work, and Charlie sent me home to get my shit together.

Self medication with alcohol seemed the obvious answer to all my woes.

I was already drinking quite heavily. Sally, Katie and I were still managing to maintain our uni-era party lifestyle. It was one of the few aspects of my life I genuinely enjoyed, so I threw myself into it wholeheartedly.

I started to let my drinking take priority over other things – not work, because I still enjoyed my job, and had too much respect for Charlie – but the smaller things, like my miniscule role in Jesus Christ Superstar.

One day, I turned up drunk for rehearsal. It must have been blatantly obvious to everyone, but the director, his hands full with other issues, turned a blind eye – until I missed my one and only queue.

One of the others sang my lines – doubtless doing a much better job than I'd have done – while someone else ducked backstage and dragged me on.

When it was over, and we all assembled on stage for the director to give us his notes, he gave me a thorough (and well-deserved) dressing down. I think it centred around the fairly reasonable admonition, "You'd better not show up drunk for rehearsals again."

Of course, I didn't feel that it was deserved at the time. Probably because I was still drunk. I stood my ground centre-stage, surrounded by the rest of the cast, and unleashed my fury. "How *dare* you talk to me like that!" I scolded him. "If you have a problem with me, you tell me in private. Not in front of all *these* people!" My indignance swelled into rage – which was probable quite funny, for anyone watching.

"Yes, alright," snapped the director.

"No! Not alright. I expect an apology!"

He glared up at me. "Tony, you're drunk."

"Drunk?" I demanded. "DRUNK? How *dare* you say that to me! *Don't you know who I am?* I do this shit for a living, you know. I'm a *professional!*"

Jacob's Ladder

You know those moments when you wish a dormant super-volcano would erupt beneath your feet without warning, completely eradicating all life in the immediate vicinity?

That's how I felt, when I slunk back into the rehearsal room a few days later.

Words can't describe just how embarrassed I felt.

I still went, though.

That's the real meaning behind the phrase, 'The Show Must Go On' – no matter what personal disasters or differences of opinion ensue, all that has to be left at the door. The show is too big and too important for any one person to derail.

So I crawled back – sober, from now on – and ate enough humble pie to feed a third world country.

I couldn't wait for that show to be over.

I had a sneaking suspicion they wouldn't be asking me back for the next one.

But my reward for sticking with it came when a pair of talent scouts showed up at rehearsal one evening. They'd come in search of actors for an upcoming TV series called *Jacob's Ladder*. Casing amateur venues for their artists was a bit of a red flag, but I'd never let that stop me before. They needed a cast and I needed a win; the speed at which they were doling out audition times meant there was bound to be a chance for me.

And TV is TV. Beggars can't be choosers.

I was getting worryingly close to being a beggar.

The scouts didn't tell us anything about the production, but I knew Jacob's Ladder well enough. A psychological horror movie from the nineties, about a Vietnam veteran suffering disturbing visions, it had been one of the first 18-rated (or 'R' rated) movies I'd seen as a kid. And it was awesome! Being in a modern remake, even in a tiny role, would be a major coup.

It would also be the perfect opportunity to test out my new audition strategy.

You remember the problem I'd been having with auditions, right?

Basically, I was bloody awful at them.

Whenever I stood in that spotlight with critical eyes upon me, I turned into a lump of wood. My self-consciousness was so profound that I couldn't get away from myself – the detachment needed to get into character was impossible to attain, and I ended up doing a brilliant impersonation of a picnic table.

I felt sure this would pass, with time and practice. But the trouble was, I didn't go to many auditions. Or any auditions, really. The ones I did get became so important to me that my nerves came screaming to the fore, my traitorous brain magnified every flaw in my technique, every crack in the dam of my self-belief, and left me... well, buggered.

So. New tack.

Although not a huge fan of watching plays, I frikkin' *loved* watching movies.

One thing I'd always loved to do, on my own in my room – minds out of the gutter, please! – was to re-enact scenes from my favourite movies. I liked to think of this as acting practice, whereas in reality it was skiving real acting practice to fantasize about being Batman. But it occurred to me that I could do a pretty good impression of most of my favourite characters. And what is acting, if not impressions? So long as

I changed the pacing of the words a bit, and added my own emphasis here and there, who's to say a scene from *Star Wars* wouldn't make just as good an audition piece as a chunk of *Richard III*? The added benefit was that I knew these scenes word for word already, thereby removing the stress of forgetting my lines.

It was, I felt, a fool-proof plan.

And now I would get to try it out.

Pulp Fiction is one of my favourite movies. Tarantino at his finest, it has some masterful pieces of dialogue. Having seen the film at least twenty or thirty times, I could recite most of it by heart. It was therefore a no-brainer to select a chunk filled with tension that featured a significant monologue.

Fans of the movie will know straight away which bit I was going for: 'The path of the righteous man is beset on all sides…'

Pure, dramatic, gold.

I arrived for my audition at the appointed time, at the HTV studios in Culverhouse Cross. I was familiar with the place – specifically, what a bastard it was to get to by public transport – so I'd left myself plenty of time. I was directed to a bare room; I knew it the right place because there was a piece of paper taped to the door, with 'Jacob's Ladder', scrawled on it in marker pen. The only equipment in evidence was a bulky video camera mounted on a tripod in the far corner.

The director sat behind a borrowed desk, a mess of papers splayed out beneath his fingertips. He looked up and smiled at me as I walked in.

"Hi Tony, nice to have you here. I'm Ciarán, I'm the director of Jacob's Ladder."

"Thank-you, I really appreciate you inviting me."

I took the only other seat in the room, a cheap school chair in front of the desk.

Ciarán shuffled a few papers around, coming up with the copy of my CV I'd sent him. "Ah, yes," he said, skimming the information. "So, this is you."

I nodded.

"Okay, so we're just going to do a basic audition. You have something prepared?"

"Certainly!"

"Great. Before we start, is there anything you'd like to ask me?"

Now, it always pays to ask questions in auditions. Not because you expect to learn anything, but because you get brownie points for appearing interested. I always made sure to have a few in-depth questions ready about the role, or the character's motivation – something that would demonstrate to the auditioner that I cared enough about their show to do my homework. This time, it was all too easy.

"Well, I got this audition because the recruiters came to my acting group. They didn't tell us much, so I'm afraid I don't know anything at all about this production. Could you give me a quick run-down?"

"Oh, of course, yes. So, *Jacob's Ladder* is going to be a seven-part series for HTV, and we're filming entirely on location in South Wales."

"Ah."

"Do you know anything about Jacob's Ladder?"

"Um, just that it's a horror film…"

"Ah, yes! That old thing. Well, what we're doing is a little different. What we're filming is a series of children's bible stories."

If I'd been drinking coffee, I would have sprayed him with it.

Holy. Shit.

They were after *holy*. And I was in the *shit*.

"Oooookaaaaaay…." I took a deep breath. This was not going to end well. "I'm afraid my audition speech may be a *little* inappropriate…"

"That's fine," said Ciarán, and gestured me up.

There was nothing else for it. So I pushed back my chair, took up a stance in the empty space next to it, and shook my head in disbelief.

Children's. Frigging. Bible stories.

You couldn't make this up.

Ciarán got up and fiddled with the camera, making sure it was focused on me. When it was running, he gave me a thumbs-up, and I took a deep, deep breath.

And then another one.

And then I began my spiel.

"What does Marsellus Wallace look like?"

I paused for a second, eyeballing the empty chair where my invisible target was sitting.

"What? Say 'what' again! Say. 'What'. Again. I dare you, I double dare you, mutherfucker! Say 'what' one more God damn time!"

My mental script called for another pause here. It took all my willpower not to sneak a look at the horrified expression Ciarán's face must be wearing. Instead, I closed my eyes. *In for a penny, in for a pound.*

"Does Marsellus Wallace look like a bitch? DOES HE LOOK LIKE A BITCH? Then why are you trying to fuck him like a bitch?"

It went on.

And on. And on.

For centuries.

I was dying inside, one expletive at a time.

As I ended my scene by miming the violent execution of invisible 'Brad', I turned to Ciarán and cringed.

He was, understandably, a bit lost for words.

"Good job though," he said, when he rediscovered the power of speech. "Very intense. Very… ah… moving!"

"Oh. Really?"

"Yes, great! I love Pulp Fiction. A bit, ah, colourful for what we're doing, but no problem."

He glanced down at his desk, shuffling some papers around and reading something on each.

I stood waiting, head down, face aflame.

"Okay," he said, "I think this would be right for you. Or, wait—" he dug through the pile of papers for a different sheet. "Can you ride a horse?"

I thought about this for a second. There's a golden rule in acting auditions, which had been drummed into me – not during my university course, but by those jaded old extras in the Coronation Street green room. *Say Yes To Everything.* It's simple, really. Can you drive? Ski? Speak Urdu? The answer must always be yes. Because if you say no, the director will thank you for your time, and go find someone else who can. If you say yes no matter what they're asking, you'll at least have a chance of getting the role – and then you can worry about how to make it work afterwards. The chances are, they won't actually *need* you to speak Urdu – and if they do, well, that's a great day to suddenly develop laryngitis.

"Yeah, of course I can ride," I told him.

"Great! How well?"

I gave a modest shrug. "Like the wind."

I couldn't help it, it just tripped out.

"Great," he said again. "I have two roles in mind for you. I'll be in touch."

So I thanked the man and made my escape.

I got as far as the car park, then tore through my bag looking for my phone.

"Mum!" I yelled, when she answered. "It's me!"

"Oh! Hi Tony! Are you done with your audition? How did it go?"

"Brilliant, Mum. Really good. But I need a favour."

"Sure! What is it?"

"Can you book me some riding lessons? As many as possible. Like, *right now!*"

I hadn't been on a horse since I was eight.

I next met Ciarán two weeks later, on a rainy, windswept Welsh hillside.

It wasn't an ideal match for Palestine a thousand years before the birth of Jesus, but he didn't seem too bothered with the technicalities.

"You're to ride up this hill, into the castle at the top," he explained.

My horse was a fine, strapping specimen, a gorgeous chestnut colour with dark eyes and mane. I love horses and have a good affinity with them; showing no fear is the key, I've always felt, as nothing makes a horse nervous like nervousness.

And I wasn't nervous. Not really.

I was shitting breeze blocks.

I'd squeezed in four riding lessons – all I could manage, nipping to Somerset on weekends between work. I'd been offered one day of work as a horse-riding messenger, and another as a guard. Both were small speaking roles, but both had the potential to get me recognised. I'd pulled out all the stops on this one – to the point of ridiculousness, you might say.

What I'd been asked to do went so far beyond my abilities as a horseman, I was almost starting to question the wisdom of the Universal Yes. What Ciarán wanted was for me to gallop this horse up the steep slope surrounding the castle, charge through the open gate and into the cobbled courtyard. There I was meant to leap from the saddle, dashing inside the keep with an urgent message for the king.

How do I get myself into these situations? I wondered, as the rain soaked through my thin velvet cloak.

Four times, I coaxed my trusty steed up that hillside.

The cobbles in the courtyard were deathly slippy, and I braced for the inevitable. Finally, realising that we'd keep repeating this until I conveyed the appropriate sense of urgency, I threw caution to the wind, kicking my horse into a dead run. The magnificent beast surged upwards, exuding power and grace. Every step flung me two feet into the air, only to come crashing down on my testicles. I barely kept hold of the reins, and hauled on them as we charged through the gateway. The horse reared up, sliding to a stop on its hind legs. I flung myself out of the saddle, nearly breaking my nose on the cobblestones as my feet went from under me. I sprawled full-length, my knee smashing into the ancient stones, but I held the King's message tube high, away from the wet ground, and dashed inside with it. I thought my fall had ruined yet another take, but Ciarán loved it. It added *gravity* to the scene, he said – I wasn't sure if he was taking the piss out of me or not.

My heart was hammering. Pride and pain warred within me.

So wet was my uniform, neither of us noticed that blood was streaming down my leg inside it and filling my boot. I was convinced that I was one take away from breaking my legs – or the horse's legs – or, more realistically, both. Somehow, I'd gotten away with it. My next scene, in which I delivered my precious message to the king, was a rare triumph. The camera focussed right in on me as I gave my memorised report, before kneeling to pass over the scroll of proof.

I even managed to avoid screaming out as I knelt down – only just, but I felt the muffled groan added to my weary messenger routine.

Maybe I am going to be famous, after all, I mused later, as I wrapped my knee in tissues and duct tape. *And it will all be worth it. I'll look back at all this, and laugh...*

Jacob's Ladder was eventually released over a year later, in 2003.

In Wales.

It was only ever shown once, never repeated, never renewed, never even reviewed, as far as I can tell. I don't even think anyone watched it; I certainly didn't, as I'd moved away from Wales by then.

When doing the research for this book, it took me hours to find the barest trace of it online. I almost convinced myself the whole episode was a hallucination.

In fact, the only place you can really find a picture of it these days is in the dictionary, under the definition of the word 'Obscurity'.

I think it's safe to say, it wasn't my big break.

A Trip To The Doctor's

My next opportunity to shine came with the revival of an obscure TV series from the 1960s. Attempts had been made before to breathe life back into the franchise, but all had failed. Now, the BBC was tentatively trying again – only, they weren't prepared to risk a large amount of money on such an experimental project.

So, where do you go to make telly on the cheap?

Wales, of course!

Luckily for me.

When I got the call, I couldn't quite believe my luck. I wanted to tell absolutely everyone – but I couldn't. A strict vow of confidentiality had been elicited from everyone working on the show. It would be a 'closed set' – meaning, no family or friends, no outsiders of any kind, would be allowed inside. For maximum impact, the revival of the show was going to be a surprise, unleashed upon the Great British public without warning. Yet another reason to film it in Wales; no-one would believe any rumours they heard, because as I'd spent the last few years discovering – *nothing good* ever gets filmed in Wales.

Until now, quite possibly.

Because this show had potential. I'd even *heard* of it.

It was a risky bet; one that could rise triumphantly from cold ashes, spreading wings of flaming influence over the known world. Or it could collapse into a puddle of embarrassment and sink without a trace.

Only time would tell.

But either way, I was going to be a part of it.

Oh, and in case you're wondering – the name of the show was *Doctor Who*.

It was a freezing cold, mid-winter morning, when I showed up at the warehouse.

Like most good sci-fi shows – most shows of any kind, really – much of Doctor Who was going to be filmed inside a nondescript warehouse on the edge of an unremarkable industrial estate. To the trained eye, the presence of a double-decker bus and a catering van within the mesh security fence gave the game away; the bus would be our home during filming hours, and the van would provide our sustenance. It was, as I may have mentioned, not a terribly glamorous life.

Talking to the other extras, I found that quite a few of them had been hired to play whatever monsters the Doctor would be fighting. Their measurements had been taken, and as the show progressed they would have a different costume made to fit them for each episode. I'd done my fair share of costume work. I'd dressed in a giant rat suit and roller-skated around Bristol city centre (it was murder on the cobblestones). I'd impersonated a six-foot tall slice of pizza. In fact, if there was a gigantic, foam-rubber something-or-other, the chances were I'd been inside it – one of the many joys of working for Fusion.

The downside of costume work is that it sucks ass. These poor buggers would be spending hours in the make-up chair, having various prosthetics grafted onto their faces, and once fastened in to their cumbersome costumes, they'd probably stay that way all day. It would be hot, claustrophobic work, especially if filming lasted until summer.

And if they needed a poo, they'd be in real trouble.

Worst of all, the same anonymity which allowed them to be in every episode also meant they'd be completely unrecognisable in all of them.

I, on the other hand, was part of a pool of background artists from whom they would draw the occasional speaking part – nothing too distinctive, or they wouldn't be able to use us again, but even being relegated to blink-and-you'll-miss-'em roles was exciting. My face would be on display, albeit for a second here and there, and there was always the slightest chance that I'd impress someone in the crew, and wind up with a proper part.

Ha! *As if.* It constantly amazed me that I could keep this kernel of hope alive, after years of proof to the contrary. Still. If it was going to happen anywhere… I couldn't think of a better place.

Doctor Who…

I could hardly believe it.

The 3rd Assistant Director asked if any of us had experience with blank-firing weapons. After making Displaced, I felt more than qualified in this area, so my hand shot straight up.

And when he asked us about military training, I kept it there, just in case.

He gave me a measuring glance, and seemed to like what he saw.

"You look like a mature, responsible individual," he said. I choked back a laugh. God knows how I'd fooled him. "We'll have you as the boss."

One thing TV shows can't afford to scrimp on is guns. It goes without saying that all kinds of health and safety legislation come into play. They'd hired a crew of supporting artists from a specialist agency called 'Bobbies and Blaggers' – everyone on their books was either ex-police or ex-military, and they provided their own costumes as part of the arrangement. These boys would be playing a sizeable squad of soldiers for this episode, and I was in make-up, being groomed as the suit in charge of them. An armourer issued me with my blank-firing Glock, and made sure I was safe using it. Then we all assembled in a section of the warehouse that had been dressed up as some kind of underground base. Stacks of wooden ammunition crates defined the space, and the concrete wall ahead of us bore a stencil that read 'Level

52'. A raised steel walkway on one side would be filled with the soldiers, whilst I'd be taking cover behind the ammo. This seemed like a spectacularly bad place to hide, but I guess I wasn't the smartest of bosses.

"What I'm about to tell you is top secret," the AD explained, "so please *do not* repeat this to anyone."

He waited for a murmur of assent before continuing.

"So, congratulations! You fine gentlemen are about to become the first victims of a Darlek in sixteen years."

Now that did start some tongues wagging.

"First we'll get some footage of you all rushing into position," the AD continued.

"Our Darlek is going to emerge from behind me. There'll be a Mexican stand-off for a little while, and then, when you get the command, you'll all open fire on the Darlek."

He paused, to check we were following.

"Then – and this bit is very hush-hush – the Darlek will rise up into the air, using its antigravity powers."

Now I understood the secrecy. Every child of my era knew that to escape a Darlek, all you have to do is run upstairs. Until now. The scriptwriting team must have been over the moon when they came up with that one. Darleks could fly? Game changer.

"The Darlek will hover right above me, here," the AD said, pointing upwards. "It will shoot a laser into the fire alarm panel, activating the sprinkler system, and soaking you all. We'll shoot that scene last, as once the floor's wet it'll stay that way. And then... the Darlek will shoot a bolt of lightening into the water, and you'll all be electrocuted."

Wow.

Not only was I going to be in Dr Who – and not only was I going to be firing a handgun on screen – I was also getting to showcase my special talent.

I was going to die.

The shoot itself was nothing spectacular. First, ex-pop singer Billy Piper ran out in front of us, being pursued by the Darlek. We stood around for a couple of hours, trying to look menacing, pointing our weapons at the alien machine. Then there was a very noisy half-hour, as we capped off clip after clip of blanks at an imaginary spot above us. This spot was where, we were assured, the Darlek would be floating, via the magic of CGI.

And after the shooting part came the dying.

This was even less comfortable than dying on Displaced, owing to the unique method the Darlek had chosen for our execution. First, the industrial sprinkler system was turned on, showering us all in icy-cold water. Then, in perfect synchronisation, we had to mime the effects of ten-thousand volts of electricity going through us.

Just in case that wasn't fun enough, we then spent the next two hours lying motionless in the puddles of freezing water, while they filmed a flying Darlek's eye view of the carnage he'd caused.

Bugger me, that was cold.

But it was worth it.

I reckoned I'd made it into just enough footage to be recognisable on screen, but hopefully not enough to jeopardize my position as a regular. Who knows – having been murdered by a Darlek on my first day, perhaps I'd be strangled by a Cyberman next week?

It was all very exciting.

Wandering around the warehouse at lunchtime, a couple of us gathered to admire the Darlek. All morning it had been hidden in a corner, a mysterious statue shrouded in a tarp. Now, prepped for filming, it had been revealed in all its glory. More than usual glory, in fact; it was completely golden, from nozzle to bumper.

"That is so cool," one of my companions said. "Hey, I gotta take a picture of this."

"How?" I said, horrified. "They told us first thing that we weren't allowed cameras on set! You didn't sneak one in, did you?"

"Nah, mate. Didn't need to." He held up his phone. "This has got a camera built into it."

"No way!"

"Yeah! Check it out. It's digital," he explained. "You just press this, and voilà!"

A grainy image of our feet appeared on the phone's tiny screen.

"Holy shit, dude! That's the future. I gotta get me one of those."

He grinned. "That's what everyone says. Hey listen, go stand by the corner and keep a look-out, would you? I wanna take a quick pic of the Darlek."

"Yeah, alright."

"Anyone coming?"

I poked my head around a stack of ammo crates. "Nah, everyone's just sitting around, chatting and eating."

"Right, hang on… *done!*"

I remember the thrill of the illicit running through me. I was never naughty on film sets – even when others mucked about and pranked each other, I generally stayed clear. No sense in jeopardizing everything I'd built up just for a joke.

But I hadn't *really* done anything wrong, I convinced myself. And anyway, who would ever know or care? So, the dude took a picture. *Big deal.* He wasn't hurting anyone, was he?

The next morning, that photo was on the front page of The Sun – the biggest newspaper in the English-speaking world.

'NEW GOLD DARLEK'S GOT MORE BLING THAN P. DIDDY!' read the headline.

I can only guess at what that guy got paid for his sneaky snapshot, but I bet it was a damn sight more than he'd expected to earn as an extra on the show.

Which was a bit of a shitter, as I got a phone call from my agent later that day. "I'm sorry, Tony," she said, "but they don't want you back on Doctor Who."

"What? But why? I… I didn't…"

"I know you didn't! I'm sorry. But it's out of my hands. They've fired everyone who worked yesterday."

Crazy, really.

It was only a *photograph* of a Darlek.

But it had managed to exterminate the entire cast.

Revelation

As the year wore on, afraid of losing my touch, I found another amateur dramatics society to join.

It was at this point, during rehearsals for 'The Secret Diary of Adrian Mole (aged 13 ¾)', that I realised I wasn't destined to find fame as an actor.

There had been indications all along, of course, but I'd mostly ignored them. Swept up in the constant busywork of chasing jobs and auditions, I'd managed to avoid looking at the cold, hard truth which now presented itself.

I was crap at acting.

People have asked me many times since then, what exactly it was about acting that I couldn't handle. I think this play provided me with final, incontrovertible proof of my problem: no matter how hard I tired, I just couldn't divorce myself from reality.

It sounds like a silly thing, some pretentious issue that borders on hypochondria. In fact, this process of separation from the here-and-now is the single most important skill for an actor to master. Without the ability to disassociate yourself from the world around you, from the body and characteristics and personality of yourself, you simply cannot create a believable portrayal of anyone else.

Put simply; if you're acting like the character you're portraying, then it just isn't going to work. You have to *become* them. Not in some intangible, metaphysical way, but in the sense that you take on their personality, their thought processes, their physicality and – most importantly of all – the circumstances surrounding them.

After all, if *you* don't believe you're in eighteenth-century Spain fighting against an army of infidels, then sure as shit no-one watching will believe you.

In all my rather limited experience to date, I'd been striving to lose myself in my characters. Trying, and failing. Essentially, that left me doing impressions; creating a caricature of the role I was playing, and acting it out whilst consciously trying not to ham it up.

No matter how hard I tried, I couldn't lose myself in my character. I couldn't flip that switch that turns off Tony Slater, with all his thoughts and feelings about whatever I was doing. Tony was always in my head, self-consciously running the show, worrying about how I looked to the audience, wondering who was watching and whether or not they liked my performance, calculating the required degree of body language, and listening for my cue whilst mentally rehearsing my next line of dialogue.

Adrian Mole was not only the catalyst for this terrible realisation; it also presented a perfect example of the problem.

I was cast as Mr Lucas, the used-car-dealer-esque character who seduces Adrian Mole's mother and lures her away from her husband, wrecking the family in the process. It should have been the perfect role; enough stage time to be considered a central member of the cast, without being too taxing. Plenty of variety, as Mr Lucas runs the gamut from anger to sadness to passion.

I looked deeper into the character and found a powerful selfishness that motivated him. It was understandable, having spent his life building his business as a salesman, that he would aggressively pursue whatever he wanted, consequences be damned. I could see that he wasn't an inherently evil character – just one whose goals ran directly counter to those of the main protagonist, Adrian Mole.

And from the script, it's plain to see that Mr Lucas really does love Adrian's mother. Or at least, he thinks he does.

So, I hear you cry, what the hell was the problem?

The problem was Adrian Mole's mum, Pauline.

Or rather, the lady cast to play Pauline.

Because she really *was* a mum.

A woman in her late forties, plain and frumpy and spreading comfortably, as middle-aged mothers tend to.

Which is fine, in middle-aged mothers. I've got nothing against that.

But I had to snog her.

Repeatedly.

And I had to make impassioned pleas, hold her sometimes tenderly and sometimes fiercely, pull her around the stage with me as though dancing, and gaze lovingly into her eyes – to basically inhabit the very soul of someone who was utterly besotted with this woman.

I just couldn't do it.

Not with any conviction, anyway.

Sure, I mouthed the words, I tried to imbue them with just the right amount of emotion, to sound breathless with desire and to stare at her with what I hoped would pass for adoration.

But I was quite obviously just going through the motions.

I couldn't get past the fact that she was quite blatantly *someone else's wife* – not just in the script, but in reality. More to the point, she was someone else's mother. Quite possibly someone my own age.

The thought of kissing her, of pressing her passionately against me, of whispering seductively in her ear about secret assignations we were plotting…

Ugh!

No matter what I did, I couldn't feel it.

And to be honest, I wasn't sure I wanted to.

But, as always, the show must go on.

I was determined to give it my all.

"Mr Lucas doesn't shuffle, he struts!" the director reprimanded me. "*Tony* shuffles, but you have to leave Tony at the door. Mr Lucas is a peacock! He's confident, impulsive, proud."

I could almost hear the unspoken end to that sentiment: *He's all the things, you're not.*

My portrayal of Mr Lucas needed to step up a notch and inherit some energy from somewhere. But here again came the problem; how could I act confident when I'm not a confident person? The director had called it accurately. As a writhing ball of insecurities and neuroses, I had no idea what true confidence felt like. I could adopt mannerisms, but I couldn't project an aura of self-belief – otherwise I'd be doing it 24/7, rather than spending my life drunk and hiding in my bedroom. How was I supposed to convince an audience of paying customers that I was a smooth-talking ladies' man, when I couldn't even get a girlfriend? Knowing how they'd be scrutinising my performance, looking for signs I wasn't committing fully to the role, I began to understand just how impossible a career in acting was for me. In the most competitive industry on the planet, where even the most talented people need phenomenal good luck just to stand a chance... I wasn't even in the running. I would never be the complete package, and no amount of bluster or bravado would carry me where I wanted to go.

Opening night came and went. I still felt the thrill of performing, but tinged with no small measure of embarrassment. James came to see the show, faithful as ever, and tried to console me afterwards with a pint. "It could always be worse," he pointed out.

"Really?" I asked him. "How?"

He thought about that for a while. "Let's get another drink," he said at last. "At least you can wash your mouth out!"

Adrian Mole ran for five nights – as always, I was staggered by the amount of preparation and sheer hard work that went into less than a week of actual performance.

On the last night, I stood waiting in the wings, congratulating myself on getting through it. For the first time,

I was actually glad of such a short run. In a little over two hours, it would all be over.

And with it, my career.

The lights came up, the introductory monologue played out, and I braced myself to step on stage.

And that's when I noticed them.

I'd managed to avoid inviting my other friends, and thought I'd gotten away without anyone else I knew seeing me.

But no. There in the audience – grinning madly in the front row – were the last two people I was ready for.

It was Gill. And sitting next to her was Mum.

Oh. My. God.

The shock hit me like a battering ram. They hadn't told me… of course they wouldn't! It was just like them. And… but… now…

Ohhh… SHIT!

The blood drained from my face. I mean, I say that phrase a lot, but I literally felt the blood retreat from my face and head for my ankles. It had the right idea; don't get caught in the open. I wished I could do the same.

In fact I seriously contemplated spontaneous human combustion right then. If it had been within my power, I would have burned the whole place down. Anything to avoid this.

What should I do? Double down on my efforts, really commit to the role, and hope Mum was proud of my acting ability?

Kiss with tongues?

The very thought of it made me shudder.

Or shrink back a little, play it cool, keep her aware that I was just playing a role? It sounds silly to say, but I was horrified by what she would think of me. Which, in essence, is exactly why I was crap.

And, you know, it didn't help that I had to smooch a middle-aged housewife. *That* was the reality I couldn't divorce myself from.

Oh no. Oh God. OH GOD!

It was time. My cue was approaching. I had to... there had to be something... some... way out...

I heard my cue line.

I squashed the rising panic.

This was it. Time to be a pro. To get serious. To separate the men from the boys.

And the boy from the person who snogs old ladies in public...

If my performance that night had been any more wooden, I could have made a bench out of it. Try as I might, I couldn't get into it. My attention was divided; part of it was sitting behind Mum and Gill with hands over its eyes, watching a train wreck develop between the gaps in its fingers; part of it was floating above me, looking down, and offering a running commentary in disbelief and four-letter words. There wasn't enough left over to give life to my character. If Mr Lucas had been a shuffler before, now he was a deadpan, shambling, lifeless zombie, as my subconscious tried desperately to distance me from a situation that my adrenal system had equated with certain death.

I delivered my lines with all the emotion of a ten year old boy press-ganged into his school nativity play.

When Pauline went in for one of our kisses, I nearly dodged her. It was instinctive; *my mother was watching*, for Chrissakes! She'd never even seen me kiss a regular girl. I don't think she even knew that I *had* kissed a girl yet. My cringe reflex went into overdrive; it was doing double duty, both reacting to the act itself, and channelling Mum's reaction. Pauline came in for another kiss, and I threw up a little in my mouth.

Luckily not in her mouth, or that really would have changed the course of the show.

Finally, it was all over.

I hadn't been so relived since my penis stopped bleeding on New Year's Eve.

At the same time, I was dreading seeing Mum and Gill.

I'd developed a reputation for being impossible to embarrass, but this... Words cannot express how badly I wanted to ground to swallow me up right then.

I made my way out into the auditorium, hoping against hope that they'd had to rush off to catch a train back home.

But no. They were waiting for me, rather forced smiles on their faces.

"Surprise!" said Mum. "We thought we'd catch the show, but we didn't want to make you nervous."

"Yeah... great to see you, though. Sorry, the show was a bit..."

"Yes, it was..." I could see her groping for words. *Groping*. Argh. "...very interesting," she finished.

"Dude!" Gill said. And that was all.

"I need a drink," I told them.

We never got chance to have an in-depth chat about the show, for which I am eternally grateful. They did have a train to catch, and I, joy of joys, had an after-show party to attend.

It wasn't the liveliest of gigs. Held in the home of the actor who played Adrian Mole's dad, it couldn't get too out of control because his family were sleeping upstairs. I didn't make much effort to be social – I hadn't really gelled with my colleagues during rehearsals, so it seemed a bit late now.

It had been an odd show. All the adult cast were significantly older than me, and all the young cast (playing Adrian's school friends) were kids. At twenty-one, I was closer in age to the kids, but they were all friends from previous shows and didn't really pay me much attention. It made for a lonely time. The only person close to my own age was a slim bloke in his thirties who came in towards the end of rehearsals to do a five-line part as Adrian's teacher. So I hung out with him at the party, and he offered to let me crash at his place afterwards to save an expensive taxi home.

Drinking largely to forget, I eventually found myself in the kitchen, chatting to a bunch of late arrivals. The band, hired only a few days before opening night, had only attended the dress rehearsal. I'd been far too preoccupied searching for Mr Lucas's elusive swagger to pay them much heed, and they'd been busy playing with themselves.

Musically speaking, of course. Traditionally, the actors and the band don't have much to do with each other, and tend to hang out in their own cliques. But I was thrilled to have someone different to talk to, and with a few drinks inside me I was doing just that.

As we were leaving, a rather cute blonde chick who played the drums tagged along with us. She'd also been facing a pricey taxi journey, and the teacher bloke who'd offered me a place to stay had extended the same offer to her.

We got back to his place tired, drunk, and happy. I was suffering a belated dose of the post-show euphoria, brought on at least in part by the certain knowledge that I never had to see any of those people again. I would never have to make the long commute across town for rehearsals, and my evenings would no longer be spent dying inside whilst my getting my shuffling mercilessly critiqued in a drab and draughty theatre.

Adrian Mole's teacher – I doubt I knew his name even then – went straight to bed, after setting up an inflatable mattress in his lounge. The blonde drummer unrolled a borrowed sleeping bag on the sofa, and eyed it dubiously.

"Which one d'ya want?" I asked her, gesturing at the bed behind me. "I'm easy."

"Really?" She raised an eyebrow. "If that's true, we might as well both take the bed."

So we did.

And later that night, when our exertions caused the bed to deflate somewhat, we took the sofa, too.

Appropriately enough, it was old Bill Shakespeare that best summed up this turn of events: All's well that ends well.

The Travel Bug

And it was the end.

There was no denying it – my acting career had stalled. No, that's not right – it had *disintegrated.* To be perfectly honest, I'd never actually had an acting career; just a whole bunch of weird jobs, loosely related. What made them seem like the rungs of a ladder leading to something better was nothing more than my own ambition – and that bizarre little voice in my head which kept telling me, in spite of all evidence to the contrary, that I had some kind of greater destiny.

Maybe I was just schizophrenic.

But surely, everyone secretly believes themselves to be different? To be special? Maybe it's something we start out with as kids, but it gets drummed out of us by the relentless onslaught of adulthood. Whatever the case, I'd never lost that conviction, and it had carried me through dizzying highs and crippling lows, from body-doubling for Robert Sean Leonard to being spat on whilst dancing semi-naked in Gateshead Metro Centre.

Until now.

Because I was starting to lose the faith.

Don't get me wrong – I was still enjoying life. I loved the

uncertainty that made it feel like an adventure. No matter what grubby, mud-encrusted trench I was lying in one day, I could be anywhere the day after – kissing hot girls in nightclubs, standing on guard in a breastplate and beard, or handing out flyers whilst dressed as a six-foot slice of pizza.

I still loved the *weirdness* of it all.

Which is no bad thing. I bet, on deathbeds around the world, no-one has ever wished their life was *less* weird.

And why would they? Weirdness is awesome.

But there had to be more. Some direction, some goal – some reason to carry on doing whatever it was I meant to be doing.

Man cannot live on weirdness alone.

Believe me – I've tried.

Katie was working in a call centre for British Gas, but she quite enjoyed her job.

I started meeting her after work, with a bottle of wine – *each*. We'd drink them on the walk home, before getting started on the heavy stuff. I can't help but wonder, in hindsight, if we were drinking just a tad too much.

Inevitably, this kind of behaviour beget more silliness. Once, heavily drunk in a sports bar in the city centre, Katie and I decided to see how far we could strip off without getting thrown out. I'm guessing it was her supermodel attractiveness that convinced the doormen to let us get completely naked, before ordering us to leave. Everyone in the bar had been cheering us on by that point, and we rewarded their attention by pressing ourselves up against the plate glass window outside. Then we decided to walk home – without bothering to get dressed again. People cheered us, cars beeped; our route home followed the main road out of town, after all. Somehow we made it, unmolested and unarrested, and we found the whole experience so amusing that 'Naked Walk Home' became one of our favourite games.

A few weeks later Sally got a frantic call from a friend, who was out in Cardiff. "You won't believe this," he said, "but there's a guy and a girl walking down the road in front of me, *in the nude!*"

"Oh," she replied, "That'll be Tony and Katie."

And it was.

But this sort of fun was not an indication of happiness and contentment. We were quite blatantly trying to revive our hedonistic student lifestyle, perhaps using it as a shield against the ugly truth: that we were lost. No clear path forward presented itself – at least, none that led anywhere we wanted to go. In my darkest moments, when the booze found me alone and unhappy, I admitted that I was fooling myself. I had a future with no prospects. It didn't take a genius to figure out that if I kept doing what I was doing, I'd keep getting what I'd got.

Which was nothing.

Sally saved me.

We'd talked about traveling the world – but in the same way I joked about being famous. Sally took this pipe-dream and brought it crashing into reality with a revelation: the *world* might be a bit out of our reach, but Europe wasn't.

Neither of us were terribly happy with the situations we were in, and the prospect of getting out of it all for some kind of mad adventure, shone so bright it completely eclipsed the mundanity of our lives.

It was still terrifying, though.

Over the next few weeks, we basically dared each other into it. She bought a backpack, so I bought a tent; our theory was that, by spending money we couldn't afford to waste, we were basically forcing ourselves to go.

When she quit her job, prompting me to tell Charlie that I was leaving Fusion, we kind of had no choice.

And so, we went.

To France.

Where the first night of our great adventure found us hopelessly lost in a town called *Angers*. We'd arrived there on the train, just after 10pm, with no accommodation booked, no food, and no clue at all about the place, beyond its ten-word write up in *Europe by Train*. We spent two hours staggering along darkened streets, bent double under the crippling weight of our backpacks. Eventually we came across a war memorial, and spent the rest of the night taking turns trying to sleep next to it on a freezing cold bench.

As first nights go, it wasn't the most successful.

Long-term readers may note that, at least in my case, it didn't really get much better.

As we shivered through the dawn, awaiting the first train back out of Angers, Sally had a revelation.

"We are really shit at this," she said.

I was inclined to agree with her.

Over the next two months, we bounced back and forth between the handful of countries where our rail passes were valid; camping where we could, sleeping on trains where we couldn't, and more often than not doing neither. I doubt we had a good night's sleep in the two months we were away.

We visited *Lourdes*, the third most sacred site in all of Christendom, to get Mum some Holy Water. I was amused to find that, rather than springing from the ground, the water was dispensed by a row of Holy Taps. Even better – the taps also supplied a Holy Swimming Pool, where people with all kinds of illness and disease could bathe in the hope of a cure.

Holy Water sort of lost its appeal after that.

In Amsterdam, whilst sampling the local, ah, *produce,* I narrowly avoided getting the shit kicked out of me by a man who I swear to this day was Harold Bishop from *Neighbours.*

A week later, in Belgium, I inadvertently smuggled a bag of drugs across an international border in the front pocket of my jeans. I'd completely forgotten it was there, until the *gendarmes* boarded the train and began strip-searching people from our carriage...

In Germany we did a tour of the Berlin Wall, which left me an emotional wreckage. Tears streamed down my face as our guide recounted the tales of families divided overnight, and East German women throwing their babies over the half-built Wall to be raised in the West, knowing they would probably never see them again.

We visited Switzerland, famed for its majestic mountains, and unable to afford a tour of them, we found a plastic shopping bag and slid down some hills on it.

I like to think we had more fun that way.

In Austria we explored fantastical ice caves, and got locked in a salt mine by accidentally staying past closing time. When we emerged, the world was a different place; 9/11 had happened, and suddenly the prospect of travelling anywhere beyond Europe seemed excessively dangerous. Half expecting a world war to be declared at any minute, we abandoned plans to visit Morocco and headed west.

We got more lost in Toledo, Spain, than I've ever been in my life, before or since. But Toledo is famous for it – and for swords, which is literally the only reason we went there. Unfortunately, it was a lust we couldn't satisfy, as they don't let you travel on trains with swords. I've never figured out why.

Finally, on the way out of Portugal, we got our train tickets stolen off us as we slept. It was an abrupt and devastating end to our trip. A frantic call to our emergency hotline revealed a nugget of wisdom I've never forgotten: travel insurance companies exist solely to screw you over. Not only would they not replace our tickets, leaving us effectively stranded in Spain, they also wouldn't help us get home. The bastards! I haven't bought travel insurance since.

And so it came to pass that, instead of eating breakfast tapas in Barcelona, we flew into Bristol Airport a few hours later, courtesy of my parents. It was a grey day in a grey country. Neither of us wanted to be there, but we had no choice. It started raining as we sneaked aboard the train to Cardiff – neither of us could afford the fare – and it carried on raining for the rest of my life.

At least, that's how it felt.

It was my first experience of the post-travel blues, and boy did it hit hard. I couldn't believe that we'd gone from gallivanting around the world, carefree and happy and masters of our own destiny, to this: cold, rainy Cardiff, sliding into the grip of winter; negative equity and unemployment, and everything else *exactly the same as we'd left it!* This was perhaps the hardest pill to swallow. Whilst it seemed like we'd grown so much, nothing else had changed. To everyone else around us, this wasn't the day that all dreams died forever; it was just Wednesday.

It's a good job I didn't live near any bridges, or I'd have jumped off one.

Predictably, we'd spent every shekel to our names, and so we moved in with Katie, all three of us living together in my room in Richmond Road.

That did wonders for my reputation.

I denied the rumours, of course, but that only made them stronger. My housemates were convinced that I'd returned from exploring exotic and far-off lands to become the master of a harem.

I don't think I've ever been held in such high esteem in my life.

And I've been married for six years.

But none of that mattered. All I thought about, all day, every day, was travelling.

Hardly surprising, when I was folding paper for a living.

I'd been forced to join a temping agency, and had been sent out as office staff to an investment bank in Cardiff. There, I sat at a spare desk in a tiny office... and folded letters into envelopes.

For *two months.*

I shit you not!

When the bank decided to extend my contract, and sent me downstairs to the filing room in the basement, I rebelled. I spent three full days and a dozen rolls of duct tape filling the entire room with a gigantic spider-web. It stretched from the central light fitting to every drawer of filing cabinet, and was, I believe, approaching art.

Obviously I was trying to get fired, but when I brought my boss down and proudly introduced my masterpiece, he merely asked, "You're going to tidy it all up again though, aren't you?"

I regretfully discontinued my representation with Pan Artists in 2003, after seven years. I'd finally been kicked out of my flat in Cardiff – the landlord apologised profusely, but there was only so long he could get away with pretending I was still a student.

Directionless, at a loss, I moved back into my parent's house in Somerset. The commute from there to Manchester was beyond ridiculous at over six hours by train, so that was the end of my tenure on Coronation Street.

I didn't miss it much.

I did miss the money however, and though I carried on doing odd days on Casualty in Bristol, I soon had to face reality and get another 'real' job. This time it took the form of gardening in a holiday park, where I spent most of my shifts asleep under a caravan. Somehow, my dedication was recognised with promotion to bar work in the on-site cabaret club.

It was whilst doing this job that I had an epiphany.

Saving up was taking forever. It would be months before I could go away again, and I'd be stuck doing crappy jobs the whole time. And what would happen when I ran out of cash halfway through my next adventure? I'd be right back to square one.

But what if I never ran out of money?

What if I could travel the world *continuously*, and do the same jobs I'd been doing at home – only, do them in exciting different countries? They wouldn't be crappy then – they'd be an adventure! I'd worked in shops, offices, one bank and now a bar. I'd done gardening (if sleeping under caravans counted), promotional work, tour guiding, and… well. I'd narrowly avoided a role *in Euroboys II*, but if worst came to worst, at least I was fairly well acquainted with the porn industry.

Could I do this?

Could I really leave home, leave my friends and family, and strike off into the unknown?

Could I work my way around the world, bartending in Bondi Beach one week, and serving coffee in Canada the next?

Could I really do something so outrageous – so ridiculous – so incredibly and awesomely terrifying?

Or, put another way... *how could I not?*

Sure, it would be challenging. Probably uncomfortable. And quite possibly dangerous.

But I would do it.

Or I would die trying.

And who knows? Maybe I'd return to acting one fine day. When years of travel had broadened my character. When foreign suns had kissed my skin and foreign women had kissed my... ah... other bits. Travel would bring me everything I'd ever wanted; happiness and strength, self reliance and wisdom, and perhaps even that most elusive trait of all: confidence.

Yes. Maybe then, I'd come back and try my hand at acting once more.

I'd still be crap though.

Epilogue

In case you're wondering what happened to the other fine individuals who were good enough to guest-star in this book, here's a quick summary:

Pete stopped working in the pub we used to drink in when his boss, a rather portly bloke, made a pass at him. He ended up getting a job at a bank, and threw himself into an impressive series of courses and qualifications. Thus, Pete – purveyor of somewhat dubious advice – eventually became a financial advisor.

The irony being, he's actually pretty good at it.

As for Mark Strange, it took him another decade of hard work to become an 'overnight success', but Mark was no stranger to hard work. He has since done stunts for *Twelve*, *Redcon-1,* and *Batman Returns.* He is still working professionally as an actor and stunt performer in the UK and internationally. Which is exactly what I hoped people would say about me one day. Ah well! You win some, you lose some – and Mark Strange is a winner through and through.

Charles and Eleanor started a family, allowing their other work to slip gracefully into the background. Charlie even went into politics – now, whenever I see him, I have to call him gov'ner. But only because it winds him up.

After university Chris went back home to Swansea, where he's been working for the DVLA.

Sally spent several years teaching English in Italy, and since returning to Cardiff has renewed her interested in the Am-Dram scene.

And Katie, after nearly twenty years of being badgered about it, has finally decided to take up modelling.

The four of us are still great friends, despite me living over 10,000 miles away.

I keep trying to persuade them to come out to Australia, maybe do a spot of travelling with me, but so far no-one's taken the bait…

Maybe this is the year?

THE END

A Message from Tony...

Hiya! Thanks so much for buying and reading my ridiculous book. If you enjoyed it, I'd REALLY appreciate a brief review on Amazon! It doesn't have to be epic, or poetic – a couple of honest words is all I need. Word of mouth is the best form of recommendation an author can get, and I love reading my reviews! Thanks in advance.

Now, if you'd like to check out the photos that accompany this book – and there are quite a few of them – just head to my website at:

www.TonyJamesSlater.com

In case you're wondering about my other books, here's a list:

It all stared with **'That Bear Ate My Pants!'**, which followed my stint as a volunteer in an exotic animal refuge in Ecuador. Spoiler alert! I got bitten by a crocodile.

This was followed by **'Don't Need The Whole Dog!'**, which chronicled myriad adventures in the UK and then me following my dreams to Thailand.

Next came **'Kamikaze Kangaroos!'** – all about the two years I spent travelling around Australia in a knackered old van. This was when I met Roo!

After that came the story of my wedding to Roo, and our ridiculous honeymoon, told in **'Can I Kiss Her Yet?'**

Last but not least, we spent six months exploring the weirder countries in Asia. For reasons I won't go into, that book is called: **'Shave My Spider!'**

You can also catch up with me on Facebook, Twitter or Instagram by searching for Tony James Slater – or check out what's happening on my crazy blog:

www.AdventureWithoutEnd.com

About the Author

Tony James Slater is a very, very strange man. He believes himself to be indestructible, despite considerable evidence to the contrary. He is often to be found making strange faces whilst pretending to be attacked by inanimate objects. And sometimes – not always, but often enough to be of concern – his testicles hang out of the holes in his trousers.

It is for this reason (amongst others) that he chooses to spend his life far from mainstream civilization, tackling ridiculous challenges and subjecting himself to constant danger. He gets hurt quite a lot.

To see pictures from his adventures, read Tony's blog, or complain about his shameless self promotion, please visit:
www.TonyJamesSlater.com
But BE WARNED! Some of the writing is in red.